EASTMAN AND LAIRD'S TALES OF THE TEENAGE MUTANT NINJA TURTLES

VOLUME 4

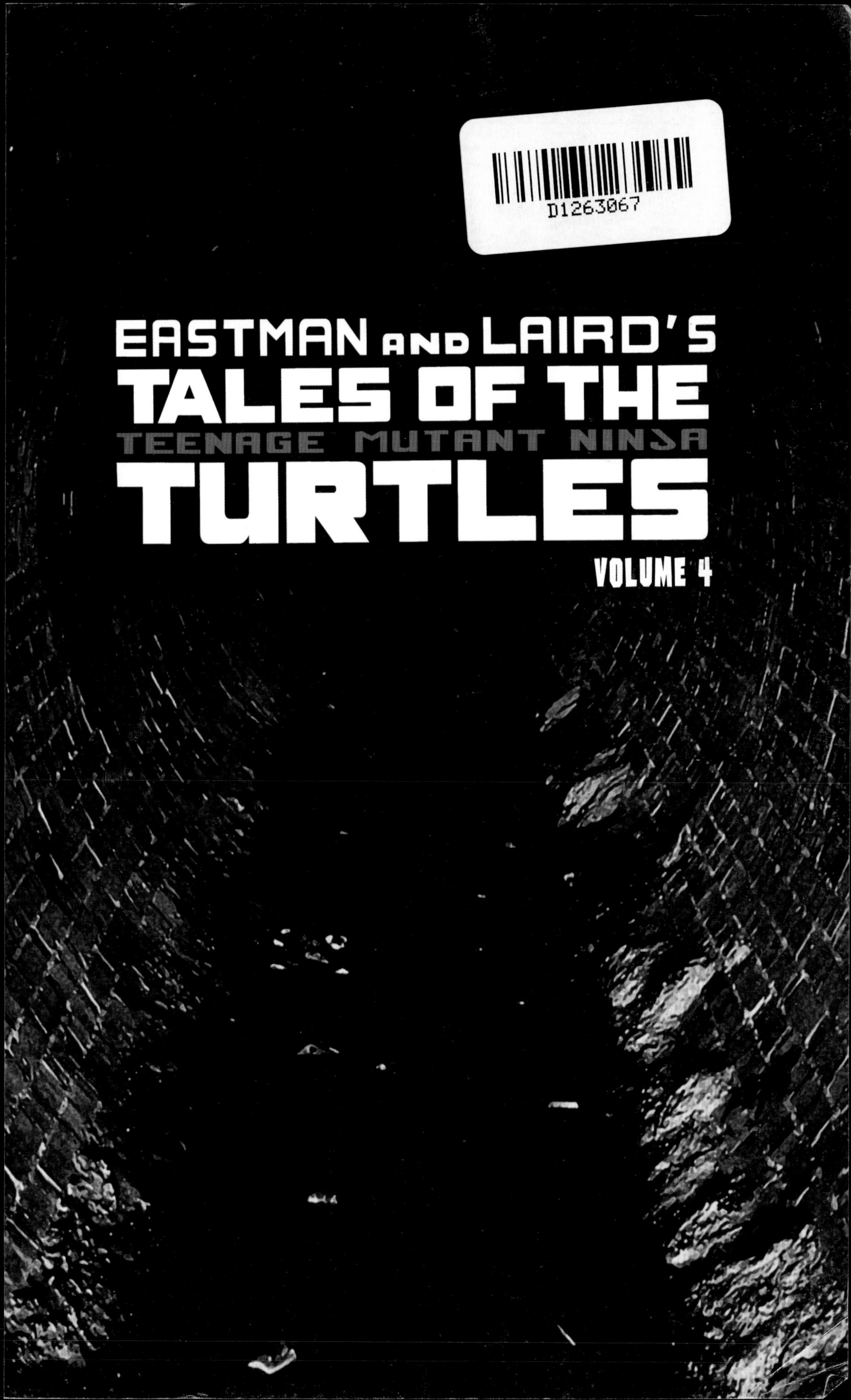

COVER BY
JIM LAWSON

COVER COLORS BY
JOANA LAFUENTE

COLLECTION EDITS BY
JUSTIN EISINGER
AND **ALONZO SIMON**

COLLECTION DESIGN BY
CLAUDIA CHONG

These reprints were intended for mature audiences and do not reflect the values of Nickelodeon or IDW Publishing. Except for the addition of color, the comics are presented here as originally published.

Special thanks to Joan Hilty, Linda Lee, and Kat Van Dam for their invaluable assistance.

ISBN: 978-1-61377-939-2

nickelodeon™

17 16 15 14   1 2 3 4

www.IDWPUBLISHING.com
IDW founded by Ted Adams, Alex Garner, Kris Oprisko, and Robbie Robbins

Ted Adams, CEO & Publisher
Greg Goldstein, President & COO
Robbie Robbins, EVP/Sr. Graphic Artist
Chris Ryall, Chief Creative Officer/Editor-in-Chief
Matthew Ruzicka, CPA, Chief Financial Officer
Alan Payne, VP of Sales
Dirk Wood, VP of Marketing
Lorelei Bunjes, VP of Digital Services
Jeff Webber, VP of Digital Publishing & Business Development

Facebook: **facebook.com/idwpublishing**
Twitter: **@idwpublishing**
YouTube: **youtube.com/idwpublishing**
Instagram: **instagram.com/idwpublishing**
deviantART: **idwpublishing.deviantart.com**
Pinterest: **pinterest.com/idwpublishing/idw-staff-faves**

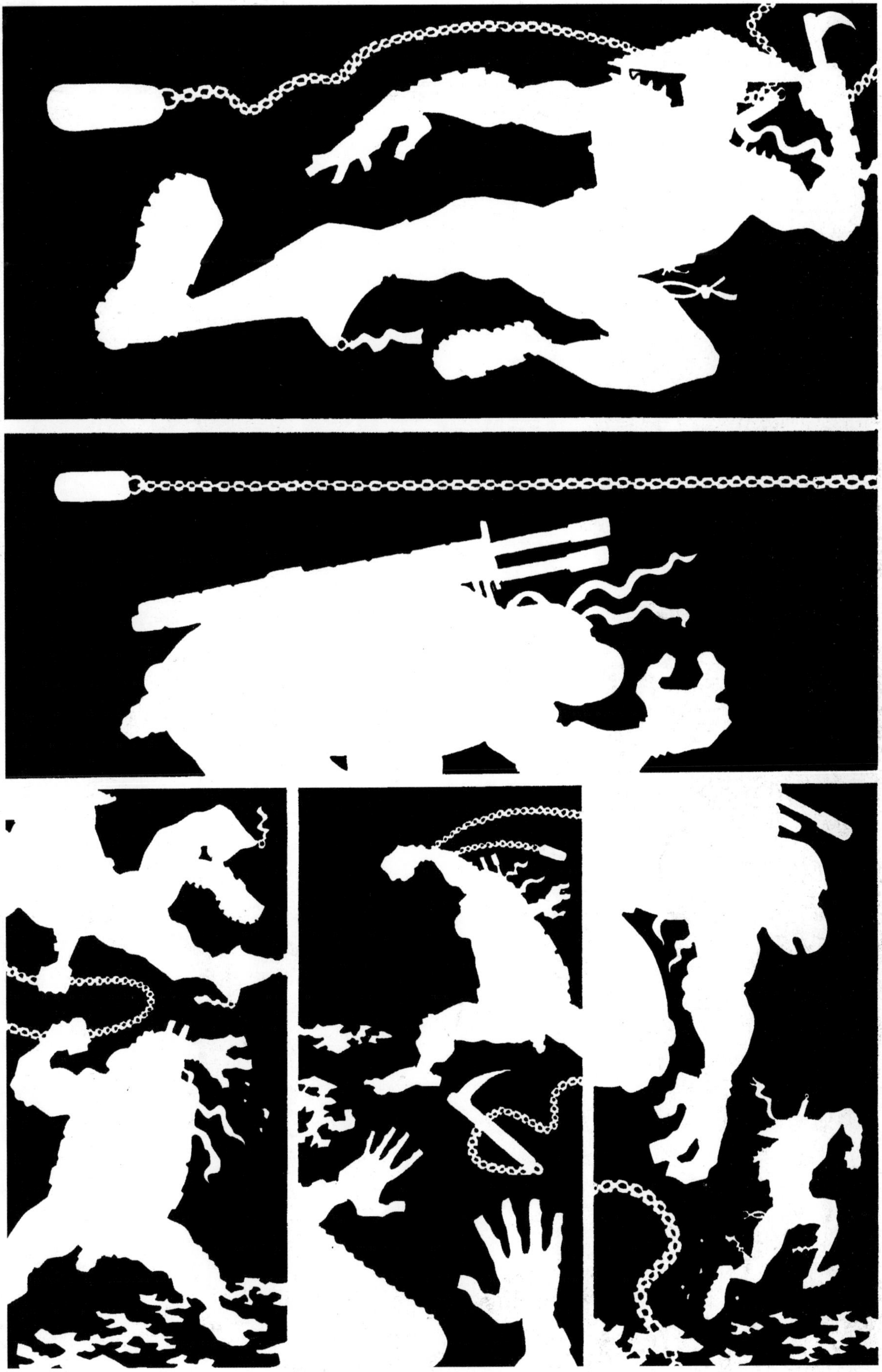

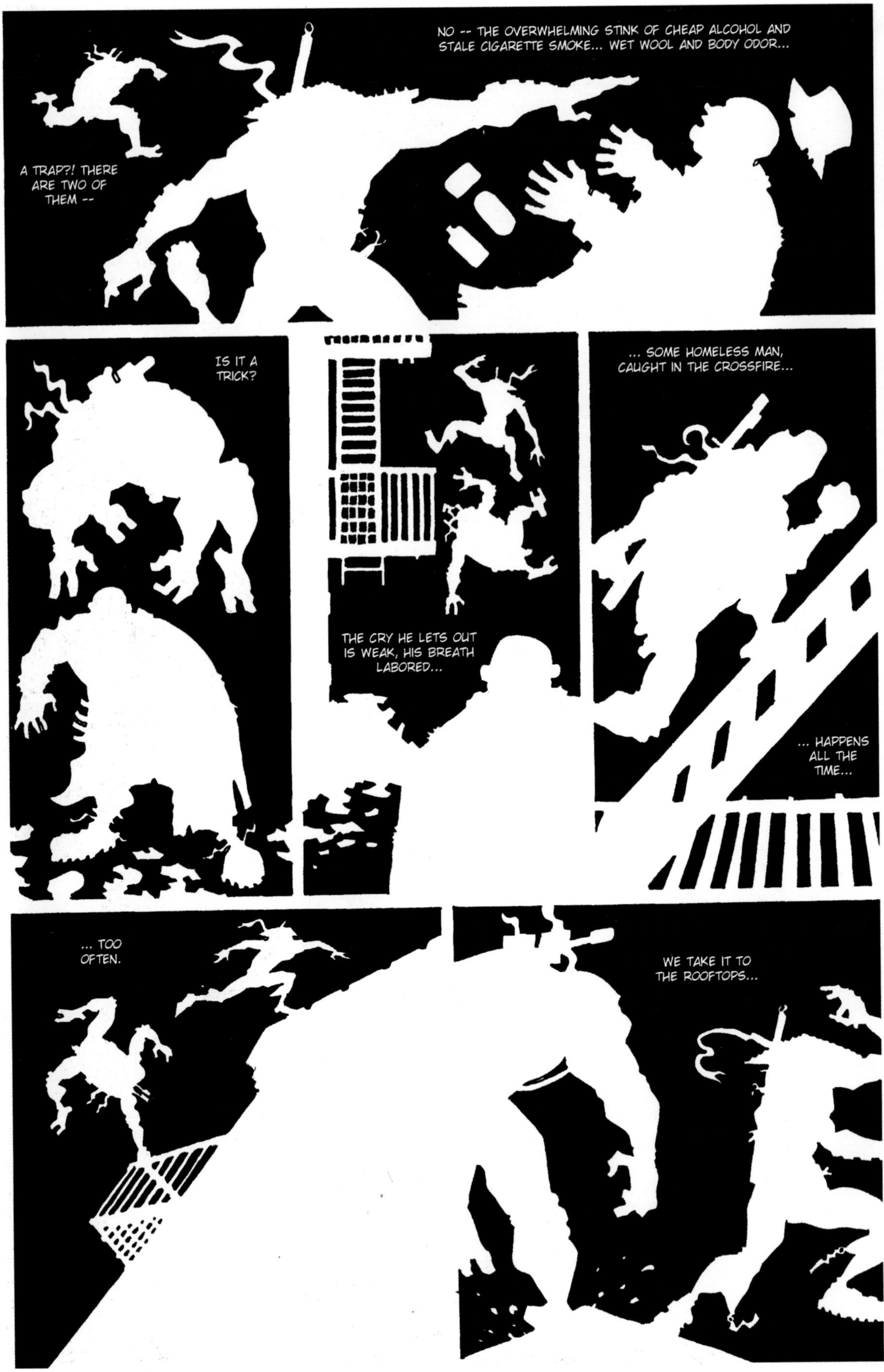
NO -- THE OVERWHELMING STINK OF CHEAP ALCOHOL AND STALE CIGARETTE SMOKE... WET WOOL AND BODY ODOR...
A TRAP?! THERE ARE TWO OF THEM --
IS IT A TRICK?
THE CRY HE LETS OUT IS WEAK, HIS BREATH LABORED...
... SOME HOMELESS MAN, CAUGHT IN THE CROSSFIRE...
... HAPPENS ALL THE TIME...
... TOO OFTEN.
WE TAKE IT TO THE ROOFTOPS...

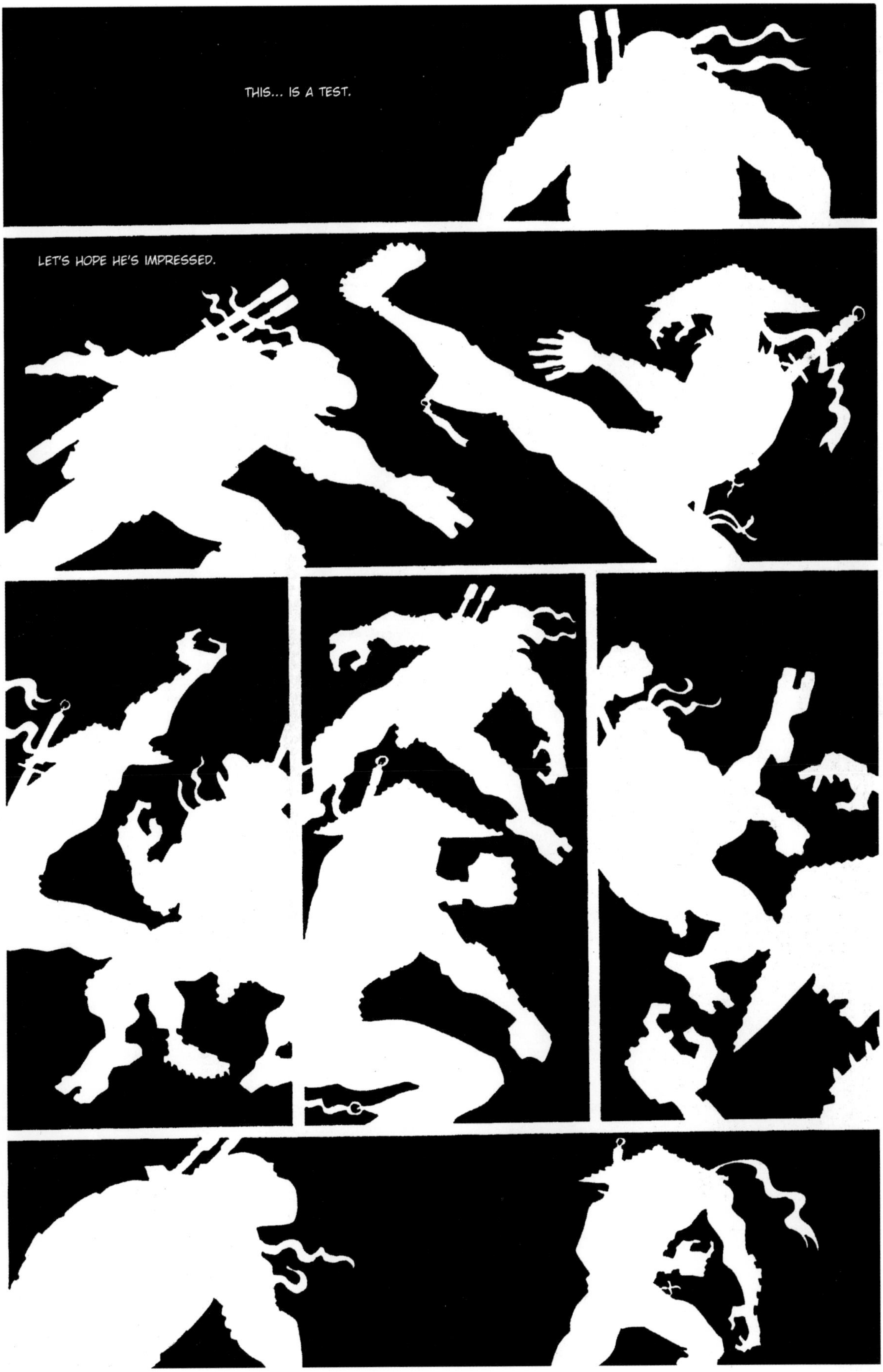
THIS... IS A TEST.
LET'S HOPE HE'S IMPRESSED.

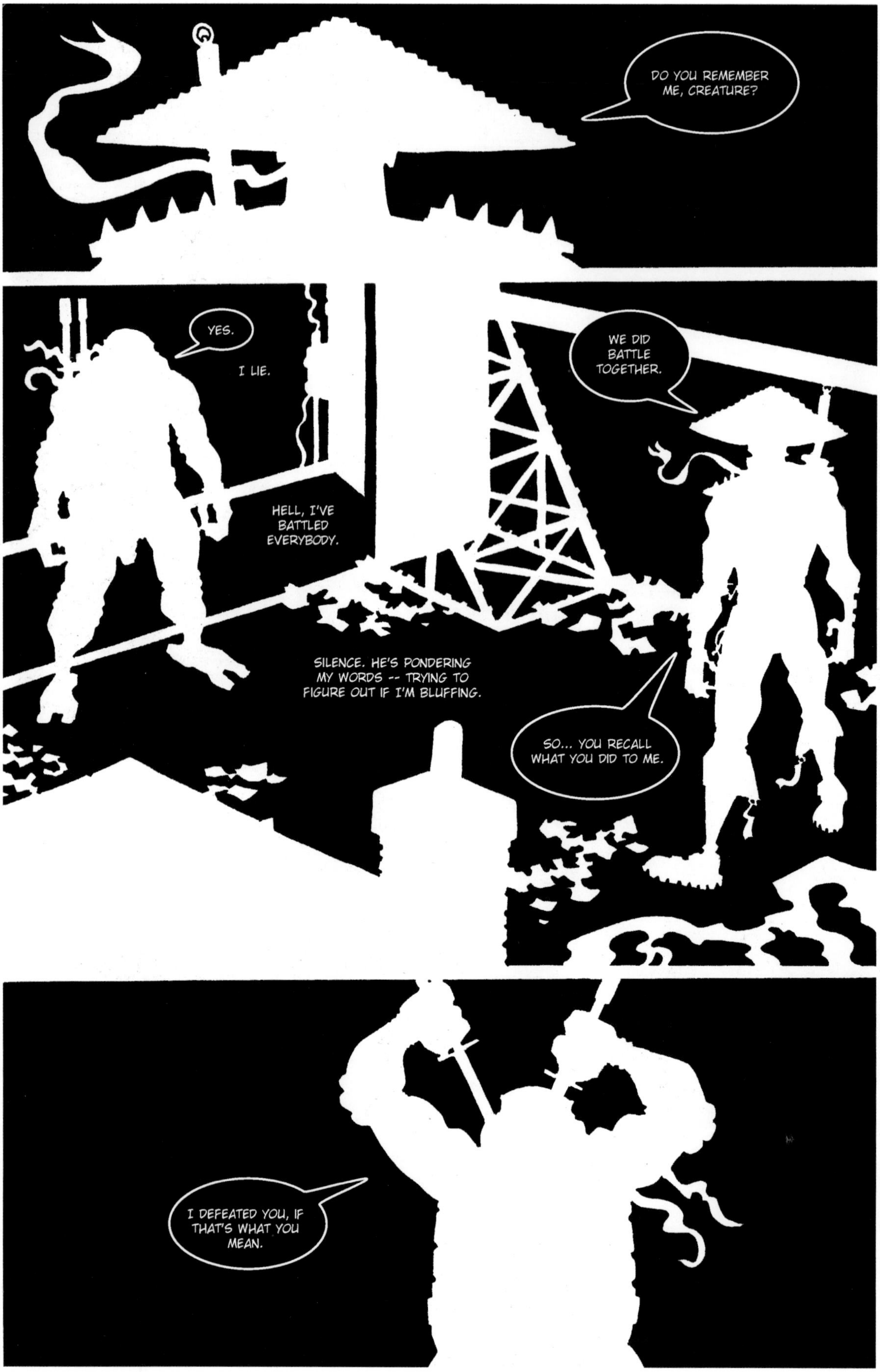
DO YOU REMEMBER ME, CREATURE?
YES.
I LIE.
WE DID BATTLE TOGETHER.
HELL, I'VE BATTLED EVERYBODY.
SILENCE. HE'S PONDERING MY WORDS -- TRYING TO FIGURE OUT IF I'M BLUFFING.
SO... YOU RECALL WHAT YOU DID TO ME.
I DEFEATED YOU, IF THAT'S WHAT YOU MEAN.

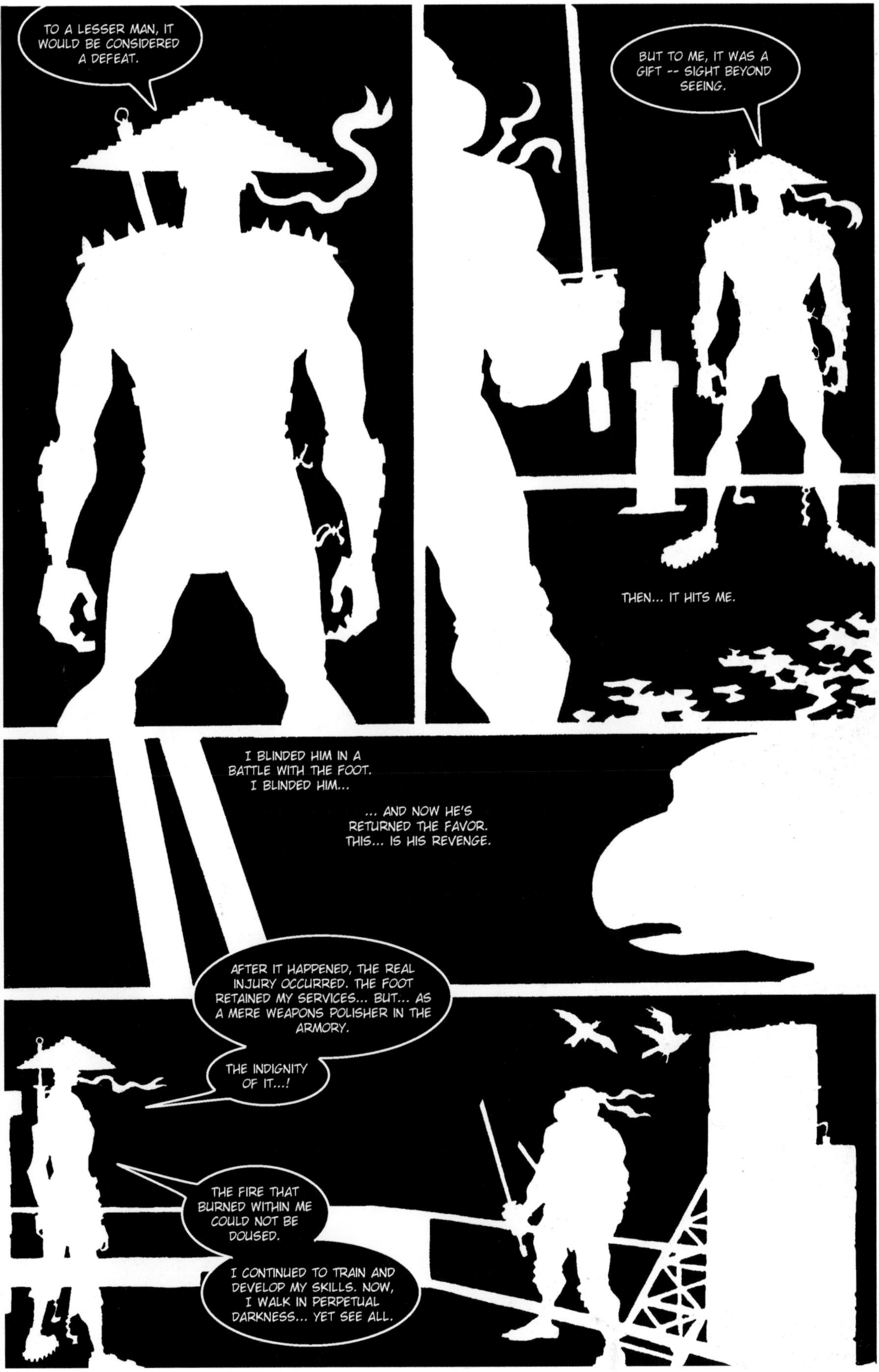
TO A LESSER MAN, IT WOULD BE CONSIDERED A DEFEAT.
BUT TO ME, IT WAS A GIFT -- SIGHT BEYOND SEEING.
THEN... IT HITS ME.
I BLINDED HIM IN A BATTLE WITH THE FOOT. I BLINDED HIM...
... AND NOW HE'S RETURNED THE FAVOR. THIS... IS HIS REVENGE.
AFTER IT HAPPENED, THE REAL INJURY OCCURRED. THE FOOT RETAINED MY SERVICES... BUT... AS A MERE WEAPONS POLISHER IN THE ARMORY.
THE INDIGNITY OF IT...!
THE FIRE THAT BURNED WITHIN ME COULD NOT BE DOUSED.
I CONTINUED TO TRAIN AND DEVELOP MY SKILLS. NOW, I WALK IN PERPETUAL DARKNESS... YET SEE ALL.

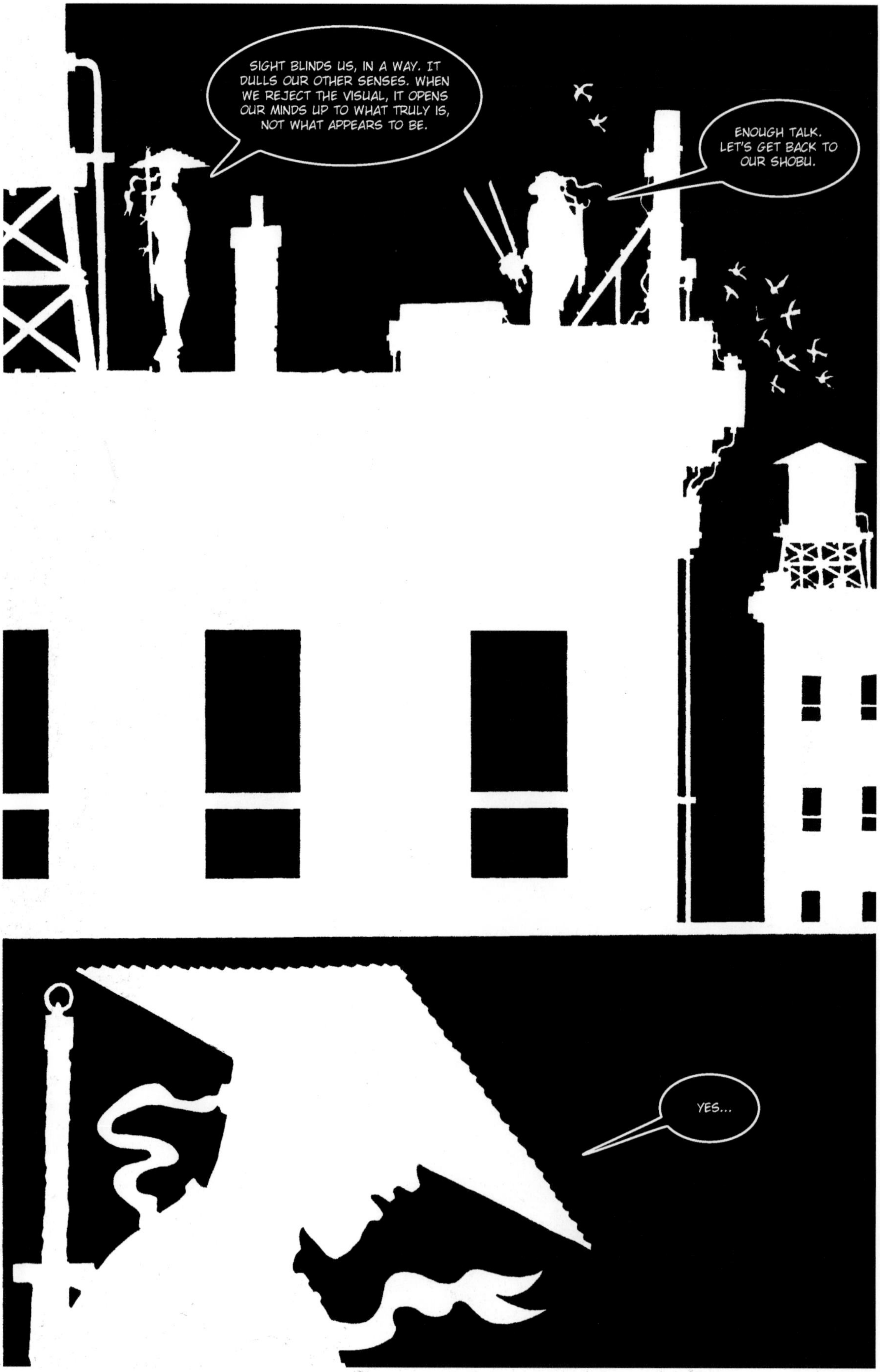
SIGHT BLINDS US, IN A WAY. IT DULLS OUR OTHER SENSES. WHEN WE REJECT THE VISUAL, IT OPENS OUR MINDS UP TO WHAT TRULY IS, NOT WHAT APPEARS TO BE.
ENOUGH TALK. LET'S GET BACK TO OUR SHOBU.
YES...

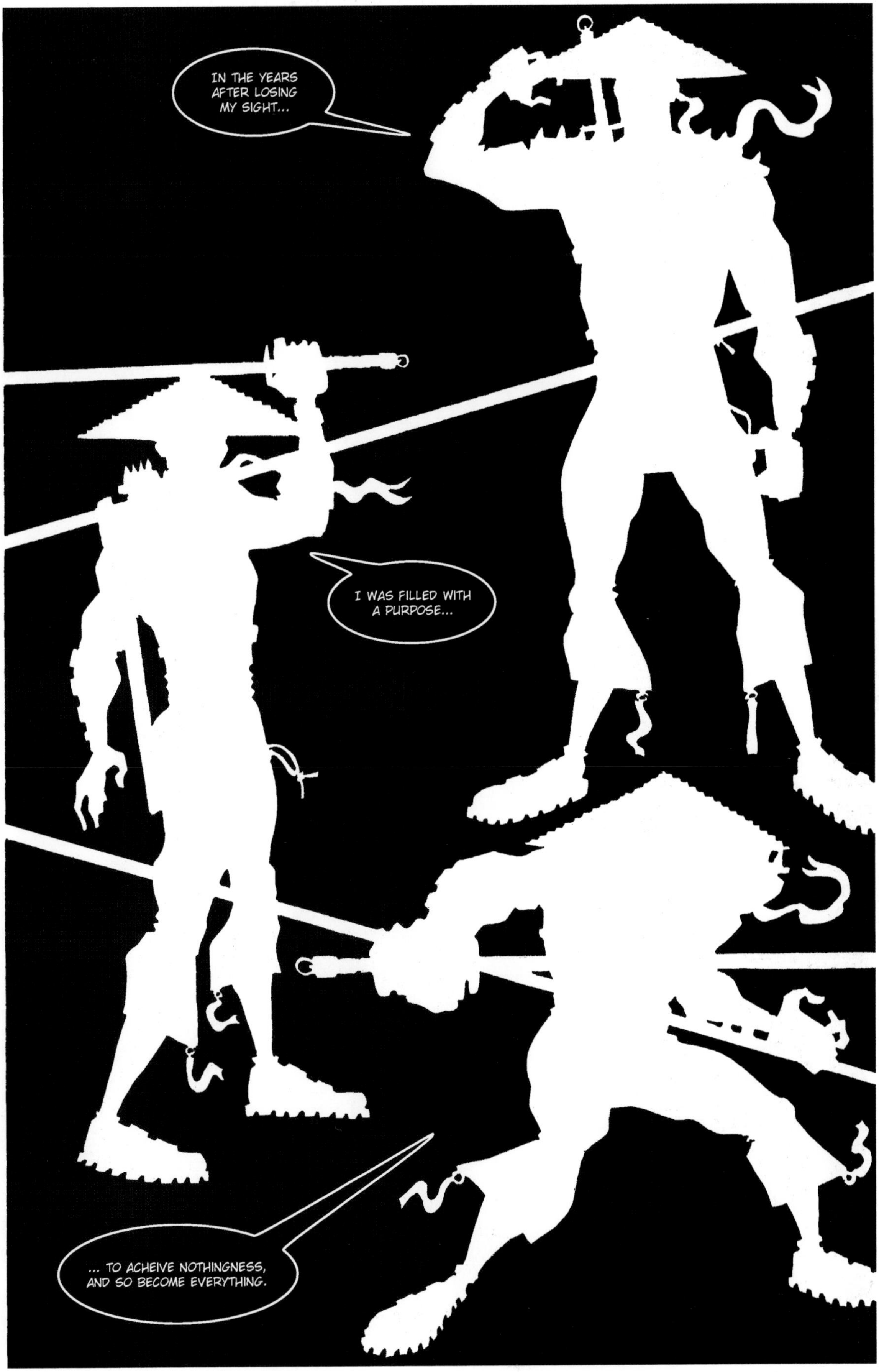
IN THE YEARS AFTER LOSING MY SIGHT...
I WAS FILLED WITH A PURPOSE...
... TO ACHEIVE NOTHINGNESS, AND SO BECOME EVERYTHING.

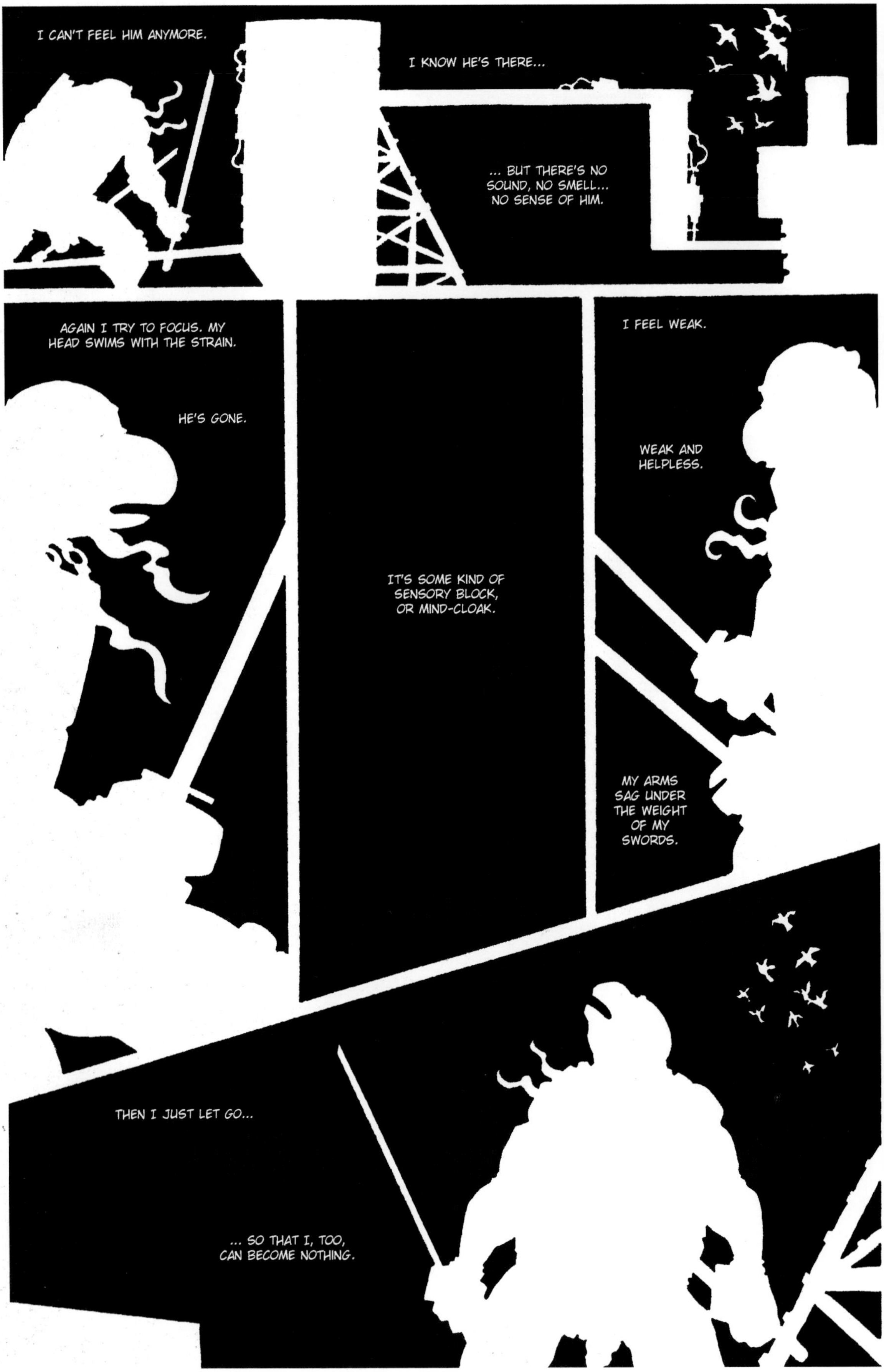
I CAN'T FEEL HIM ANYMORE.
I KNOW HE'S THERE...
... BUT THERE'S NO SOUND, NO SMELL... NO SENSE OF HIM.
AGAIN I TRY TO FOCUS. MY HEAD SWIMS WITH THE STRAIN.
HE'S GONE.
IT'S SOME KIND OF SENSORY BLOCK, OR MIND-CLOAK.
I FEEL WEAK.
WEAK AND HELPLESS.
MY ARMS SAG UNDER THE WEIGHT OF MY SWORDS.
THEN I JUST LET GO...
... SO THAT I, TOO, CAN BECOME NOTHING.

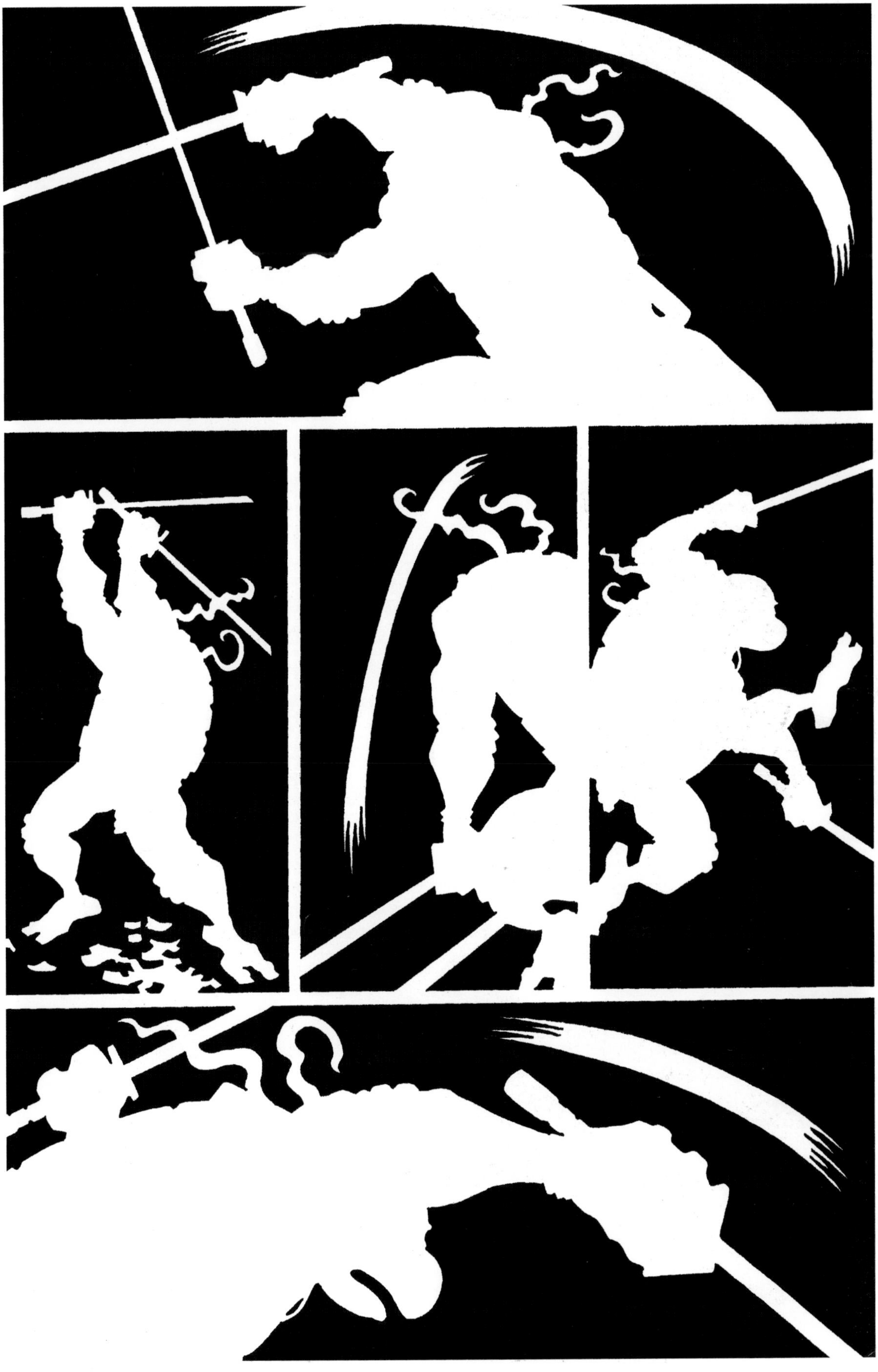

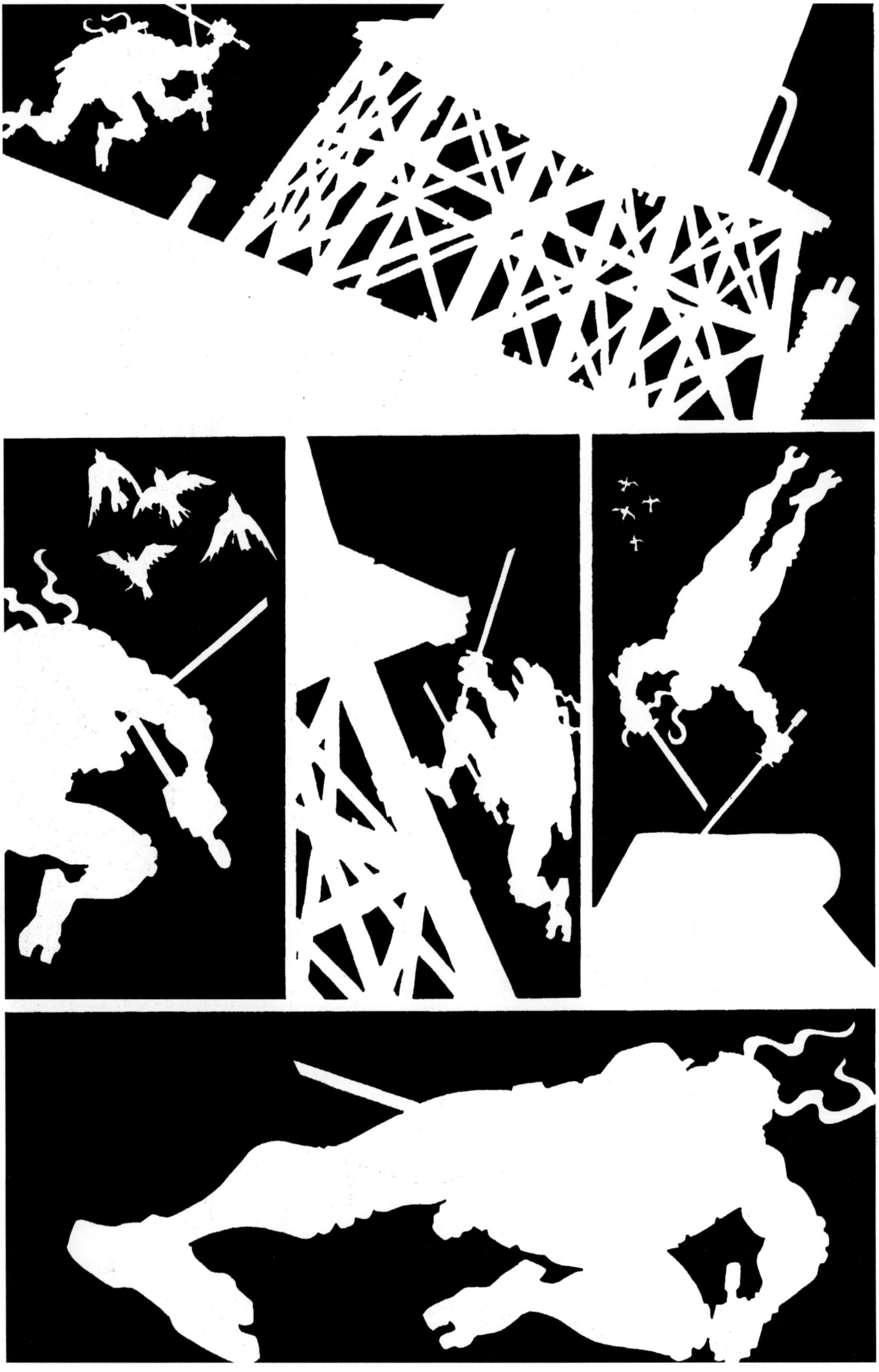

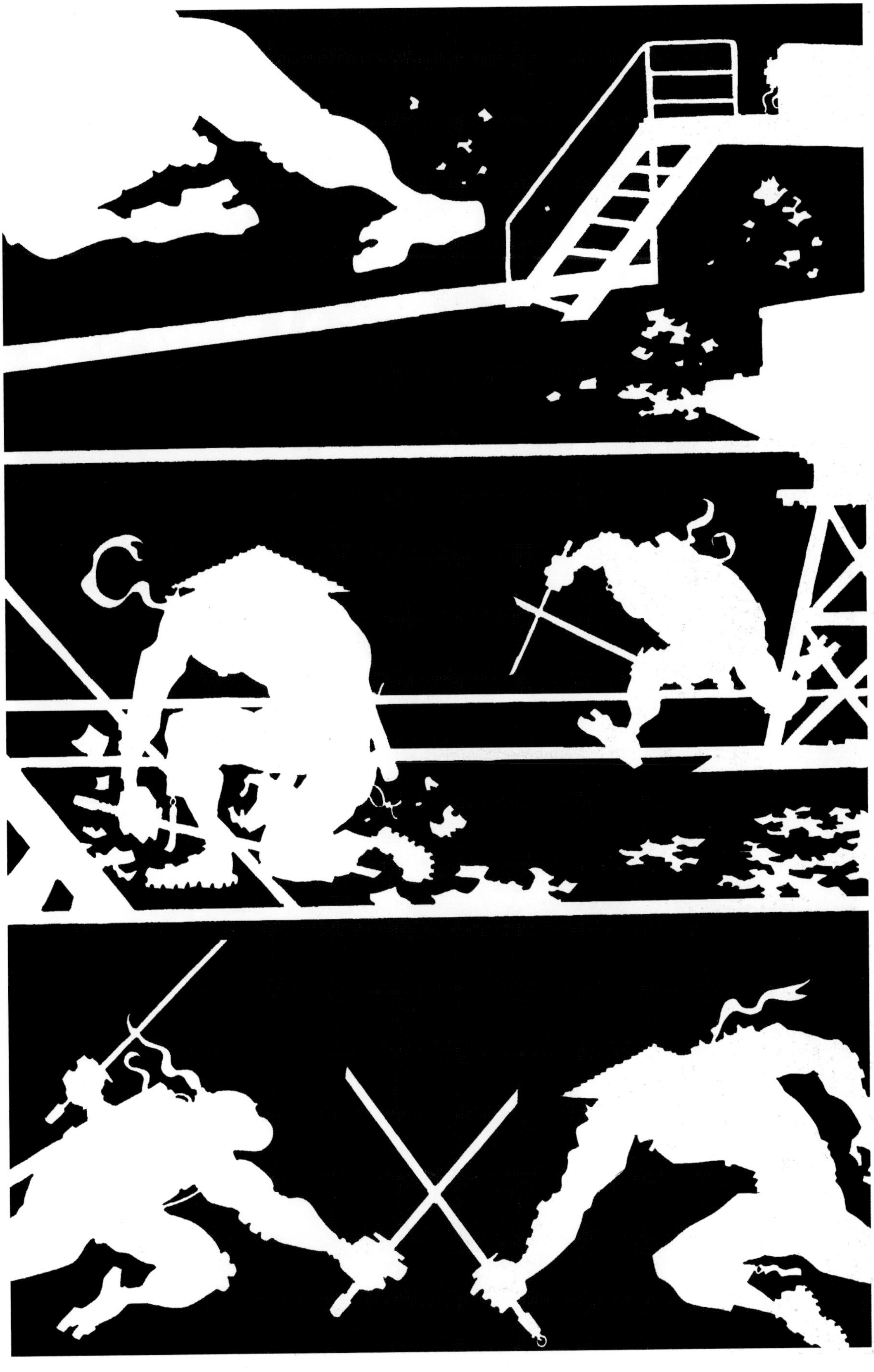

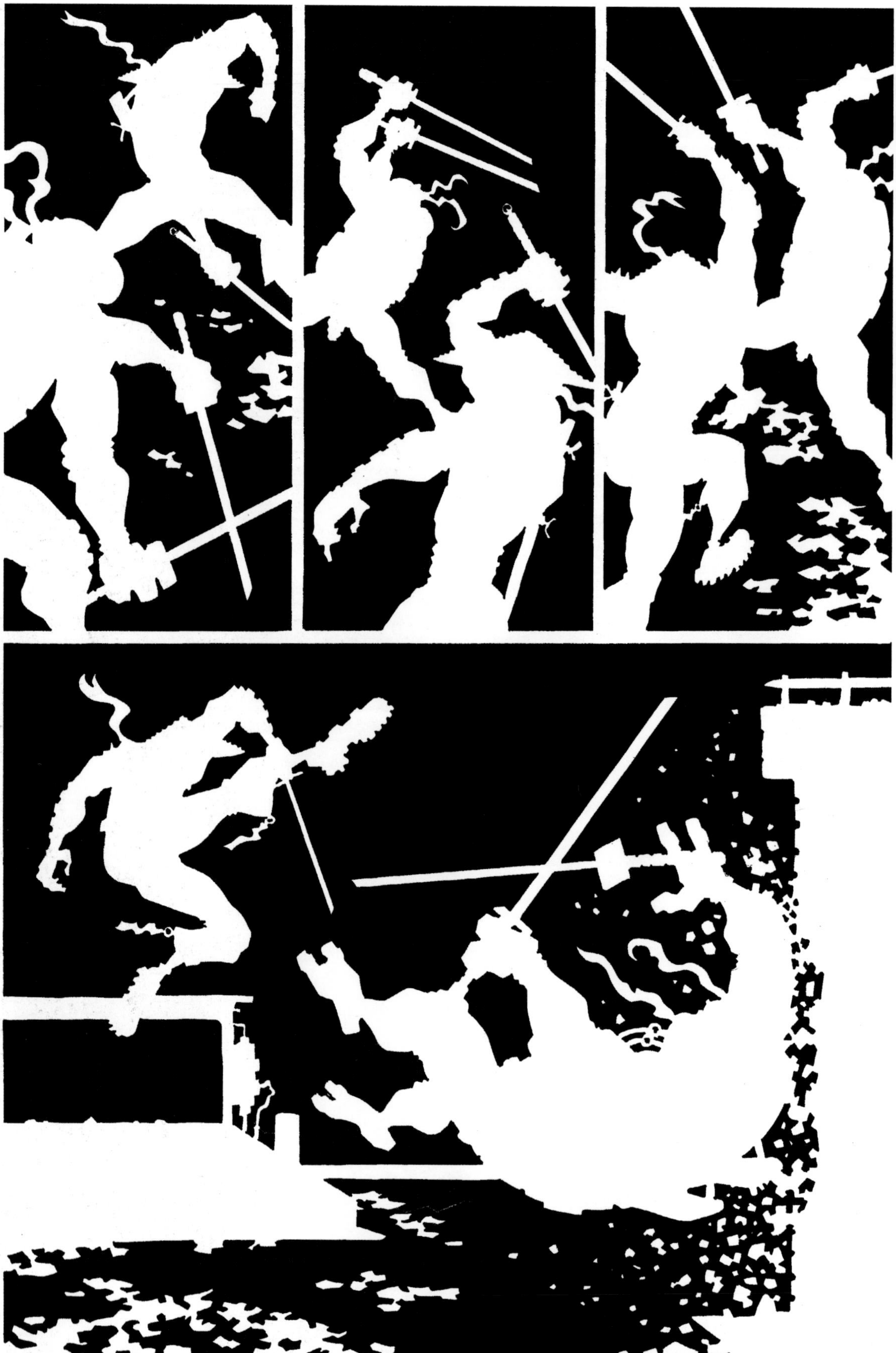

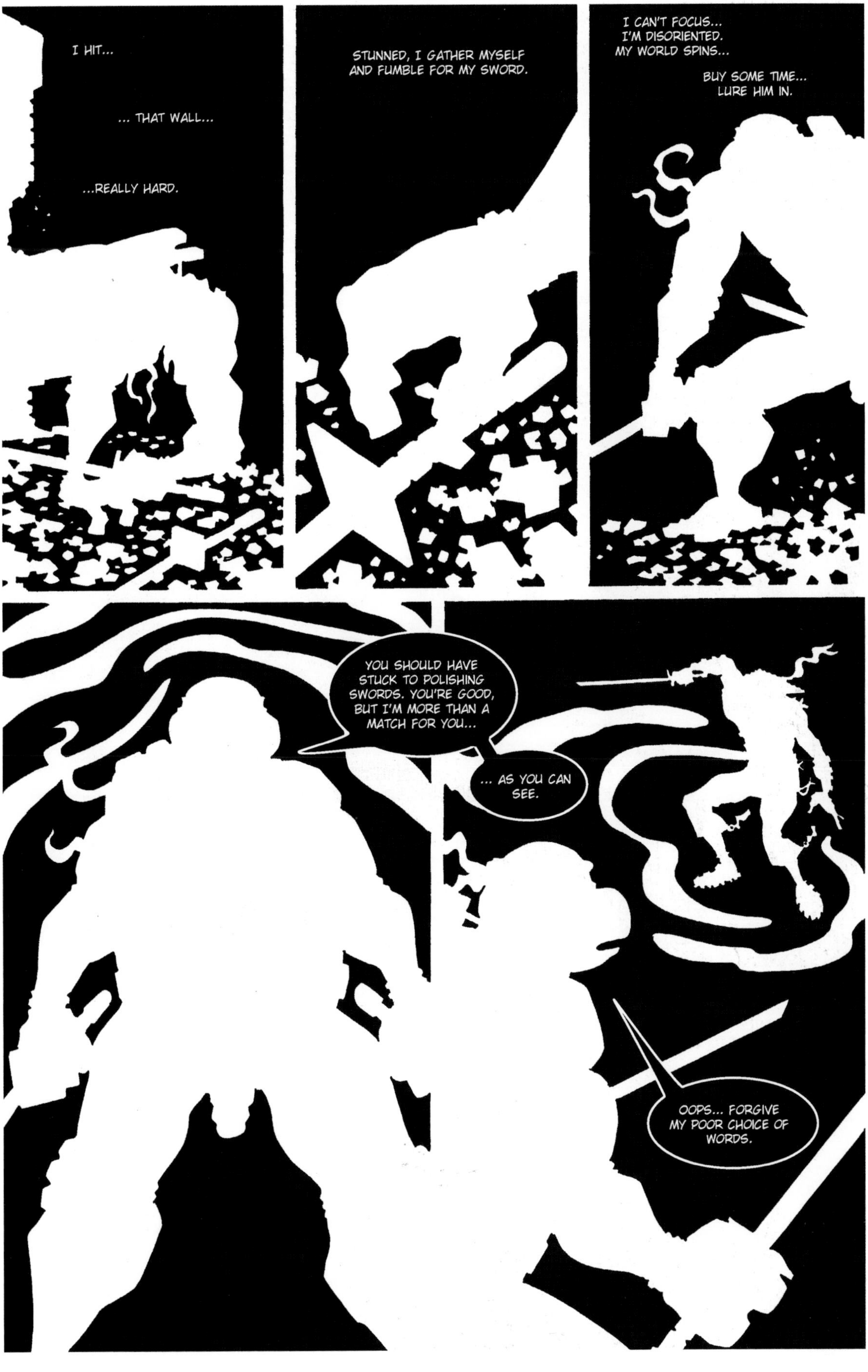
I HIT...
... THAT WALL...
...REALLY HARD.
STUNNED, I GATHER MYSELF AND FUMBLE FOR MY SWORD.
I CAN'T FOCUS... I'M DISORIENTED. MY WORLD SPINS...
BUY SOME TIME... LURE HIM IN.
YOU SHOULD HAVE STUCK TO POLISHING SWORDS. YOU'RE GOOD, BUT I'M MORE THAN A MATCH FOR YOU...
... AS YOU CAN SEE.
OOPS... FORGIVE MY POOR CHOICE OF WORDS.

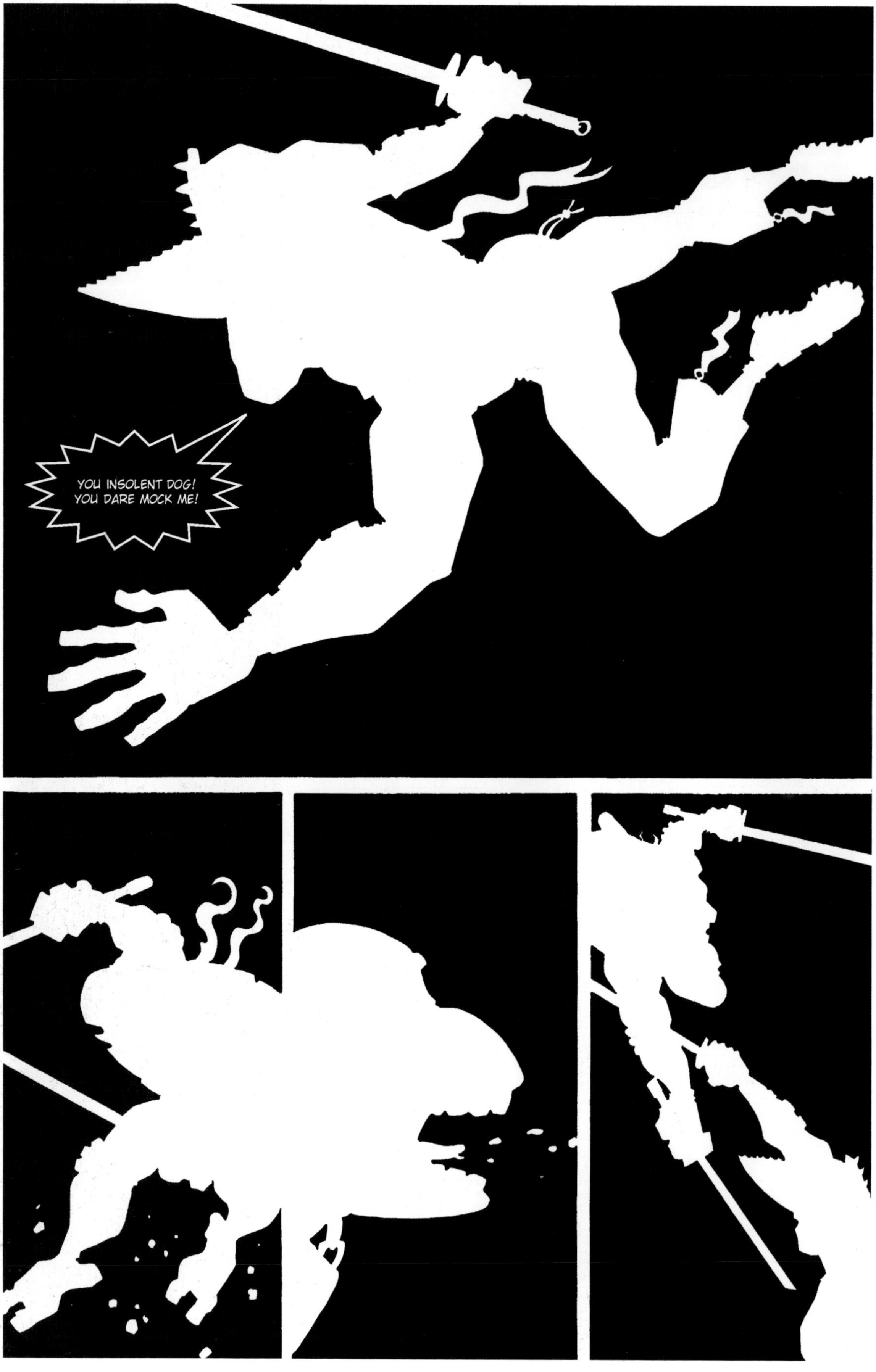
YOU INSOLENT DOG! YOU DARE MOCK ME!

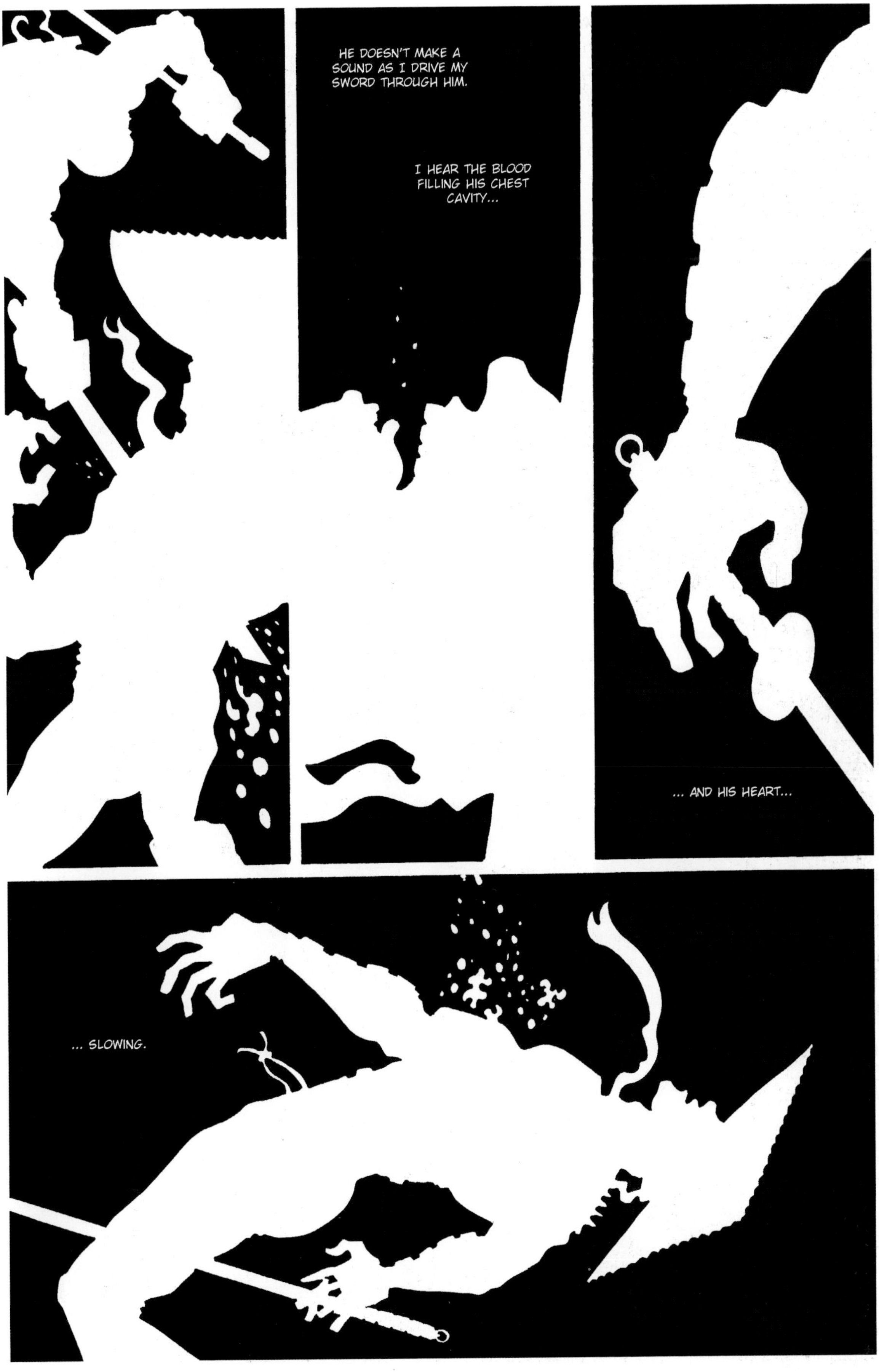
HE DOESN'T MAKE A SOUND AS I DRIVE MY SWORD THROUGH HIM.
I HEAR THE BLOOD FILLING HIS CHEST CAVITY...
... AND HIS HEART...
... SLOWING.

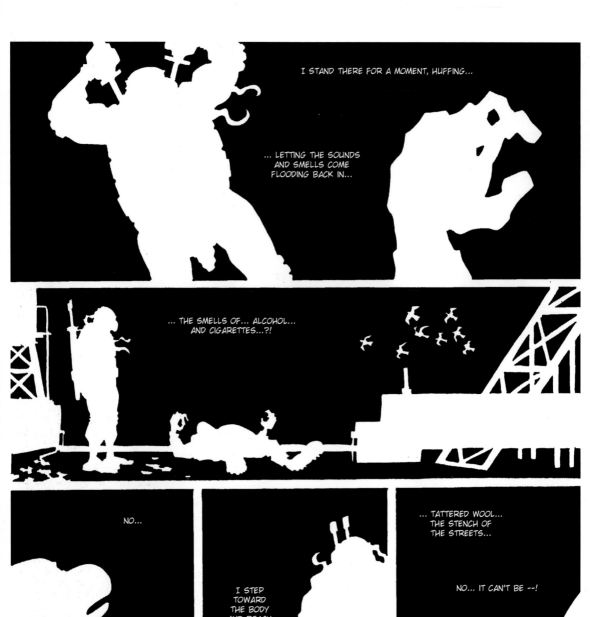

I STAND THERE FOR A MOMENT, HUFFING...

... LETTING THE SOUNDS AND SMELLS COME FLOODING BACK IN...

... THE SMELLS OF... ALCOHOL... AND CIGARETTES...?!

NO...

I STEP TOWARD THE BODY AND REACH DOWN...

... TATTERED WOOL... THE STENCH OF THE STREETS...

NO... IT CAN'T BE --!

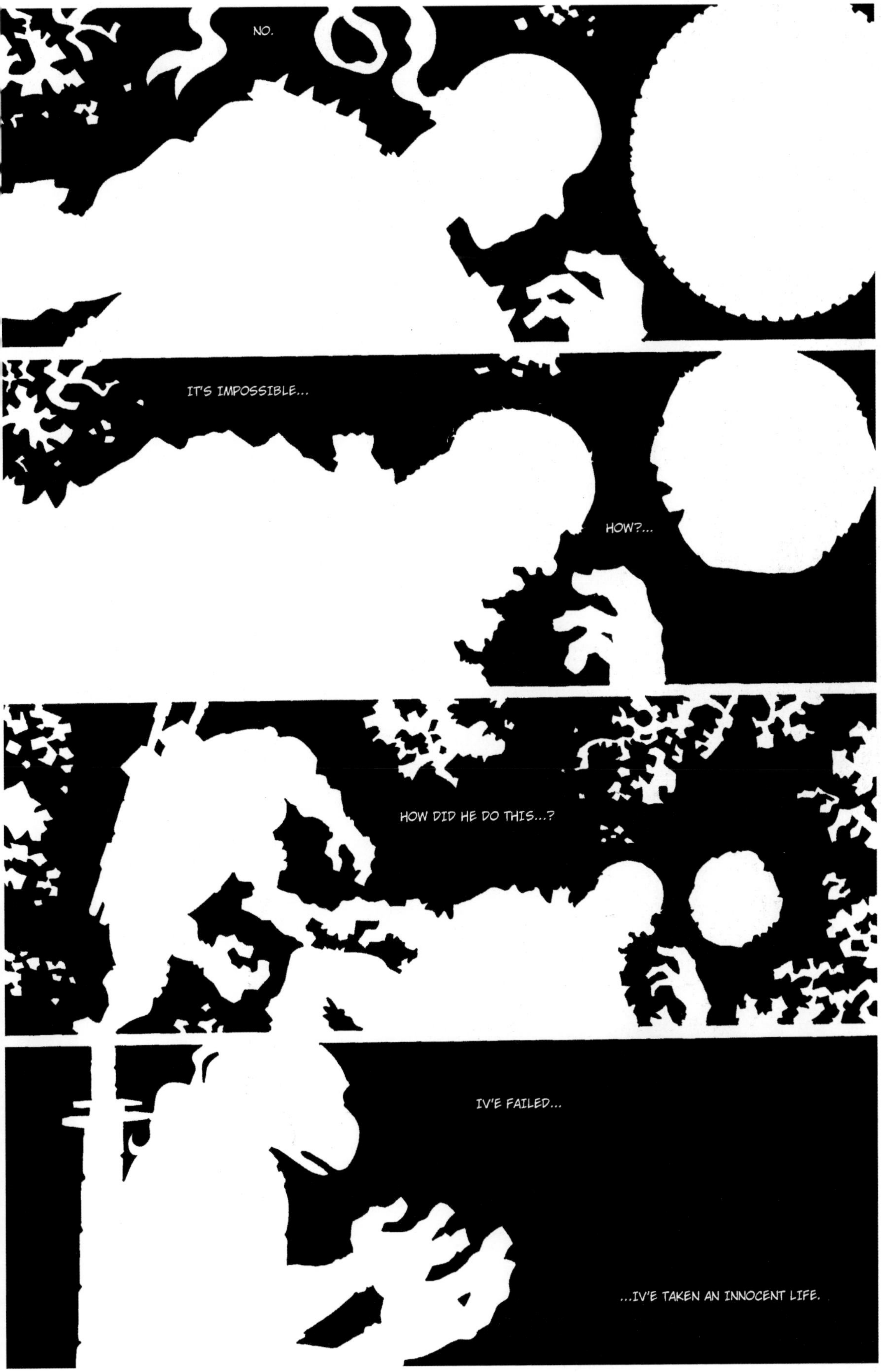
NO.
IT'S IMPOSSIBLE...
HOW?...
HOW DID HE DO THIS...?
IV'E FAILED...
...IV'E TAKEN AN INNOCENT LIFE.

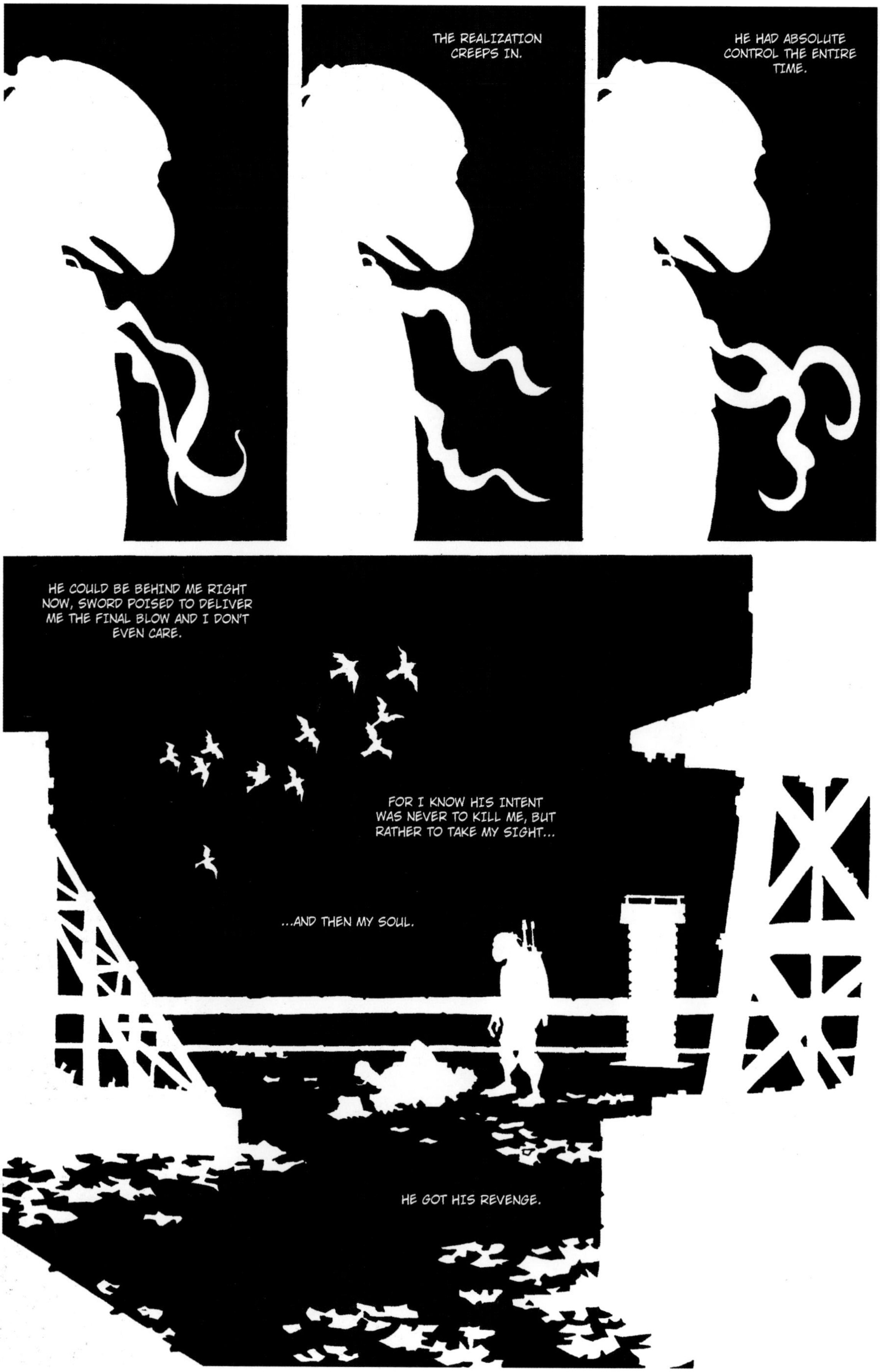
THE REALIZATION CREEPS IN.
HE HAD ABSOLUTE CONTROL THE ENTIRE TIME.
HE COULD BE BEHIND ME RIGHT NOW, SWORD POISED TO DELIVER ME THE FINAL BLOW AND I DON'T EVEN CARE.
FOR I KNOW HIS INTENT WAS NEVER TO KILL ME, BUT RATHER TO TAKE MY SIGHT...
...AND THEN MY SOUL.
HE GOT HIS REVENGE.

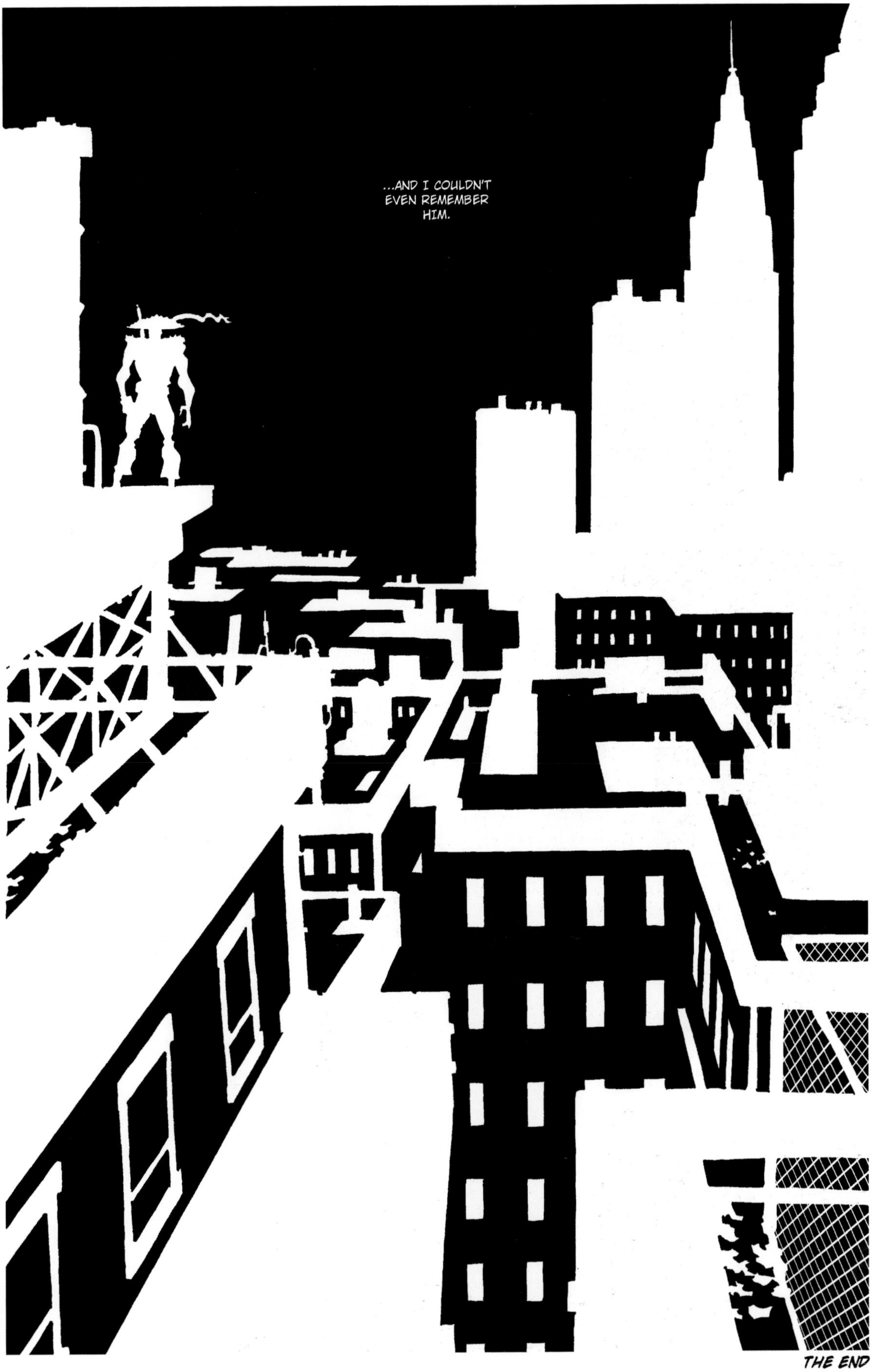
...AND I COULDN'T EVEN REMEMBER HIM.

THE END

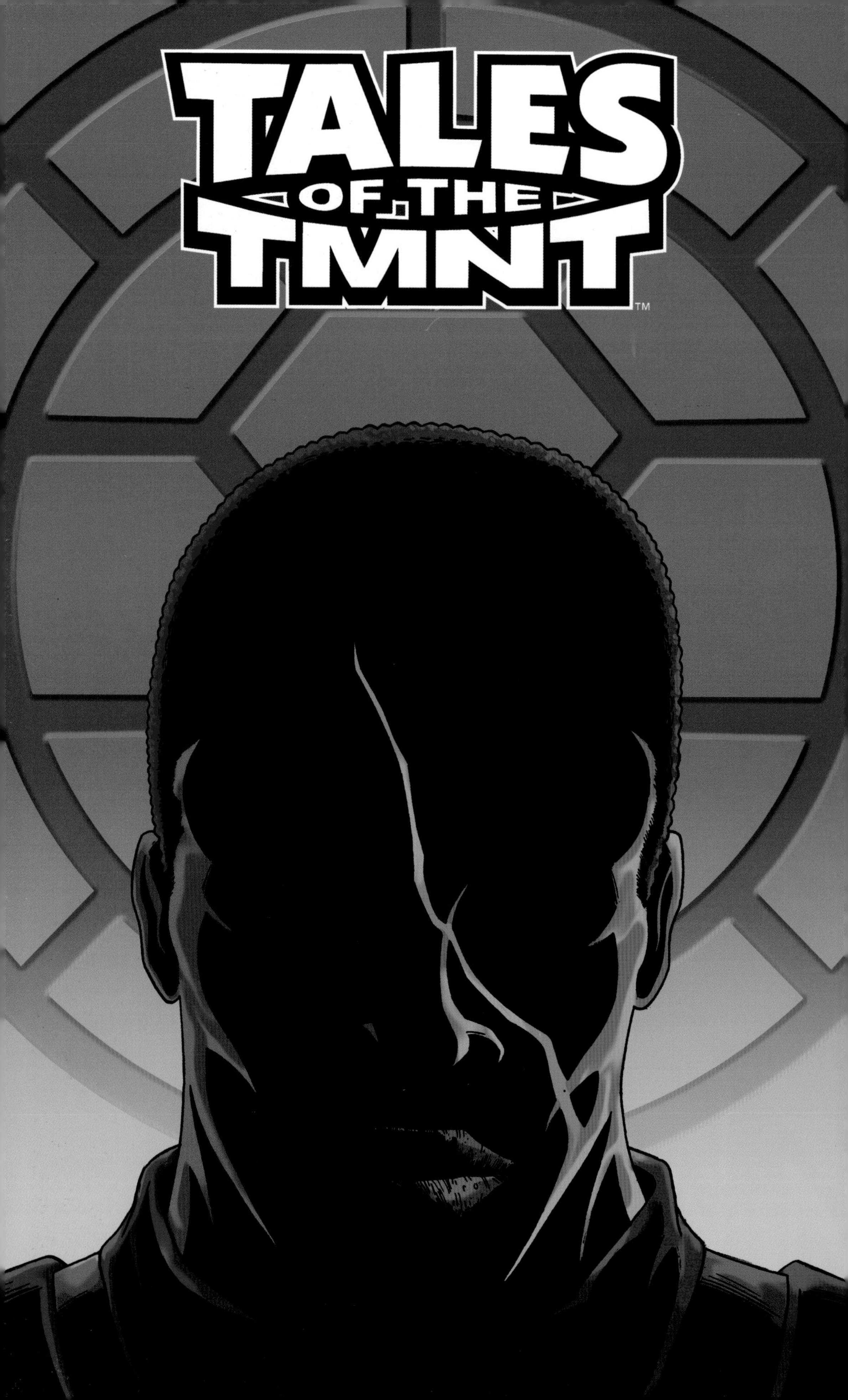
TALES
OF THE
TMNT™

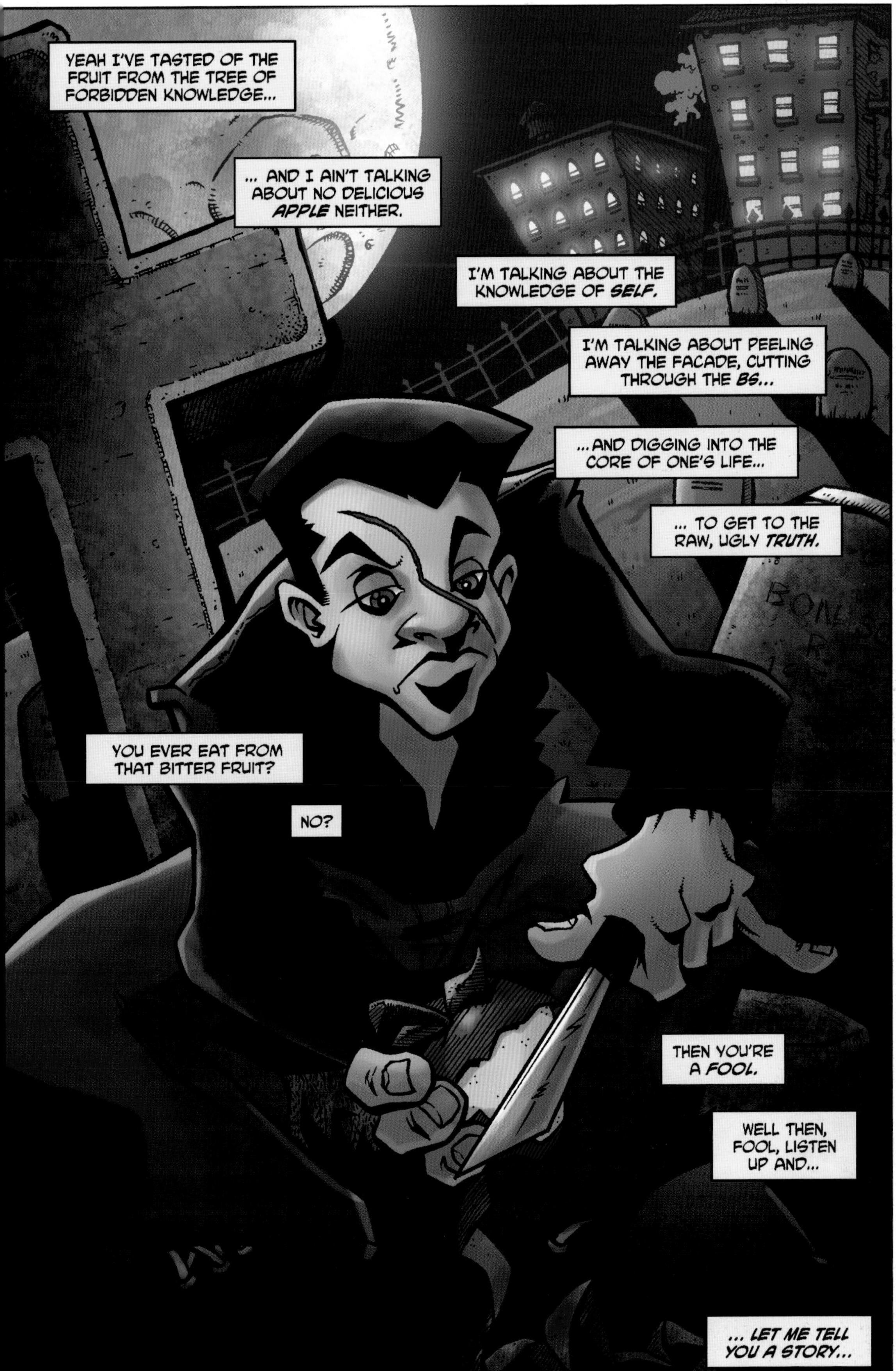
YEAH I'VE TASTED OF THE FRUIT FROM THE TREE OF FORBIDDEN KNOWLEDGE...
... AND I AIN'T TALKING ABOUT NO DELICIOUS *APPLE* NEITHER.
I'M TALKING ABOUT THE KNOWLEDGE OF *SELF.*
I'M TALKING ABOUT PEELING AWAY THE FACADE, CUTTING THROUGH THE *BS...*
...AND DIGGING INTO THE CORE OF ONE'S LIFE...
... TO GET TO THE RAW, UGLY *TRUTH.*
YOU EVER EAT FROM THAT BITTER FRUIT?
NO?
THEN YOU'RE A *FOOL.*
WELL THEN, FOOL, LISTEN UP AND...
... LET ME TELL YOU A STORY...

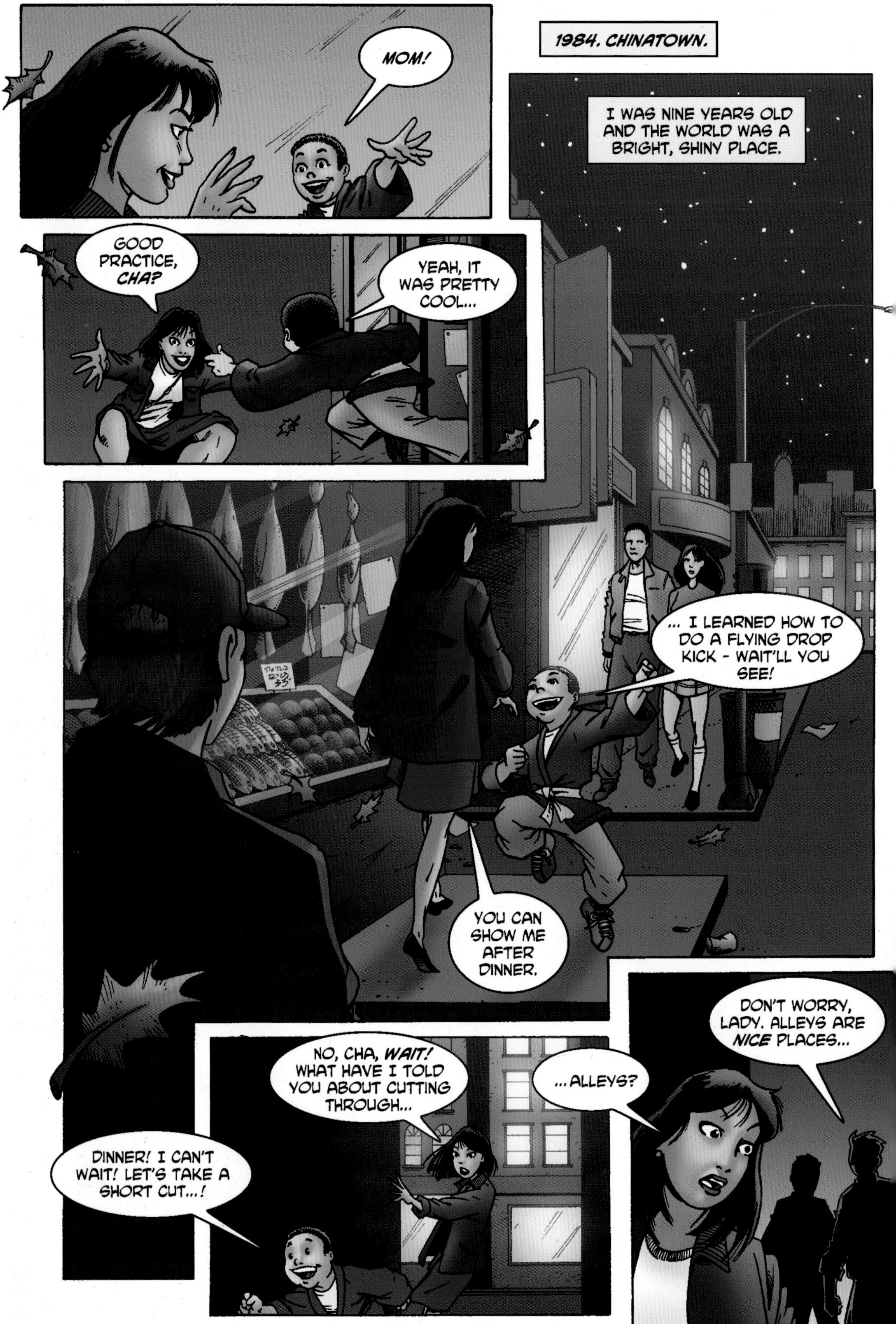
1984. CHINATOWN.
MOM!
GOOD PRACTICE, CHA?
YEAH, IT WAS PRETTY COOL...
I WAS NINE YEARS OLD AND THE WORLD WAS A BRIGHT, SHINY PLACE.
... I LEARNED HOW TO DO A FLYING DROP KICK - WAIT'LL YOU SEE!
YOU CAN SHOW ME AFTER DINNER.
DINNER! I CAN'T WAIT! LET'S TAKE A SHORT CUT...!
NO, CHA, WAIT! WHAT HAVE I TOLD YOU ABOUT CUTTING THROUGH...
...ALLEYS?
DON'T WORRY, LADY. ALLEYS ARE NICE PLACES...

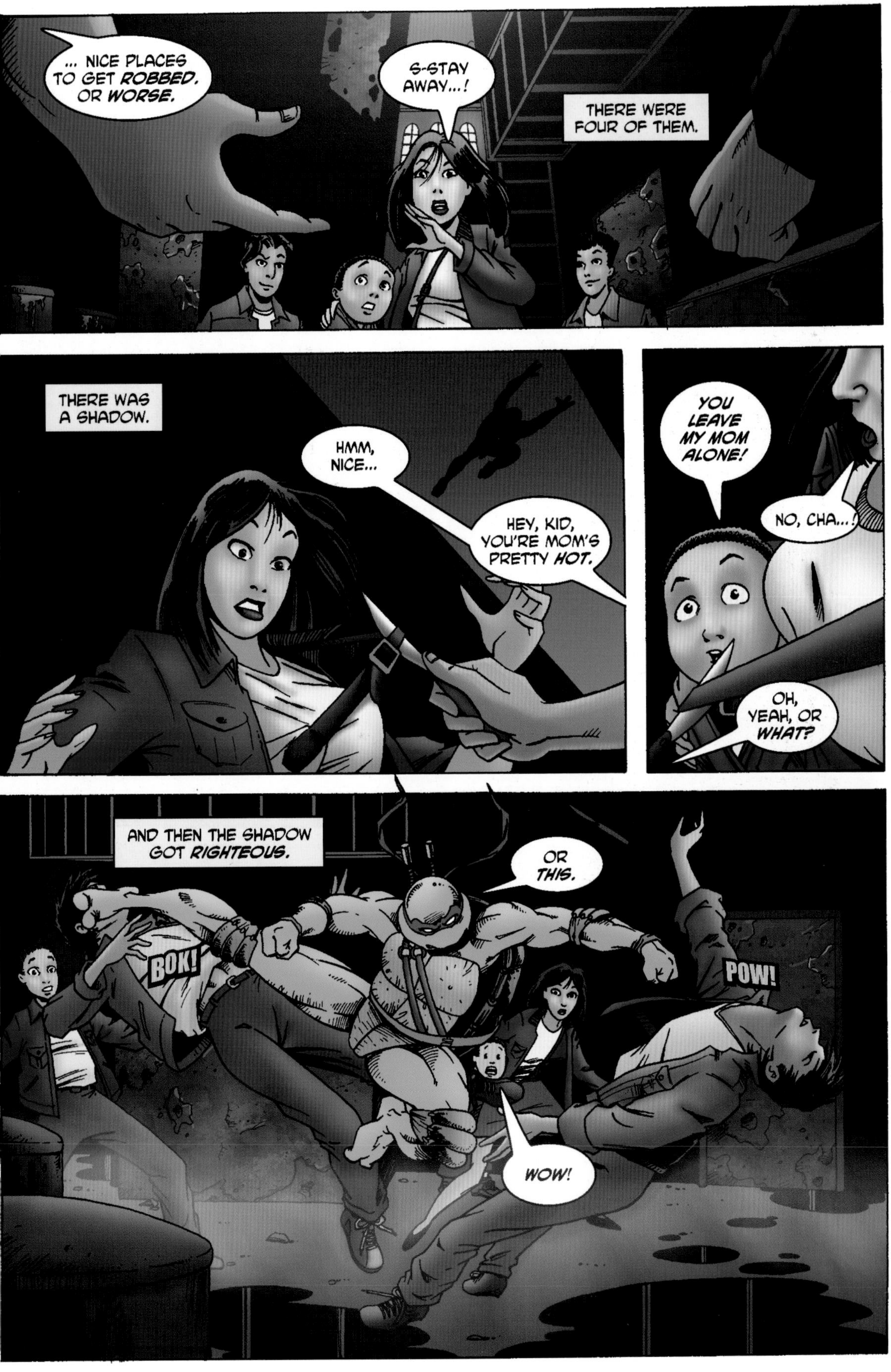
... NICE PLACES TO GET ROBBED. OR WORSE.
S-STAY AWAY...!
THERE WERE FOUR OF THEM.
THERE WAS A SHADOW.
HMM, NICE...
HEY, KID, YOU'RE MOM'S PRETTY HOT.
YOU LEAVE MY MOM ALONE!
NO, CHA...!
OH, YEAH, OR WHAT?
AND THEN THE SHADOW GOT RIGHTEOUS.
OR THIS.
BOK!
POW!
WOW!

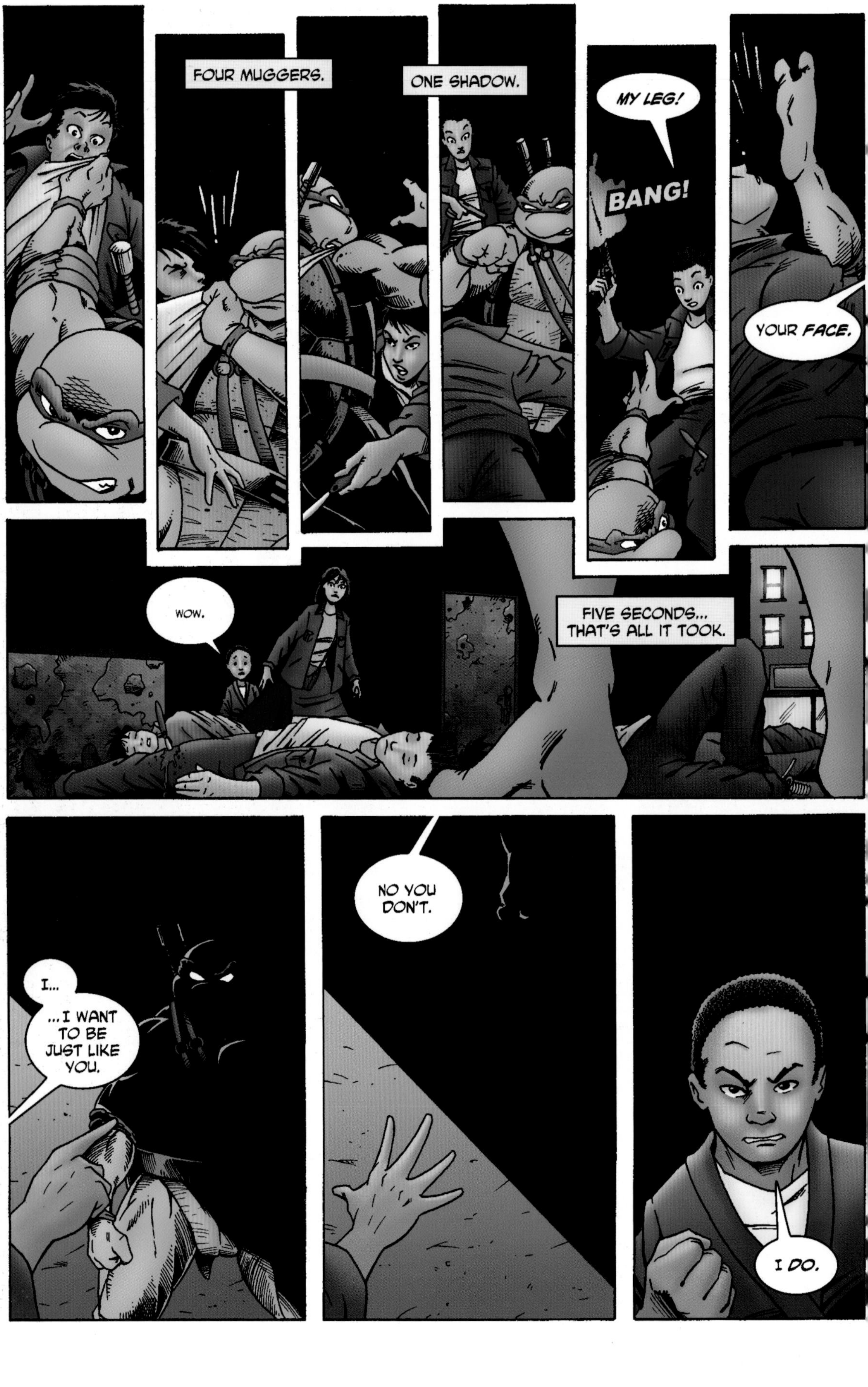
FOUR MUGGERS.
ONE SHADOW.
MY LEG!
BANG!
YOUR FACE.
WOW.
FIVE SECONDS... THAT'S ALL IT TOOK.
I...
...I WANT TO BE JUST LIKE YOU.
NO YOU DON'T.
I DO.

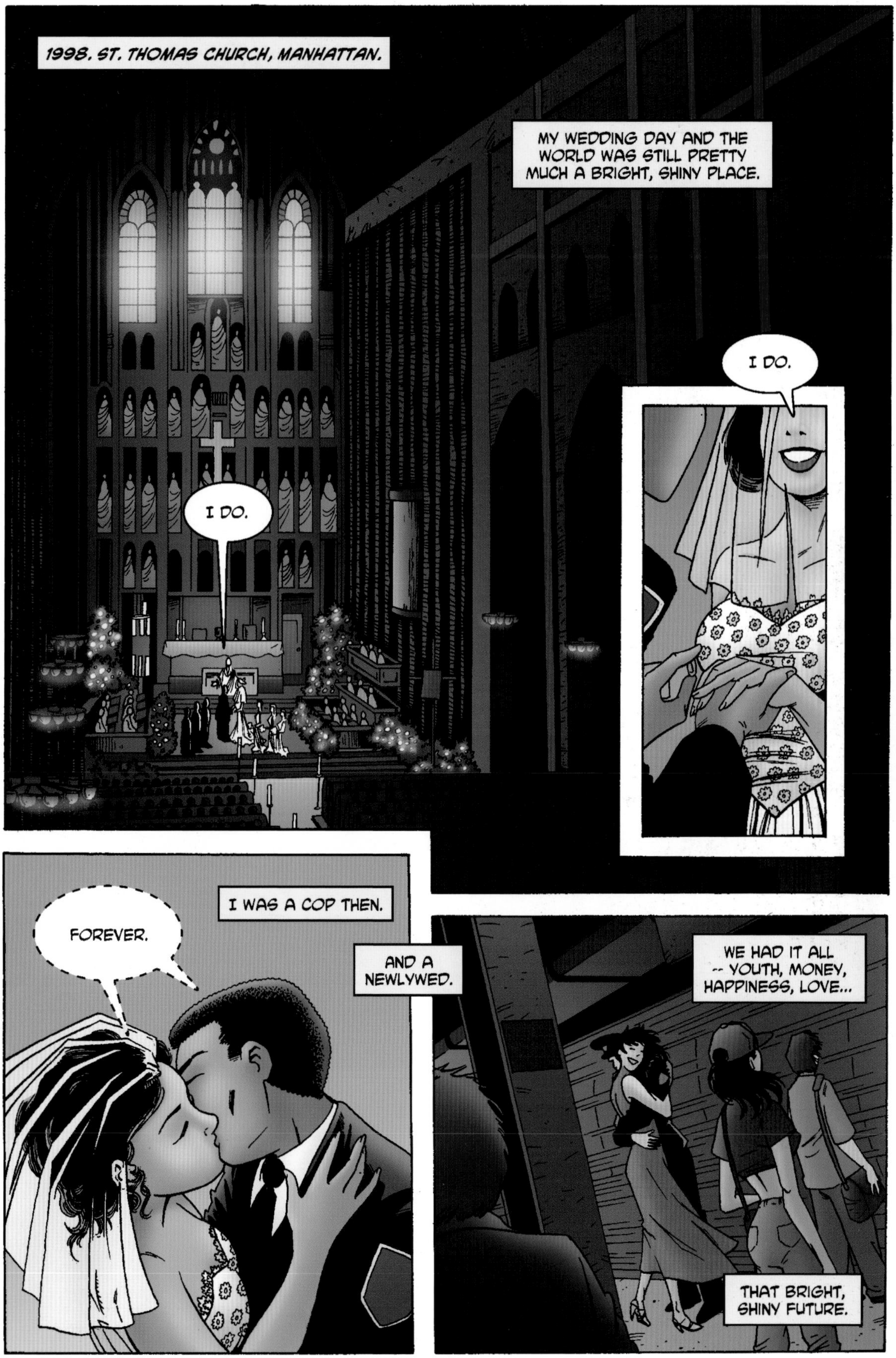
1998. ST. THOMAS CHURCH, MANHATTAN.
MY WEDDING DAY AND THE WORLD WAS STILL PRETTY MUCH A BRIGHT, SHINY PLACE.
I DO.
I DO.
I WAS A COP THEN.
AND A NEWLYWED.
FOREVER.
WE HAD IT ALL -- YOUTH, MONEY, HAPPINESS, LOVE...
THAT BRIGHT, SHINY FUTURE.

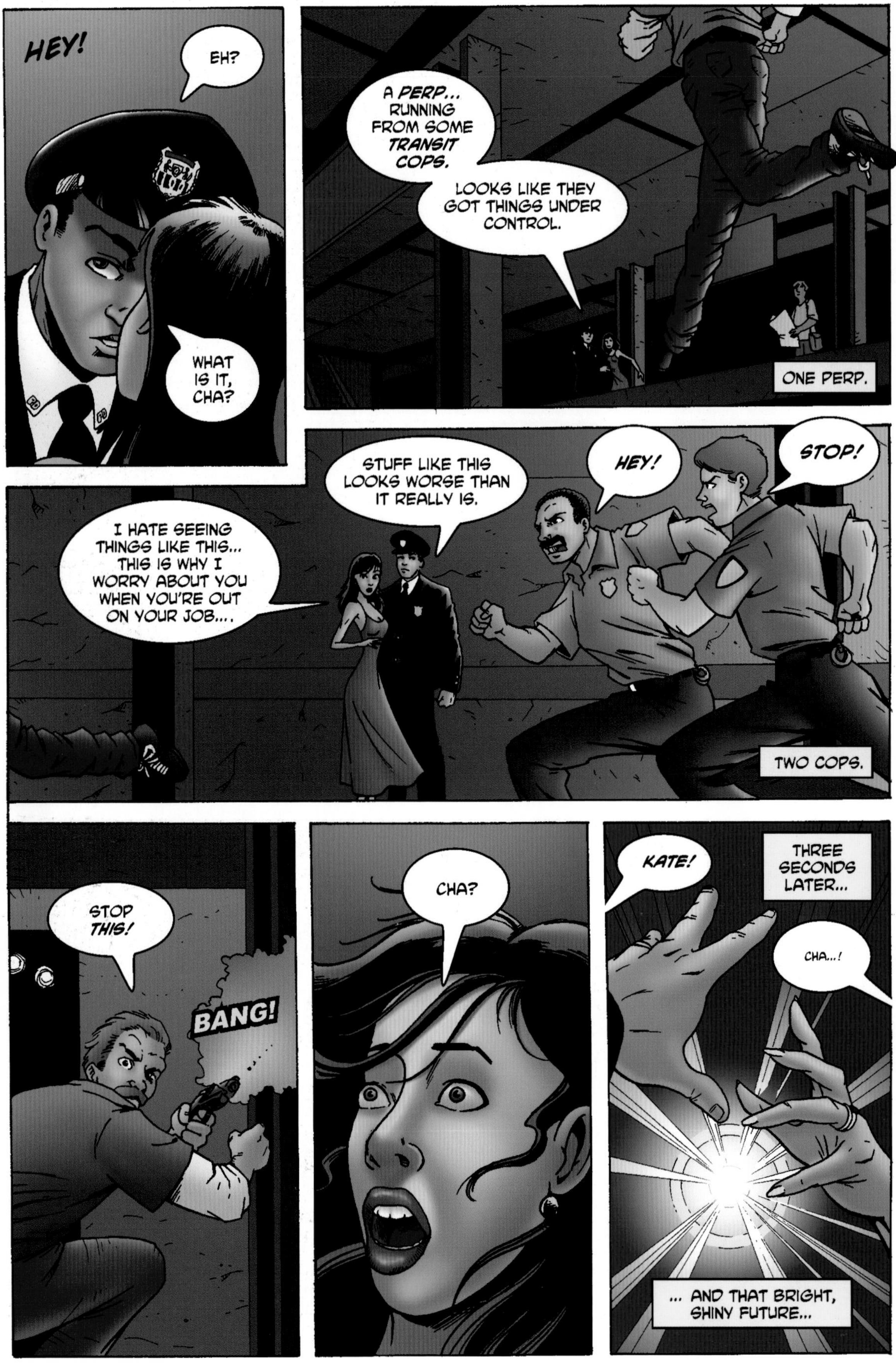
HEY!
EH?
WHAT IS IT, CHA?
A PERP... RUNNING FROM SOME TRANSIT COPS.
LOOKS LIKE THEY GOT THINGS UNDER CONTROL.
ONE PERP.
I HATE SEEING THINGS LIKE THIS... THIS IS WHY I WORRY ABOUT YOU WHEN YOU'RE OUT ON YOUR JOB....
STUFF LIKE THIS LOOKS WORSE THAN IT REALLY IS.
HEY!
STOP!
TWO COPS.
STOP THIS!
BANG!
CHA?
KATE!
THREE SECONDS LATER...
CHA...!
... AND THAT BRIGHT, SHINY FUTURE...

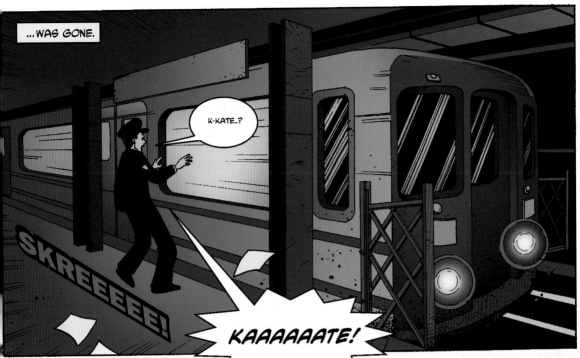

...WAS GONE.

K-KATE..?

SKREEEEE!

KAAAAAATE!

OMIGOD – THAT WOMAN...!

YEAH, FORGET THE PERP – CALL 911!

GONE.

I'M SO SORRY, CHA...

KATE...

GONE.

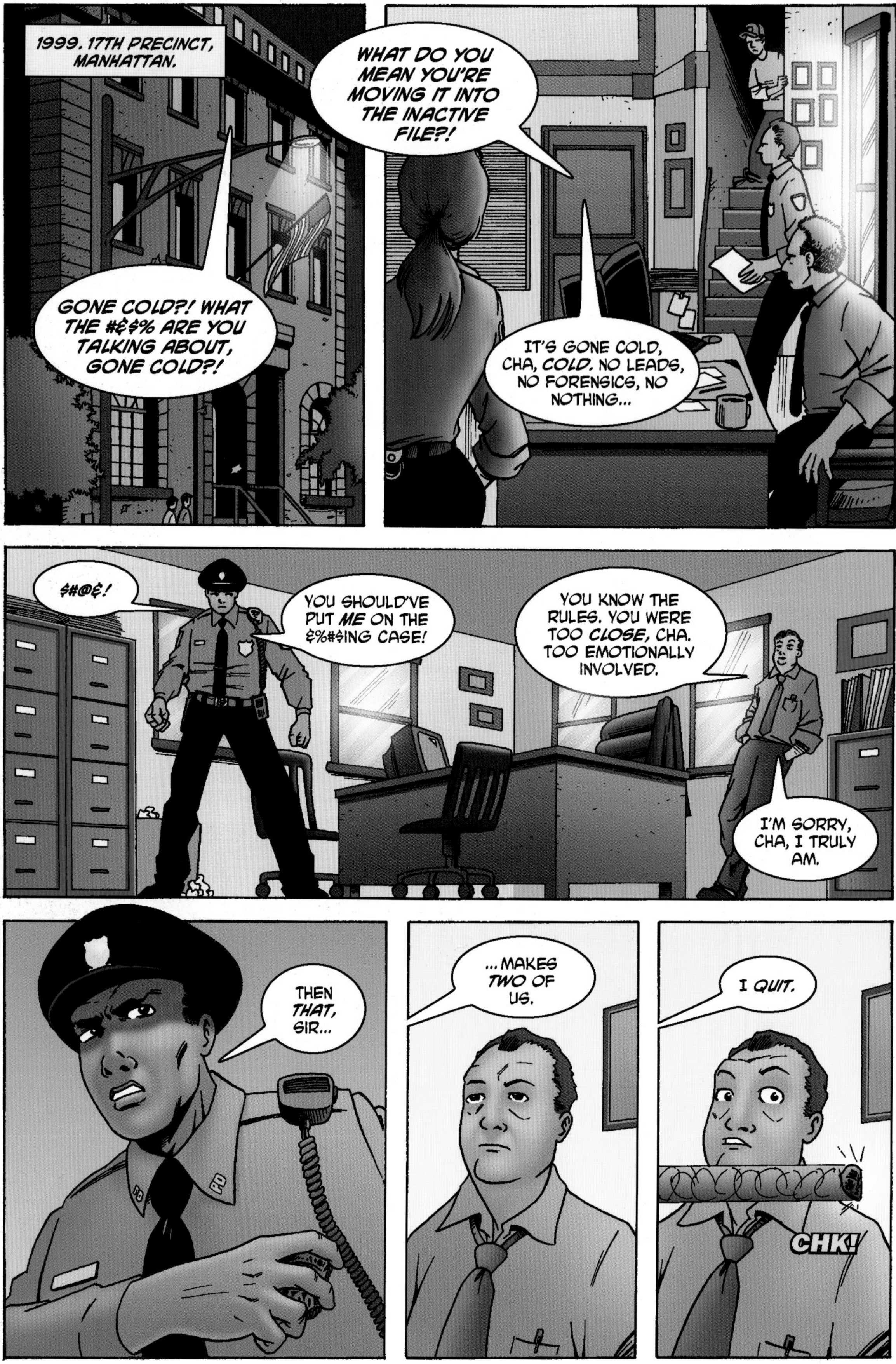
1999. 17TH PRECINCT, MANHATTAN.
WHAT DO YOU MEAN YOU'RE MOVING IT INTO THE INACTIVE FILE?!
IT'S GONE COLD, CHA, *COLD.* NO LEADS, NO FORENSICS, NO NOTHING...
GONE COLD?! WHAT THE #&$% ARE YOU TALKING ABOUT, GONE COLD?!
$#@&!
YOU SHOULD'VE PUT *ME* ON THE &%#$ING CASE!
YOU KNOW THE RULES. YOU WERE TOO *CLOSE,* CHA. TOO EMOTIONALLY INVOLVED.
I'M SORRY, CHA, I TRULY AM.
THEN *THAT,* SIR...
...MAKES *TWO* OF US.
I *QUIT.*
CHK!

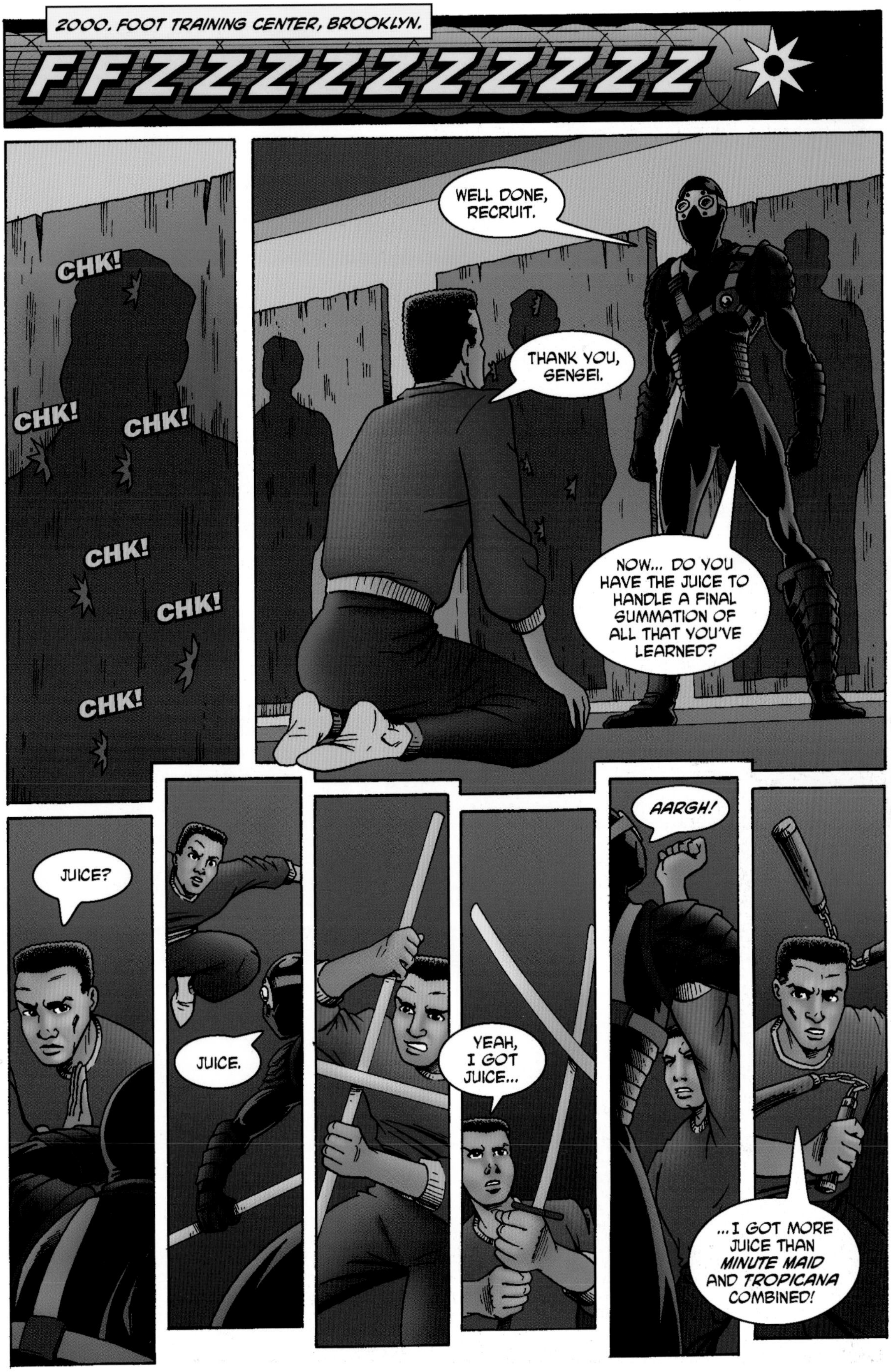
2000. FOOT TRAINING CENTER, BROOKLYN.
FFZZZZZZZZZZZ
CHK!
CHK!
CHK!
CHK!
CHK!
CHK!
WELL DONE, RECRUIT.
THANK YOU, SENSEI.
NOW... DO YOU HAVE THE JUICE TO HANDLE A FINAL SUMMATION OF ALL THAT YOU'VE LEARNED?
JUICE?
JUICE.
YEAH, I GOT JUICE...
AARGH!
...I GOT MORE JUICE THAN *MINUTE MAID* AND *TROPICANA* COMBINED!

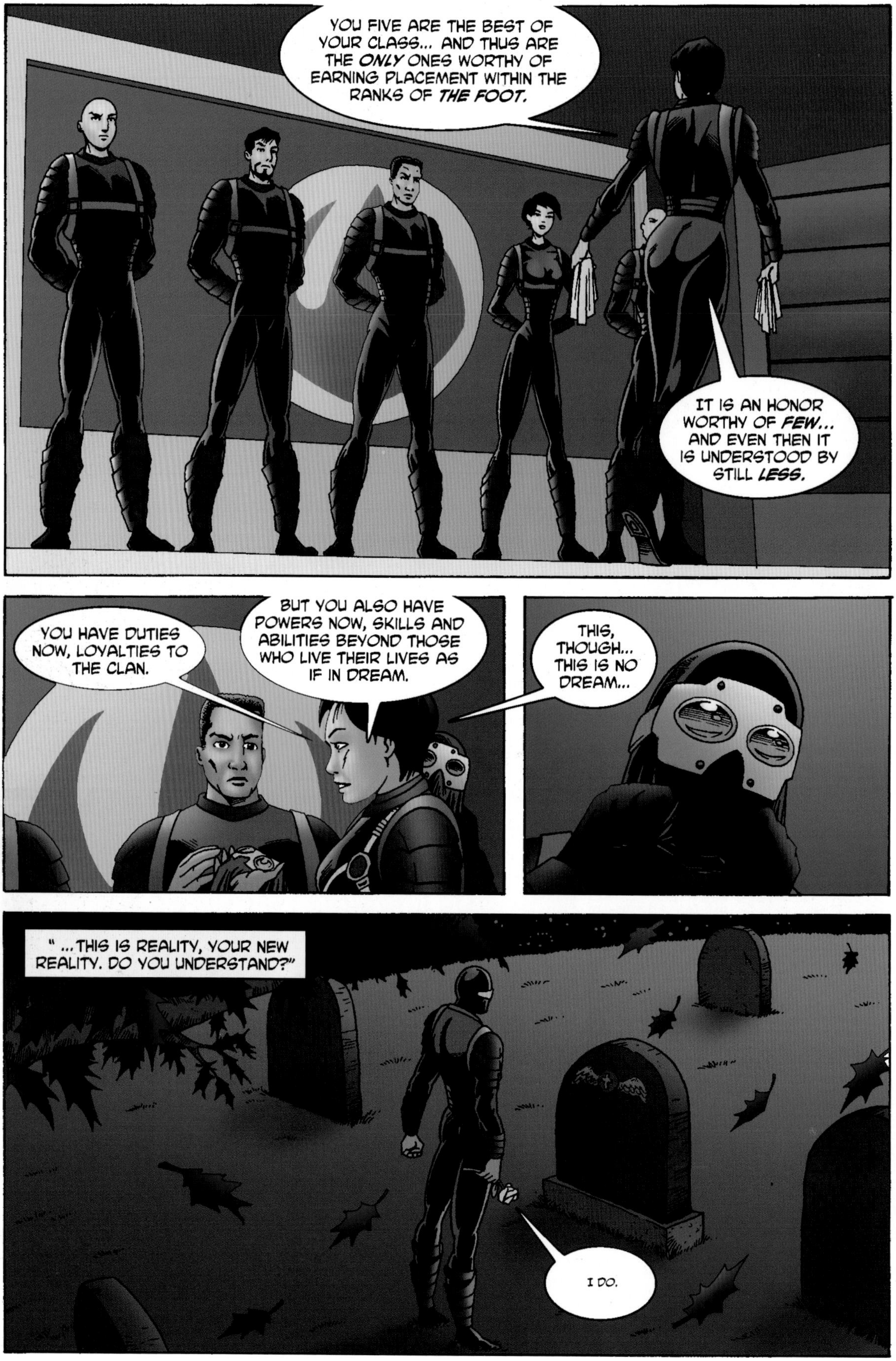
YOU FIVE ARE THE BEST OF YOUR CLASS... AND THUS ARE THE *ONLY* ONES WORTHY OF EARNING PLACEMENT WITHIN THE RANKS OF *THE FOOT.*
IT IS AN HONOR WORTHY OF *FEW...* AND EVEN THEN IT IS UNDERSTOOD BY STILL *LESS.*
YOU HAVE DUTIES NOW, LOYALTIES TO THE CLAN.
BUT YOU ALSO HAVE POWERS NOW, SKILLS AND ABILITIES BEYOND THOSE WHO LIVE THEIR LIVES AS IF IN DREAM.
THIS, THOUGH... THIS IS NO DREAM...
" ...THIS IS REALITY, YOUR NEW REALITY. DO YOU UNDERSTAND?"
I DO.

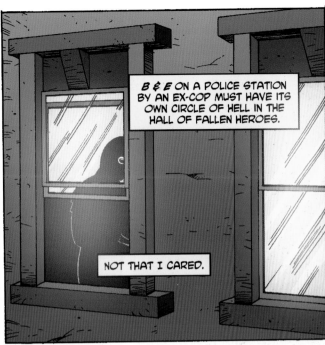

2001. 17TH PRECINCT, MANHATTAN.

B & E ON A POLICE STATION BY AN EX-COP MUST HAVE ITS OWN CIRCLE OF HELL IN THE HALL OF FALLEN HEROES.

NOT THAT I CARED.

FOR TWO YEARS I HAD BUT ONE GOAL, ONE THOUGHT:

KATE.

ocho, kate

TO FIND MY WIFE'S *KILLER*.

AND *TO KILL* IN RETURN.

MY, MY, MY, A FOOT SOLDIER BREAKING INTO A POLICE STATION.

I KNEW YOU GUYS WERE FULL OF IT WHEN YOU CLAIMED TO GO LEGIT.

WHA-? *YOU?!*

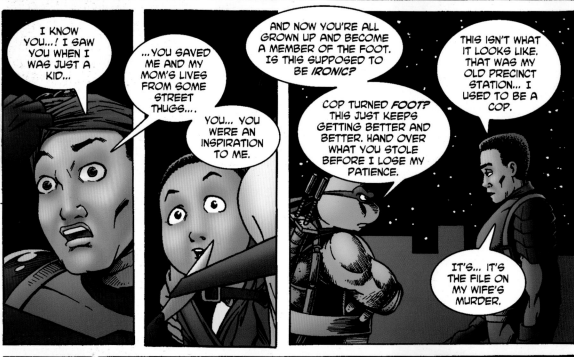

I KNOW YOU...! I SAW YOU WHEN I WAS JUST A KID...

...YOU SAVED ME AND MY MOM'S LIVES FROM SOME STREET THUGS....

YOU... YOU WERE AN INSPIRATION TO ME.

AND NOW YOU'RE ALL GROWN UP AND BECOME A MEMBER OF THE FOOT. IS THIS SUPPOSED TO BE *IRONIC?*

COP TURNED *FOOT?* THIS JUST KEEPS GETTING BETTER AND BETTER. HAND OVER WHAT YOU STOLE BEFORE I LOSE MY PATIENCE.

THIS ISN'T WHAT IT LOOKS LIKE. THAT WAS MY OLD PRECINCT STATION... I USED TO BE A COP.

IT'S... IT'S THE FILE ON MY WIFE'S MURDER.

WHAT..?

THE CASE WAS CLOSED... BUT STILL UNSOLVED. GONE COLD WE CALL THEM. I WAS GOING TO REOPEN IT... ON MY OWN. HER KILLER'S STILL OUT THERE SOMEWHERE...

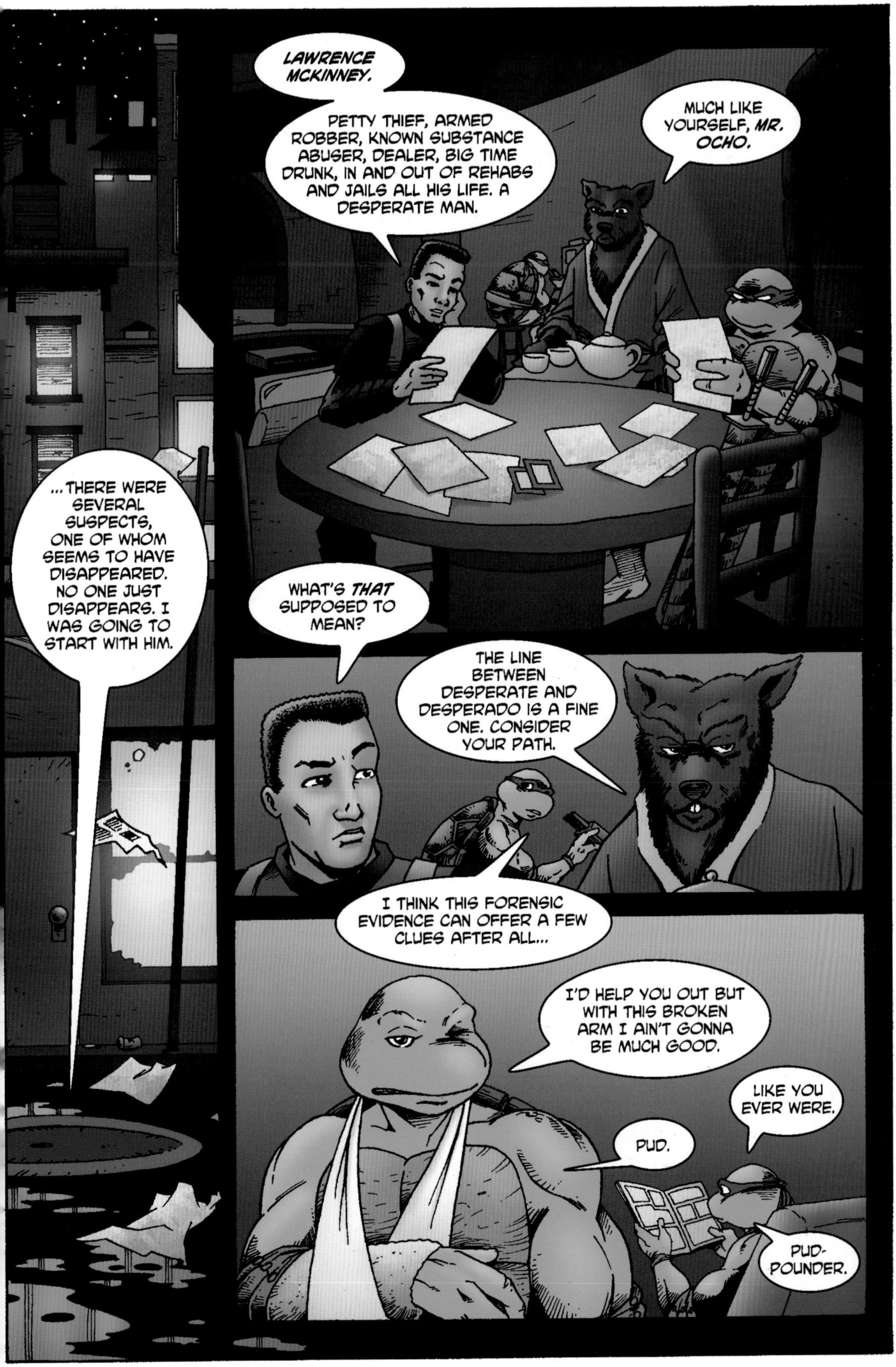
LAWRENCE MCKINNEY.
PETTY THIEF, ARMED ROBBER, KNOWN SUBSTANCE ABUSER, DEALER, BIG TIME DRUNK, IN AND OUT OF REHABS AND JAILS ALL HIS LIFE. A DESPERATE MAN.
MUCH LIKE YOURSELF, MR. OCHO.
...THERE WERE SEVERAL SUSPECTS, ONE OF WHOM SEEMS TO HAVE DISAPPEARED. NO ONE JUST DISAPPEARS. I WAS GOING TO START WITH HIM.
WHAT'S THAT SUPPOSED TO MEAN?
THE LINE BETWEEN DESPERATE AND DESPERADO IS A FINE ONE. CONSIDER YOUR PATH.
I THINK THIS FORENSIC EVIDENCE CAN OFFER A FEW CLUES AFTER ALL...
I'D HELP YOU OUT BUT WITH THIS BROKEN ARM I AIN'T GONNA BE MUCH GOOD.
LIKE YOU EVER WERE.
PUD.
PUD-POUNDER.

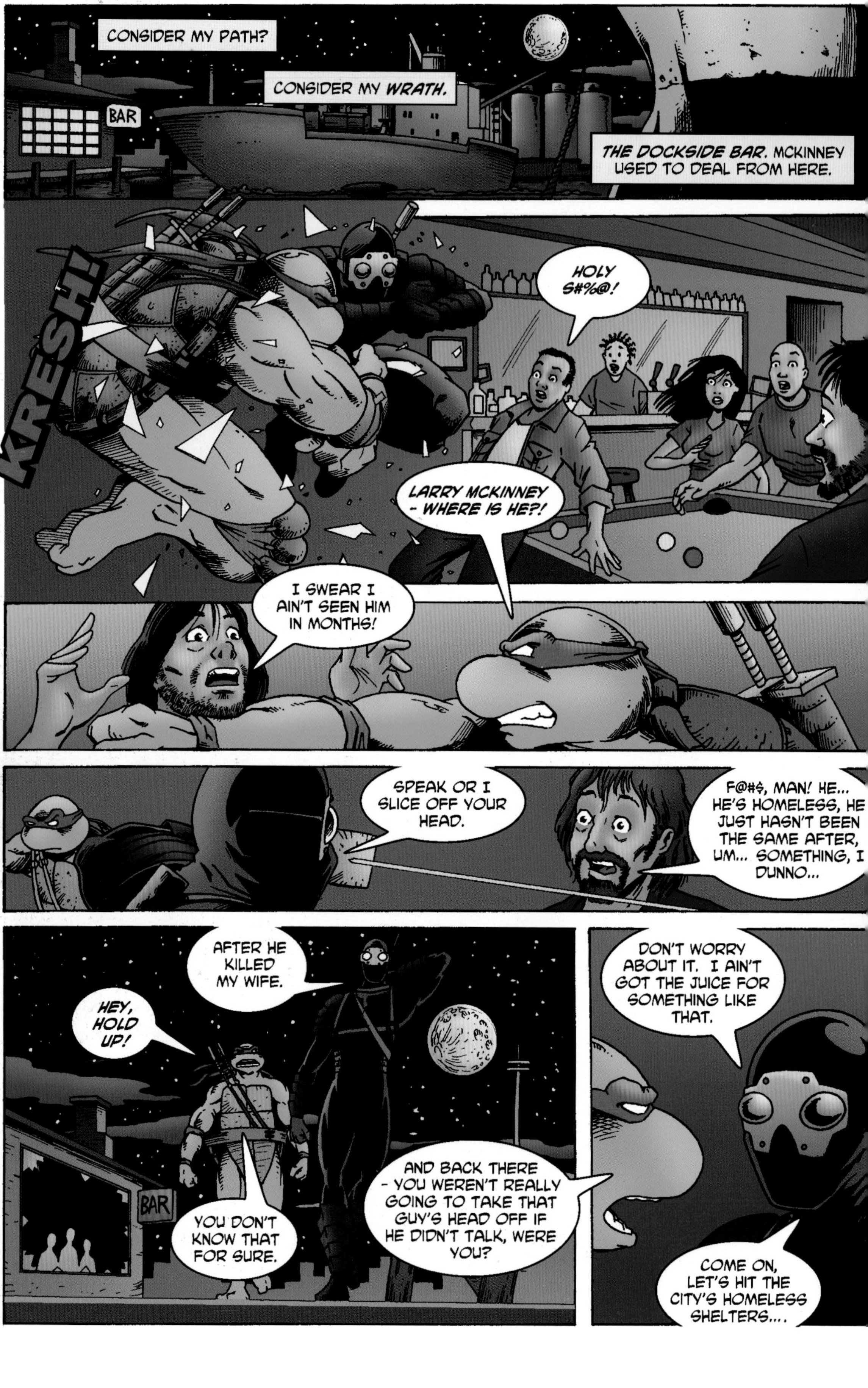
CONSIDER MY PATH?
CONSIDER MY WRATH.
BAR
THE DOCKSIDE BAR. MCKINNEY USED TO DEAL FROM HERE.
KRESH!
HOLY S#%@!
LARRY MCKINNEY - WHERE IS HE?!
I SWEAR I AIN'T SEEN HIM IN MONTHS!
SPEAK OR I SLICE OFF YOUR HEAD.
F@#$, MAN! HE... HE'S HOMELESS, HE JUST HASN'T BEEN THE SAME AFTER, UM... SOMETHING, I DUNNO...
AFTER HE KILLED MY WIFE.
HEY, HOLD UP!
BAR
YOU DON'T KNOW THAT FOR SURE.
AND BACK THERE - YOU WEREN'T REALLY GOING TO TAKE THAT GUY'S HEAD OFF IF HE DIDN'T TALK, WERE YOU?
DON'T WORRY ABOUT IT. I AIN'T GOT THE JUICE FOR SOMETHING LIKE THAT.
COME ON, LET'S HIT THE CITY'S HOMELESS SHELTERS....

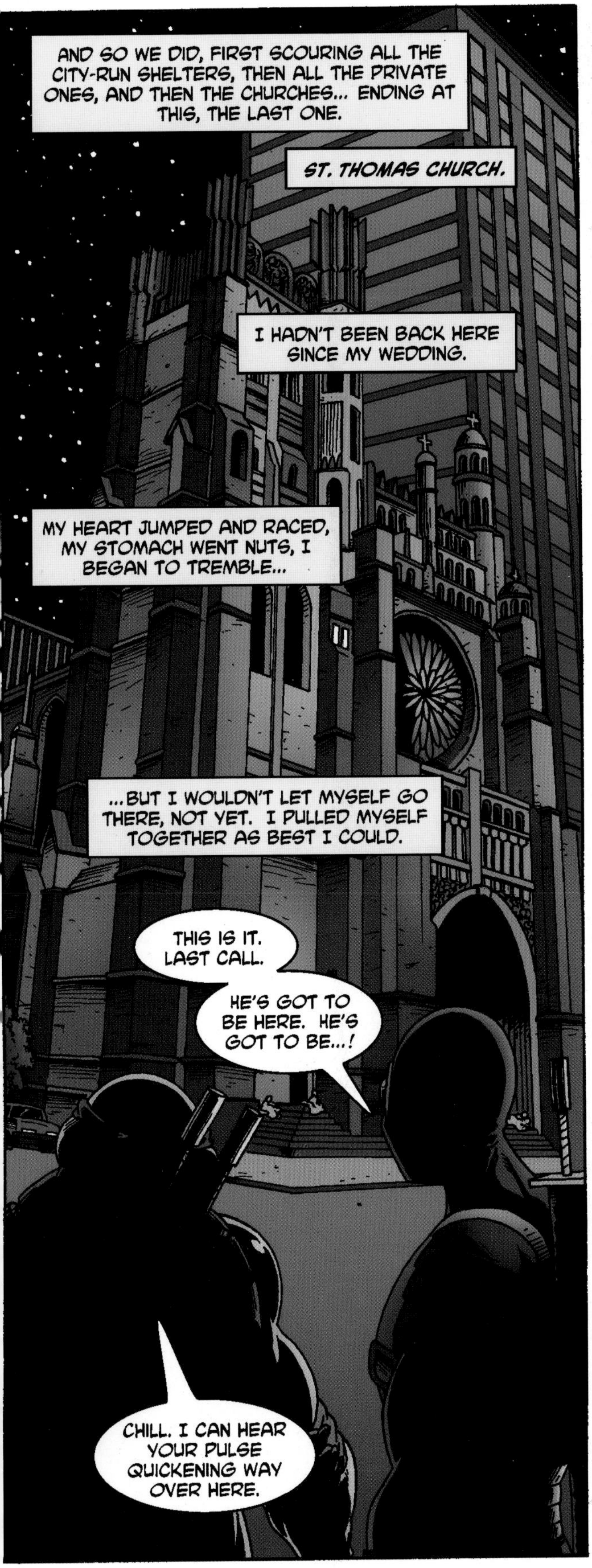
AND SO WE DID, FIRST SCOURING ALL THE CITY-RUN SHELTERS, THEN ALL THE PRIVATE ONES, AND THEN THE CHURCHES... ENDING AT THIS, THE LAST ONE.
ST. THOMAS CHURCH.
I HADN'T BEEN BACK HERE SINCE MY WEDDING.
MY HEART JUMPED AND RACED, MY STOMACH WENT NUTS, I BEGAN TO TREMBLE...
...BUT I WOULDN'T LET MYSELF GO THERE, NOT YET. I PULLED MYSELF TOGETHER AS BEST I COULD.
THIS IS IT. LAST CALL.
HE'S GOT TO BE HERE. HE'S GOT TO BE...!
CHILL. I CAN HEAR YOUR PULSE QUICKENING WAY OVER HERE.

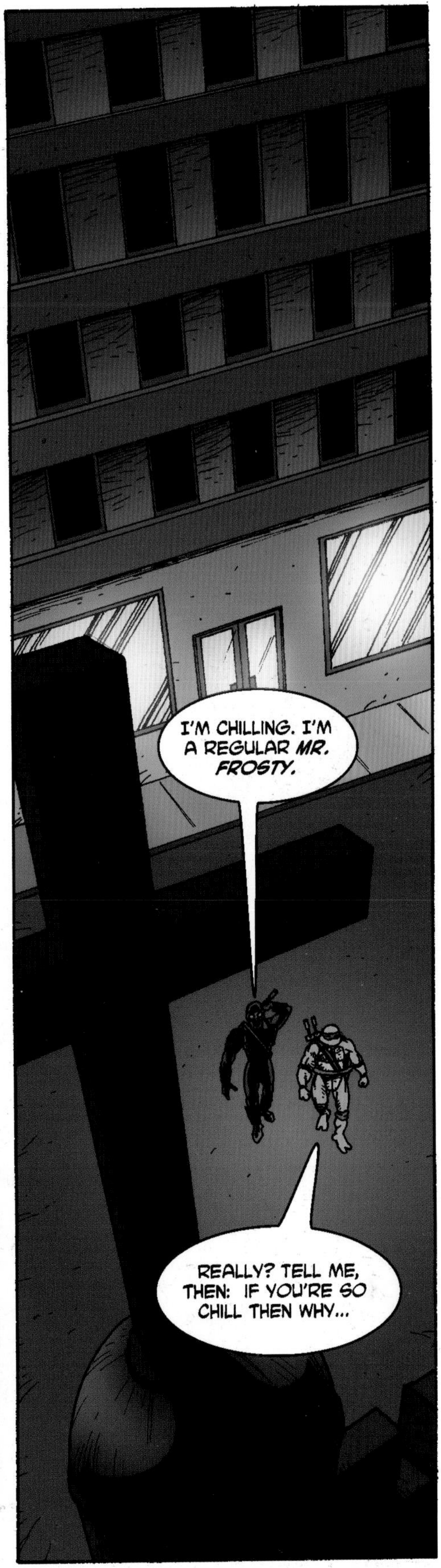
I'M CHILLING. I'M A REGULAR MR. FROSTY.
REALLY? TELL ME, THEN: IF YOU'RE SO CHILL THEN WHY...

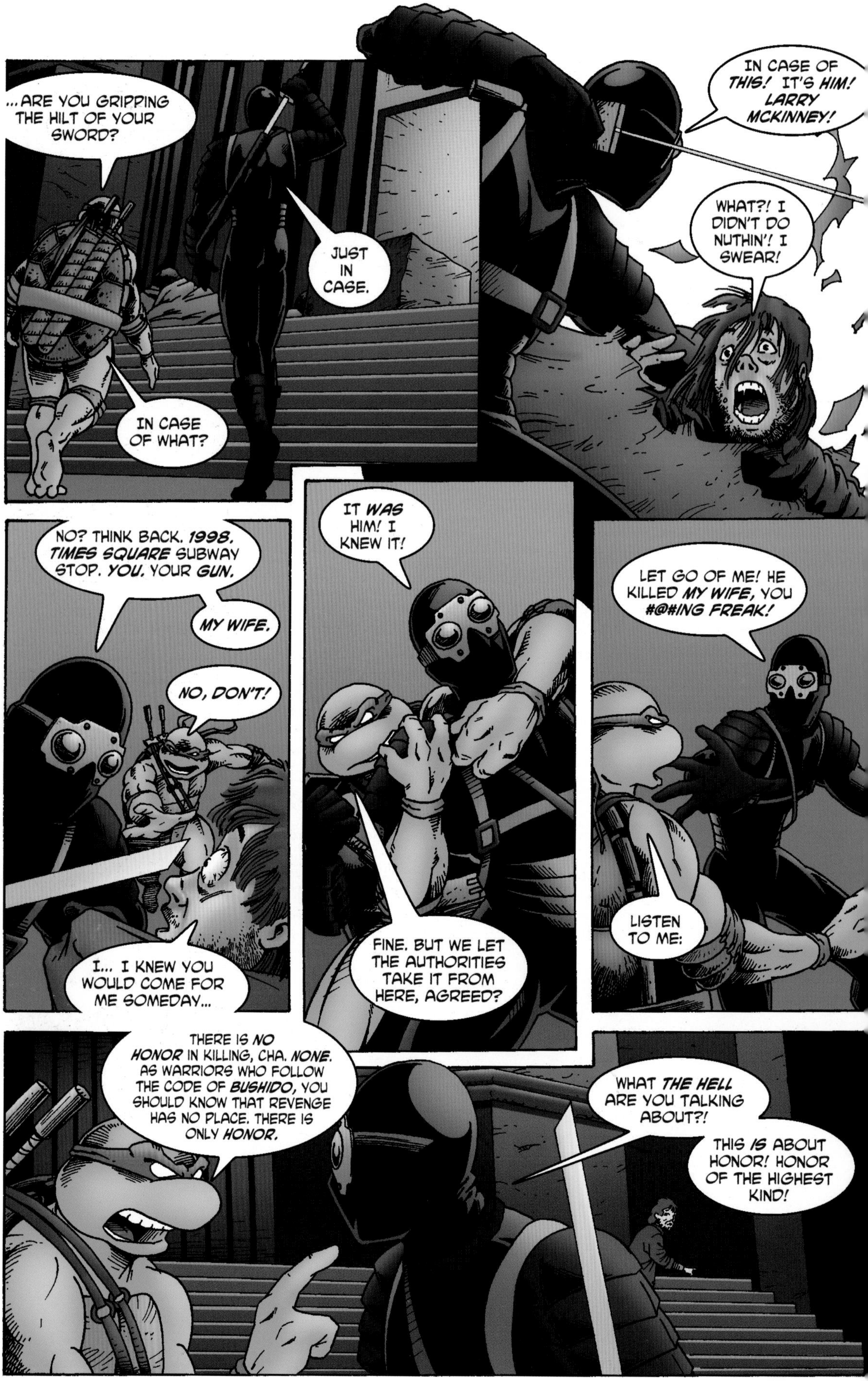
...ARE YOU GRIPPING THE HILT OF YOUR SWORD?
JUST IN CASE.
IN CASE OF WHAT?
IN CASE OF THIS! IT'S HIM! LARRY MCKINNEY!
WHAT?! I DIDN'T DO NUTHIN'! I SWEAR!
NO? THINK BACK. 1998. TIMES SQUARE SUBWAY STOP. YOU. YOUR GUN.
MY WIFE.
NO, DON'T!
I... I KNEW YOU WOULD COME FOR ME SOMEDAY...
IT WAS HIM! I KNEW IT!
FINE. BUT WE LET THE AUTHORITIES TAKE IT FROM HERE, AGREED?
LET GO OF ME! HE KILLED MY WIFE, YOU #@#ING FREAK!
LISTEN TO ME:
THERE IS NO HONOR IN KILLING, CHA. NONE. AS WARRIORS WHO FOLLOW THE CODE OF BUSHIDO, YOU SHOULD KNOW THAT REVENGE HAS NO PLACE. THERE IS ONLY HONOR.
WHAT THE HELL ARE YOU TALKING ABOUT?!
THIS IS ABOUT HONOR! HONOR OF THE HIGHEST KIND!

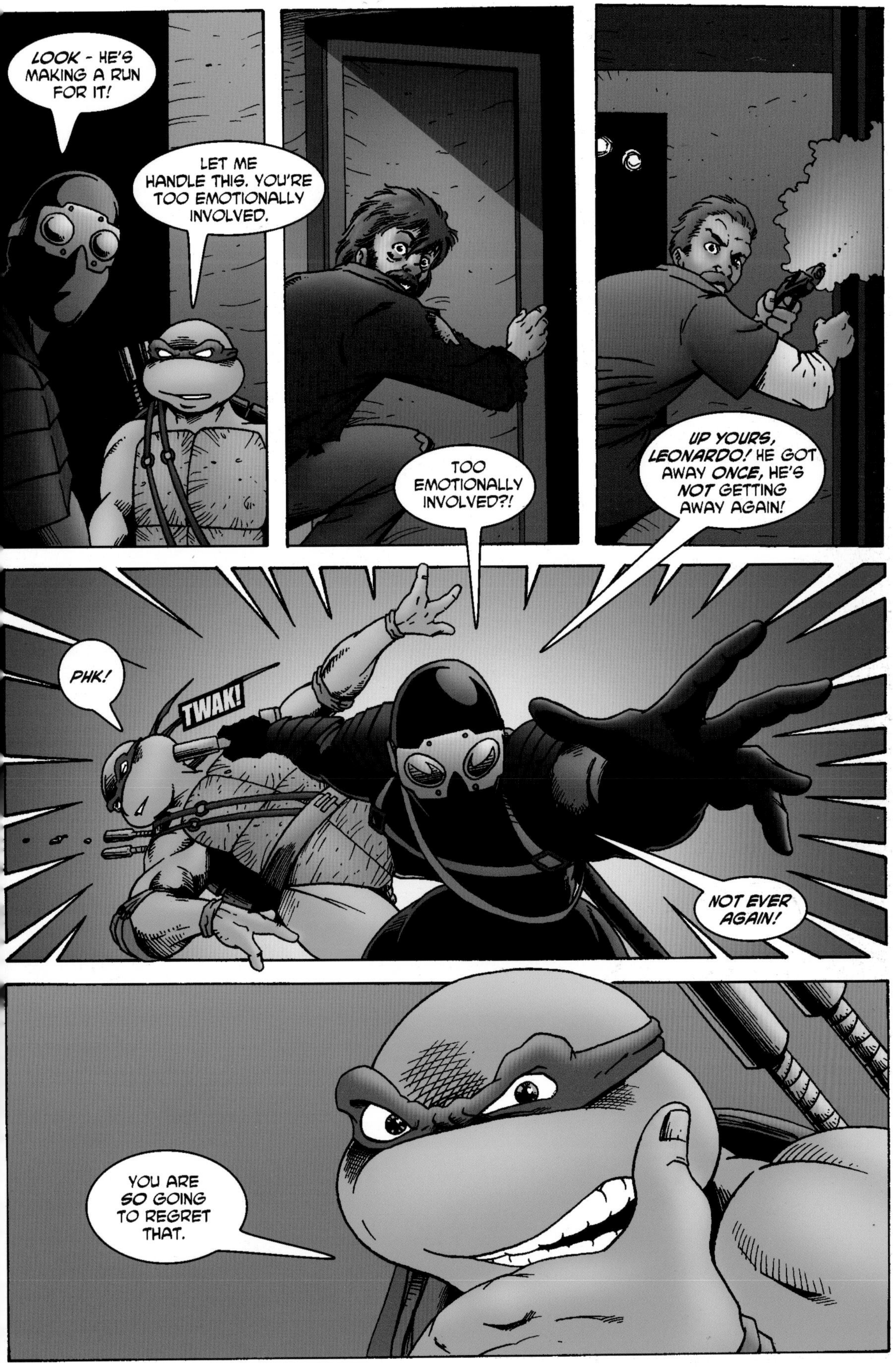
LOOK - HE'S MAKING A RUN FOR IT!
LET ME HANDLE THIS. YOU'RE TOO EMOTIONALLY INVOLVED.
TOO EMOTIONALLY INVOLVED?!
UP YOURS, LEONARDO! HE GOT AWAY ONCE, HE'S NOT GETTING AWAY AGAIN!
PHK!
TWAK!
NOT EVER AGAIN!
YOU ARE SO GOING TO REGRET THAT.

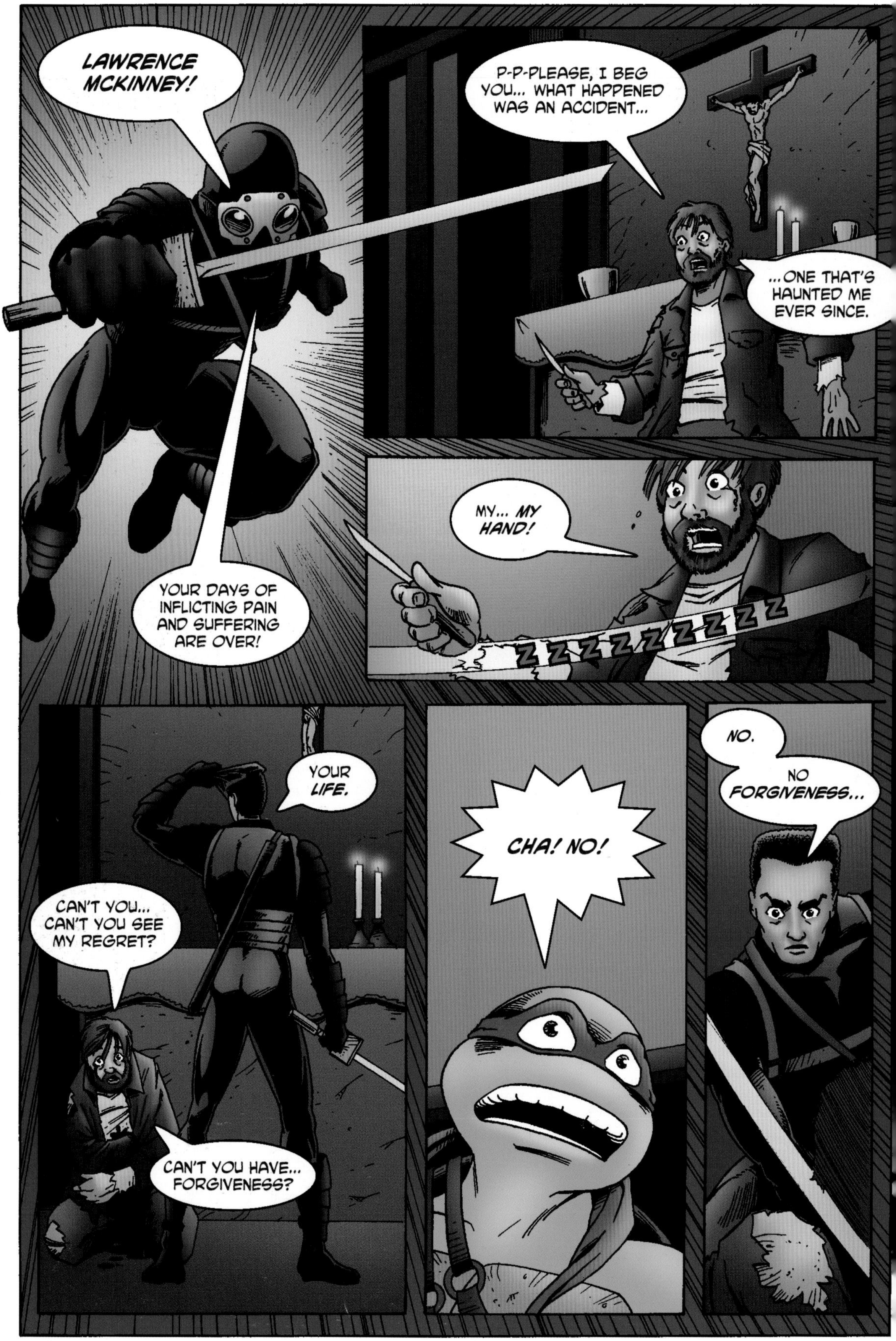
LAWRENCE MCKINNEY!
P-P-PLEASE, I BEG YOU... WHAT HAPPENED WAS AN ACCIDENT...
...ONE THAT'S HAUNTED ME EVER SINCE.
YOUR DAYS OF INFLICTING PAIN AND SUFFERING ARE OVER!
MY... MY HAND!
ZZZZZZZZZZZ
YOUR LIFE.
CAN'T YOU... CAN'T YOU SEE MY REGRET?
CAN'T YOU HAVE... FORGIVENESS?
CHA! NO!
NO.
NO FORGIVENESS...

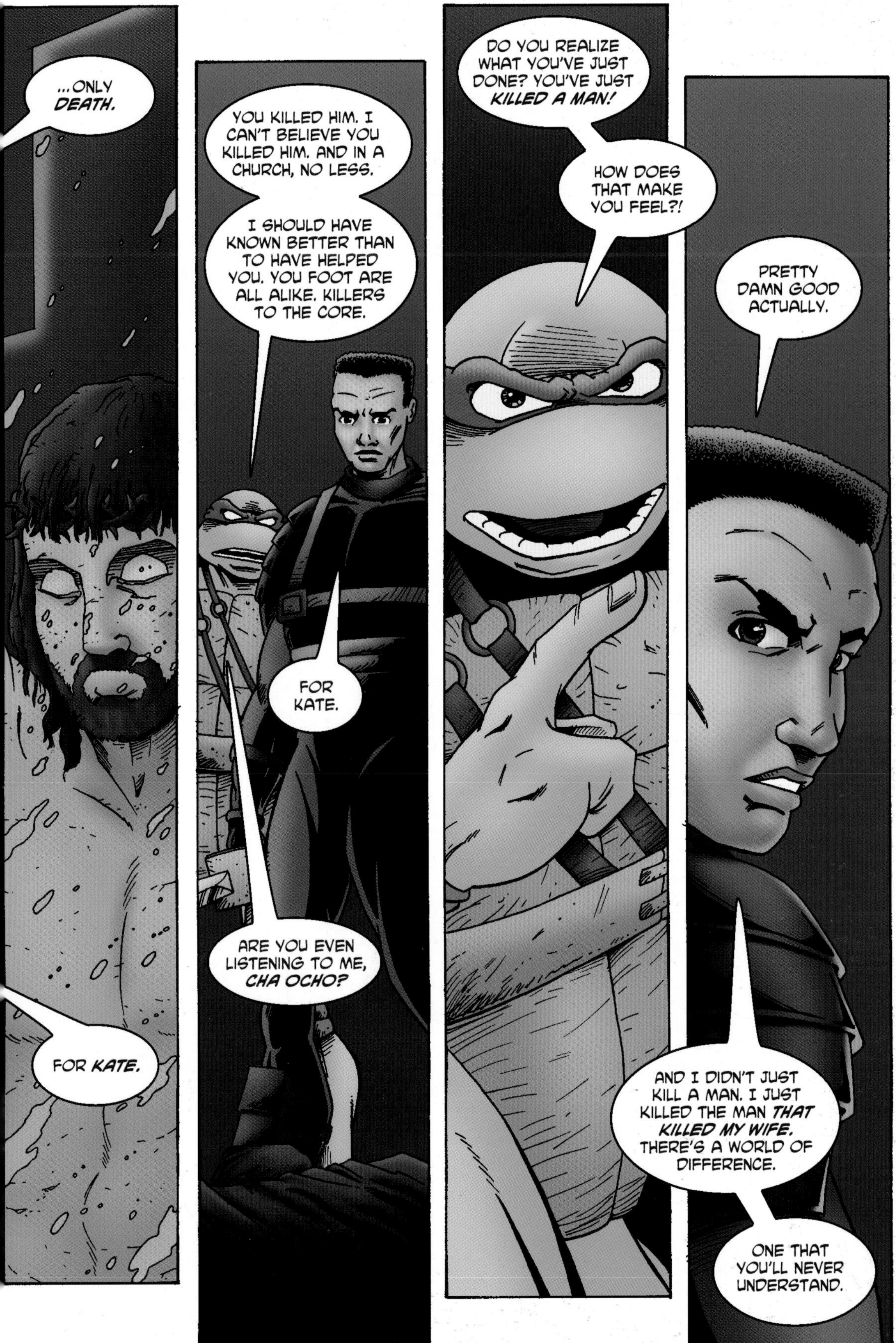
...ONLY *DEATH.*
FOR *KATE.*
YOU KILLED HIM. I CAN'T BELIEVE YOU KILLED HIM. AND IN A CHURCH, NO LESS.
I SHOULD HAVE KNOWN BETTER THAN TO HAVE HELPED YOU. YOU FOOT ARE ALL ALIKE. KILLERS TO THE CORE.
FOR KATE.
ARE YOU EVEN LISTENING TO ME, *CHA OCHO?*
DO YOU REALIZE WHAT YOU'VE JUST DONE? YOU'VE JUST *KILLED A MAN!*
HOW DOES THAT MAKE YOU FEEL?!
PRETTY DAMN GOOD ACTUALLY.
AND I DIDN'T JUST KILL A MAN. I JUST KILLED THE MAN *THAT KILLED MY WIFE.* THERE'S A WORLD OF DIFFERENCE.
ONE THAT YOU'LL NEVER UNDERSTAND.

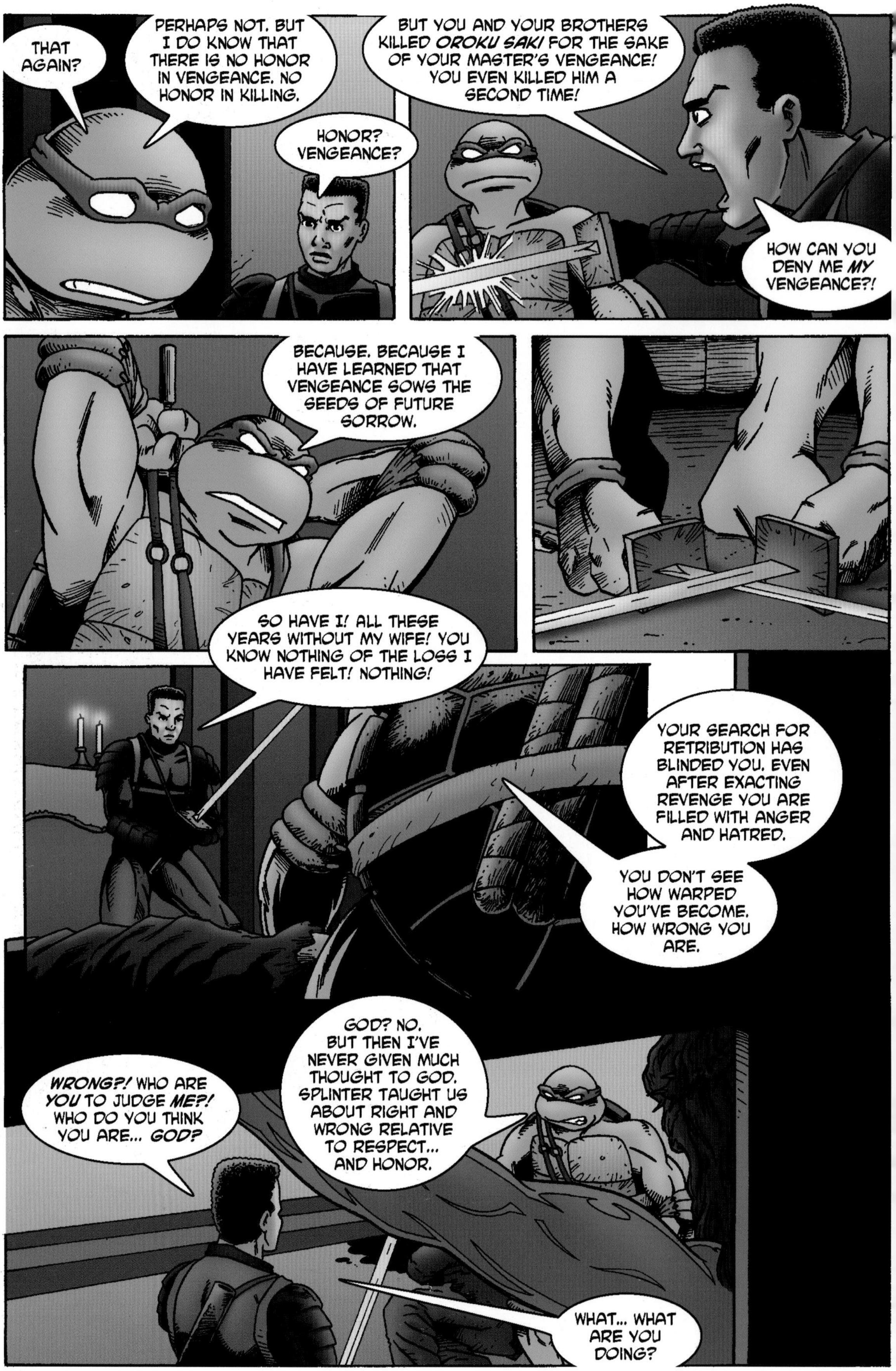
THAT AGAIN?
PERHAPS NOT. BUT I DO KNOW THAT THERE IS NO HONOR IN VENGEANCE. NO HONOR IN KILLING.
HONOR? VENGEANCE?
BUT YOU AND YOUR BROTHERS KILLED OROKU SAKI FOR THE SAKE OF YOUR MASTER'S VENGEANCE! YOU EVEN KILLED HIM A SECOND TIME!
HOW CAN YOU DENY ME MY VENGEANCE?!
BECAUSE. BECAUSE I HAVE LEARNED THAT VENGEANCE SOWS THE SEEDS OF FUTURE SORROW.
SO HAVE I! ALL THESE YEARS WITHOUT MY WIFE! YOU KNOW NOTHING OF THE LOSS I HAVE FELT! NOTHING!
YOUR SEARCH FOR RETRIBUTION HAS BLINDED YOU. EVEN AFTER EXACTING REVENGE YOU ARE FILLED WITH ANGER AND HATRED.
YOU DON'T SEE HOW WARPED YOU'VE BECOME. HOW WRONG YOU ARE.
WRONG?! WHO ARE YOU TO JUDGE ME?! WHO DO YOU THINK YOU ARE... GOD?
GOD? NO. BUT THEN I'VE NEVER GIVEN MUCH THOUGHT TO GOD. SPLINTER TAUGHT US ABOUT RIGHT AND WRONG RELATIVE TO RESPECT... AND HONOR.
WHAT... WHAT ARE YOU DOING?

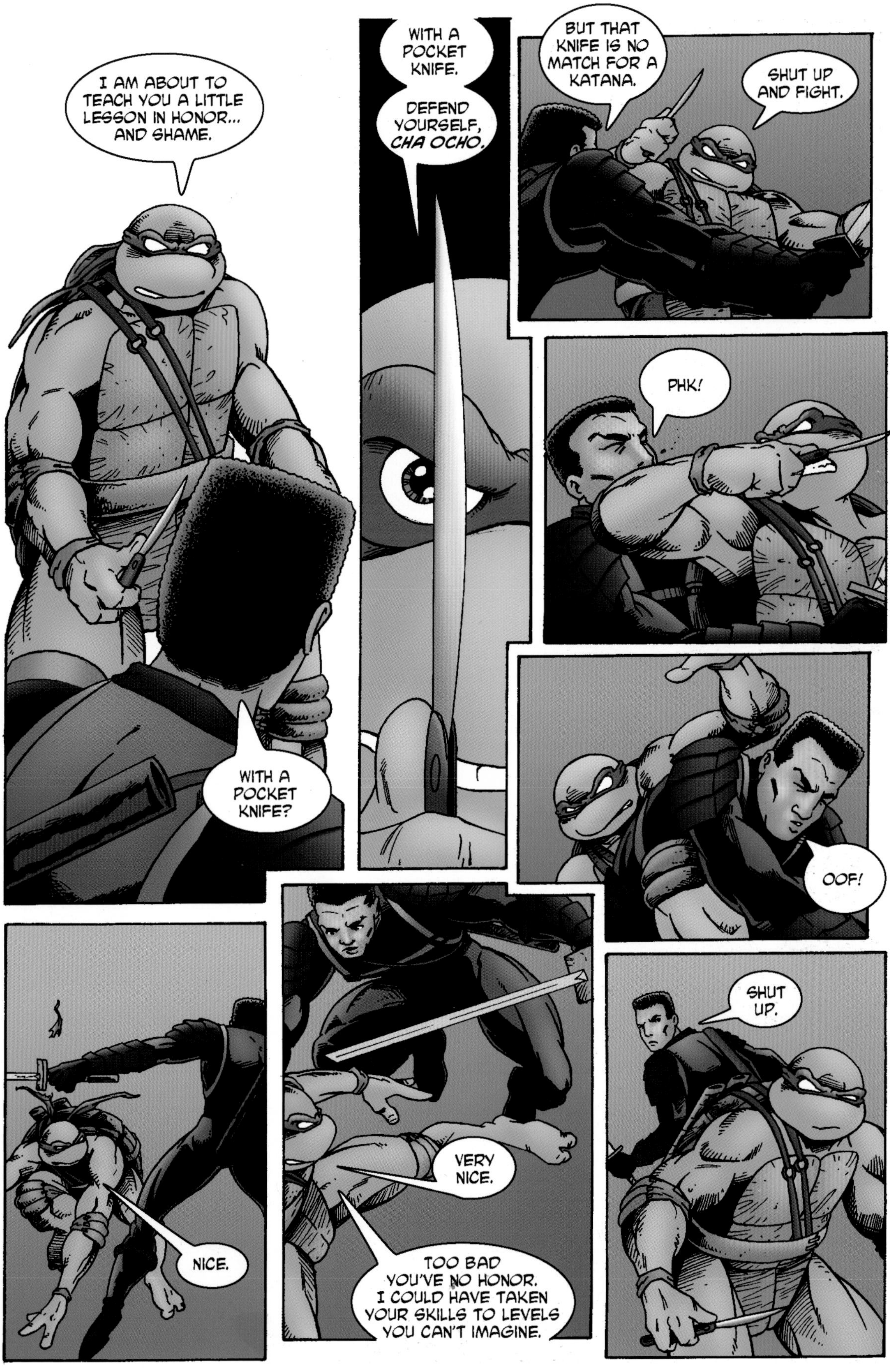
I AM ABOUT TO TEACH YOU A LITTLE LESSON IN HONOR... AND SHAME.
WITH A POCKET KNIFE?
WITH A POCKET KNIFE.
DEFEND YOURSELF, *CHA OCHO.*
BUT THAT KNIFE IS NO MATCH FOR A KATANA.
SHUT UP AND FIGHT.
PHK!
OOF!
NICE.
VERY NICE.
TOO BAD YOU'VE NO HONOR. I COULD HAVE TAKEN YOUR SKILLS TO LEVELS YOU CAN'T IMAGINE.
SHUT UP.

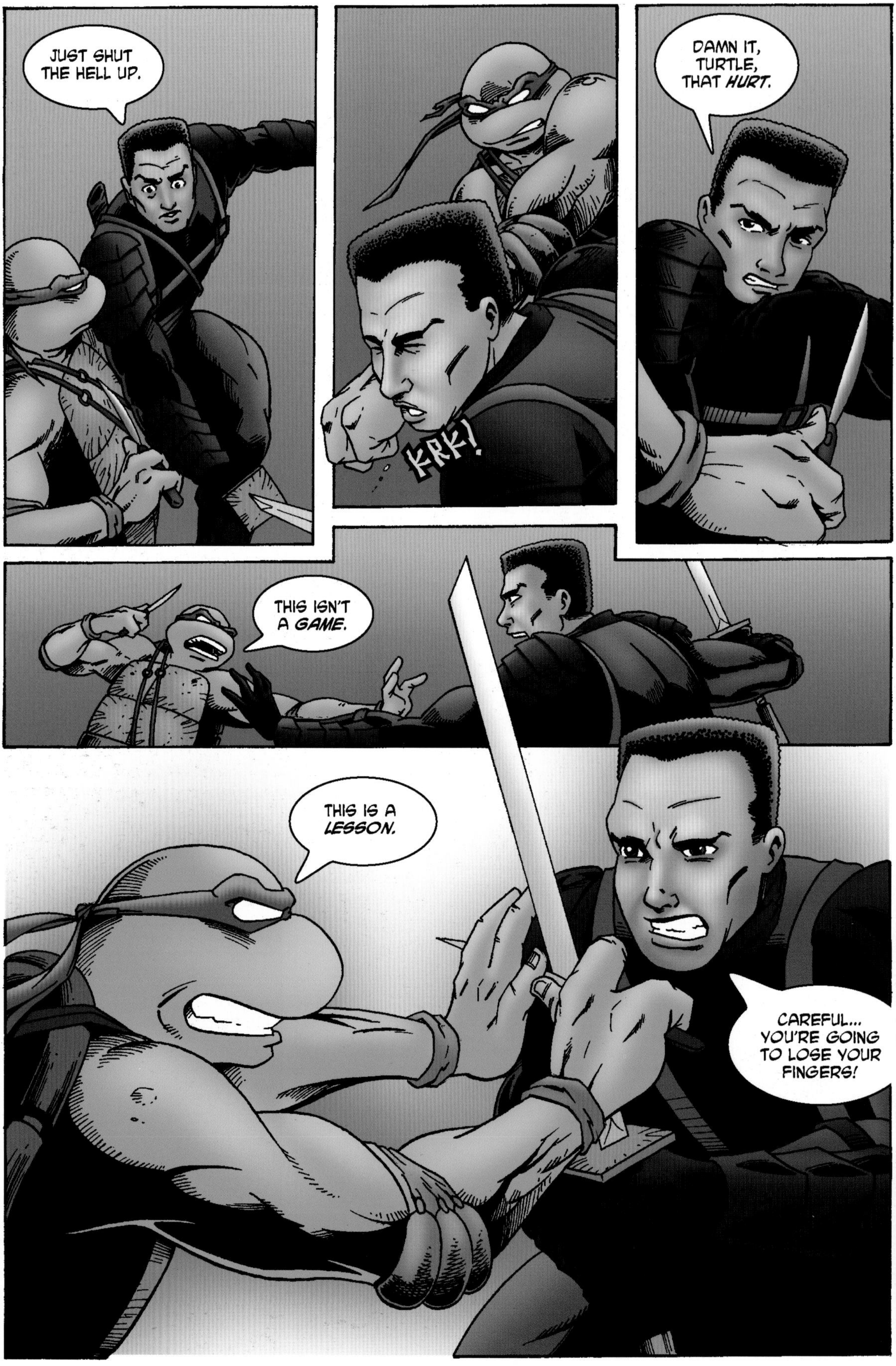
JUST SHUT THE HELL UP.
KRK!
DAMN IT, TURTLE, THAT *HURT*.
THIS ISN'T A *GAME*.
THIS IS A *LESSON*.
CAREFUL... YOU'RE GOING TO LOSE YOUR FINGERS!

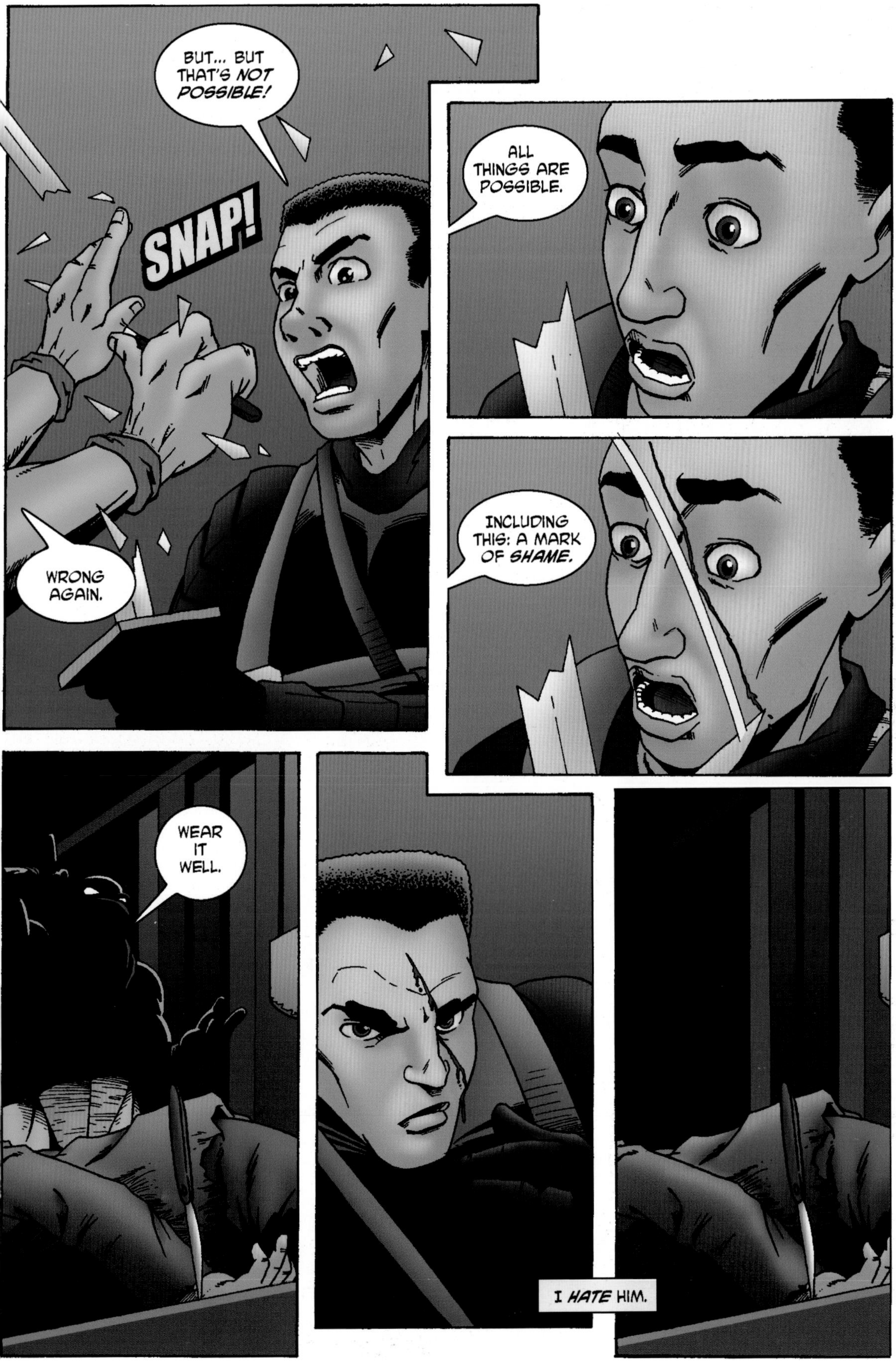
BUT... BUT THAT'S *NOT POSSIBLE!*
SNAP!
WRONG AGAIN.
ALL THINGS ARE POSSIBLE.
INCLUDING THIS: A MARK OF *SHAME.*
WEAR IT WELL.
I *HATE* HIM.

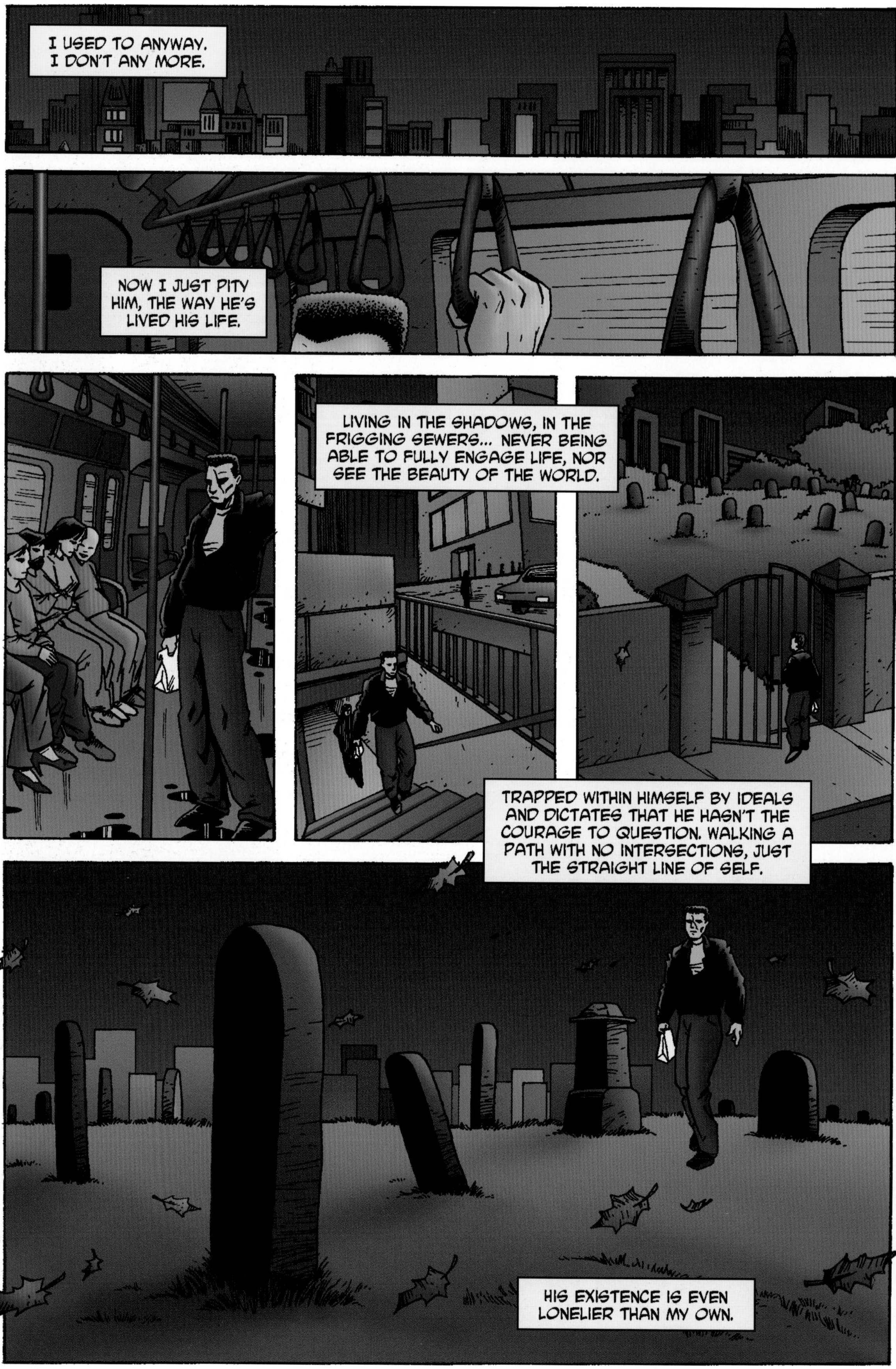
I USED TO ANYWAY.
I DON'T ANY MORE.
NOW I JUST PITY HIM, THE WAY HE'S LIVED HIS LIFE.
LIVING IN THE SHADOWS, IN THE FRIGGING SEWERS... NEVER BEING ABLE TO FULLY ENGAGE LIFE, NOR SEE THE BEAUTY OF THE WORLD.
TRAPPED WITHIN HIMSELF BY IDEALS AND DICTATES THAT HE HASN'T THE COURAGE TO QUESTION. WALKING A PATH WITH NO INTERSECTIONS, JUST THE STRAIGHT LINE OF SELF.
HIS EXISTENCE IS EVEN LONELIER THAN MY OWN.

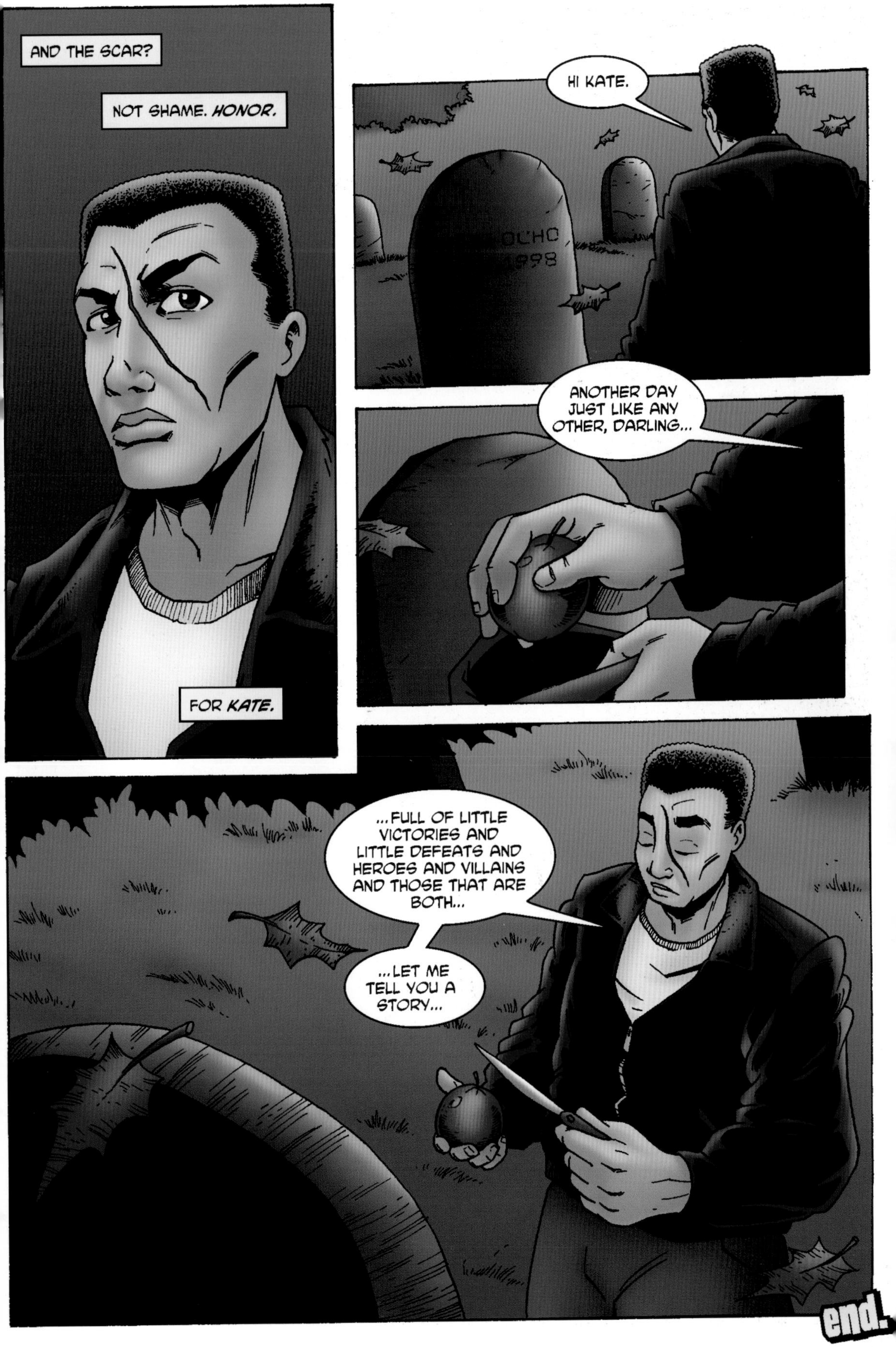
AND THE SCAR?
NOT SHAME. HONOR.
FOR KATE.
HI KATE.
OLHO
1998
ANOTHER DAY JUST LIKE ANY OTHER, DARLING...
...FULL OF LITTLE VICTORIES AND LITTLE DEFEATS AND HEROES AND VILLAINS AND THOSE THAT ARE BOTH...
...LET ME TELL YOU A STORY...
end.

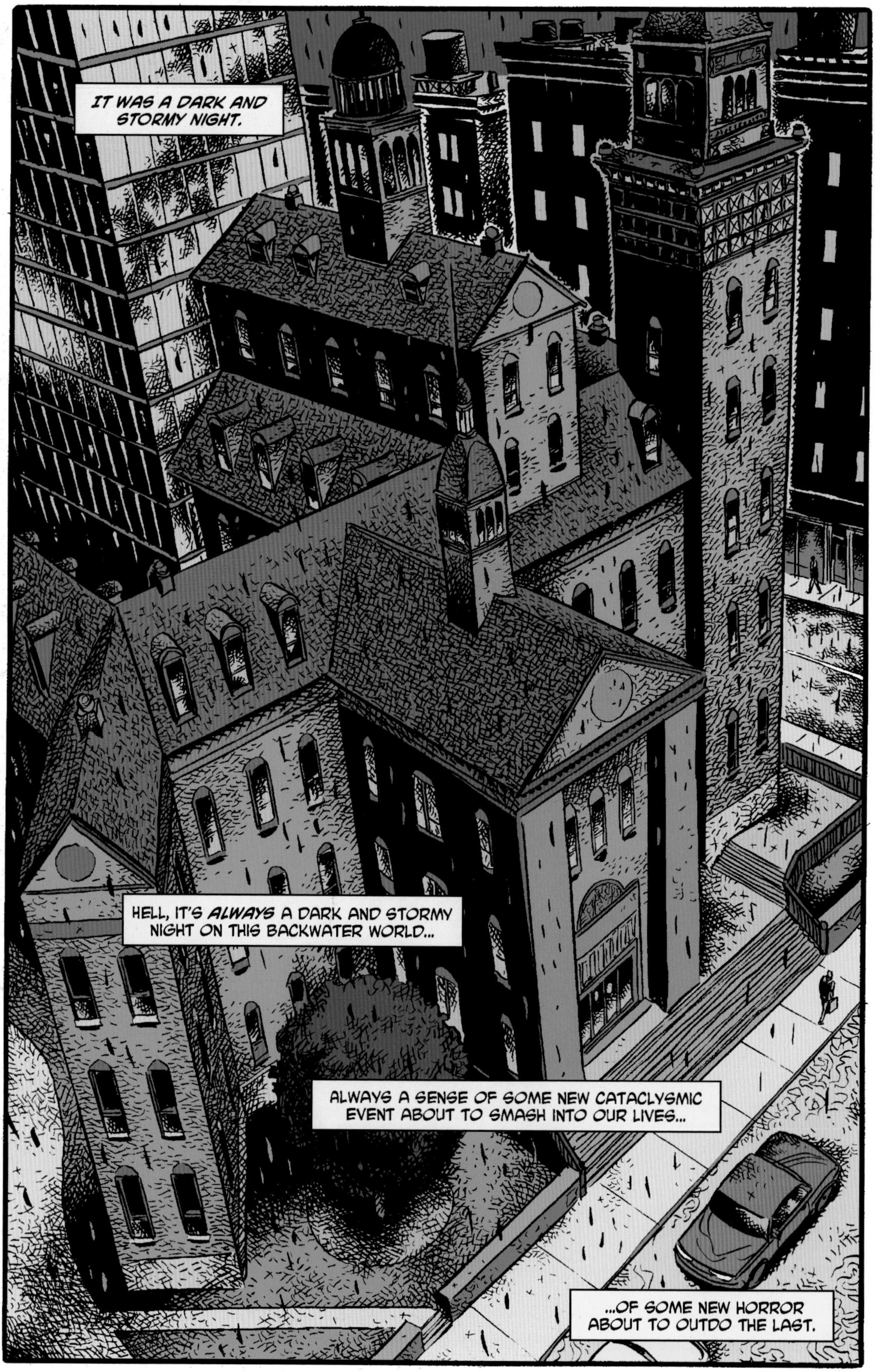
IT WAS A DARK AND STORMY NIGHT.
HELL, IT'S *ALWAYS* A DARK AND STORMY NIGHT ON THIS BACKWATER WORLD...
ALWAYS A SENSE OF SOME NEW CATACLYSMIC EVENT ABOUT TO SMASH INTO OUR LIVES...
...OF SOME NEW HORROR ABOUT TO OUTDO THE LAST.

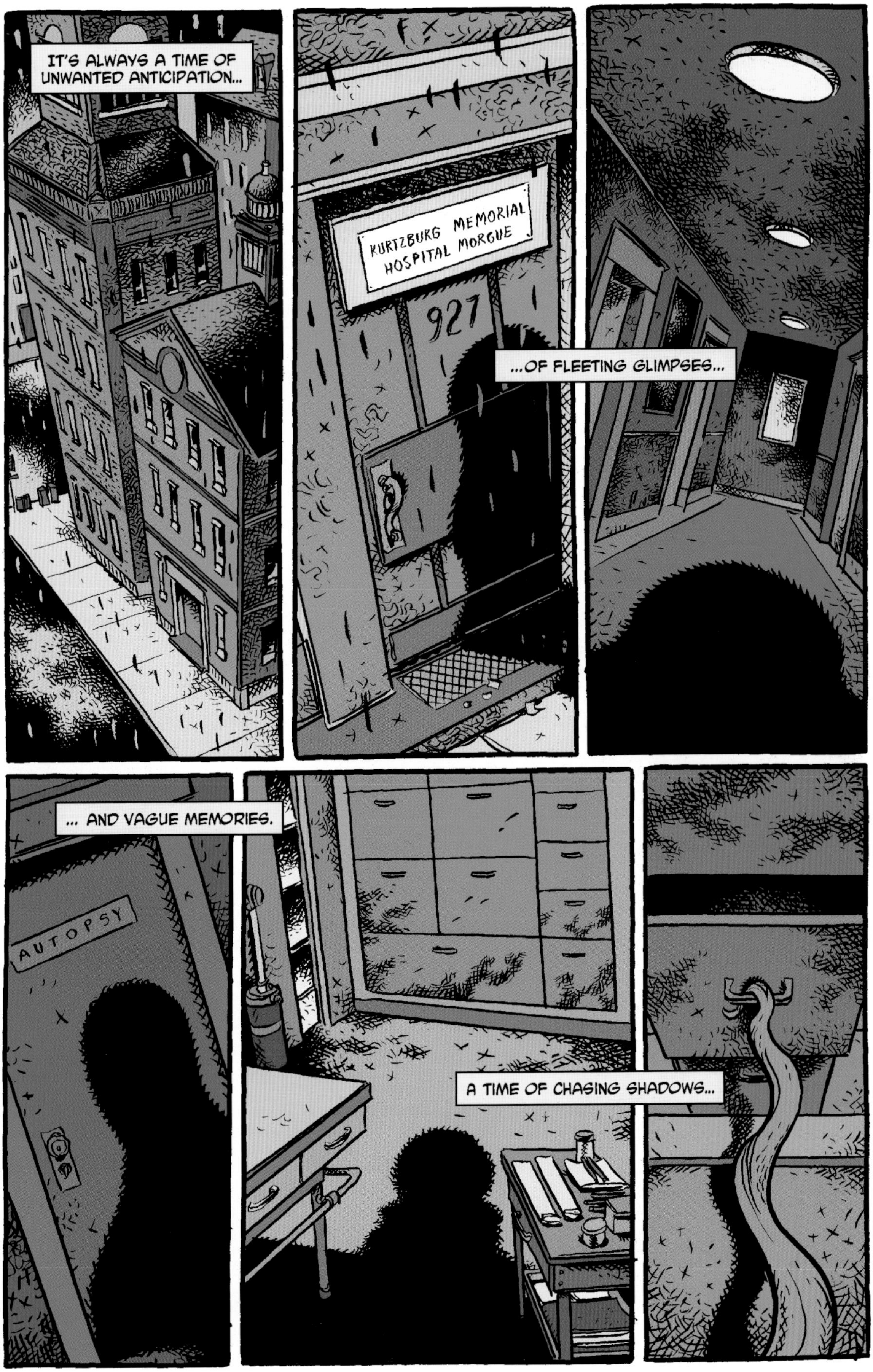
IT'S ALWAYS A TIME OF UNWANTED ANTICIPATION...
KURTZBURG MEMORIAL HOSPITAL MORGUE
927
...OF FLEETING GLIMPSES...
... AND VAGUE MEMORIES.
AUTOPSY
A TIME OF CHASING SHADOWS...

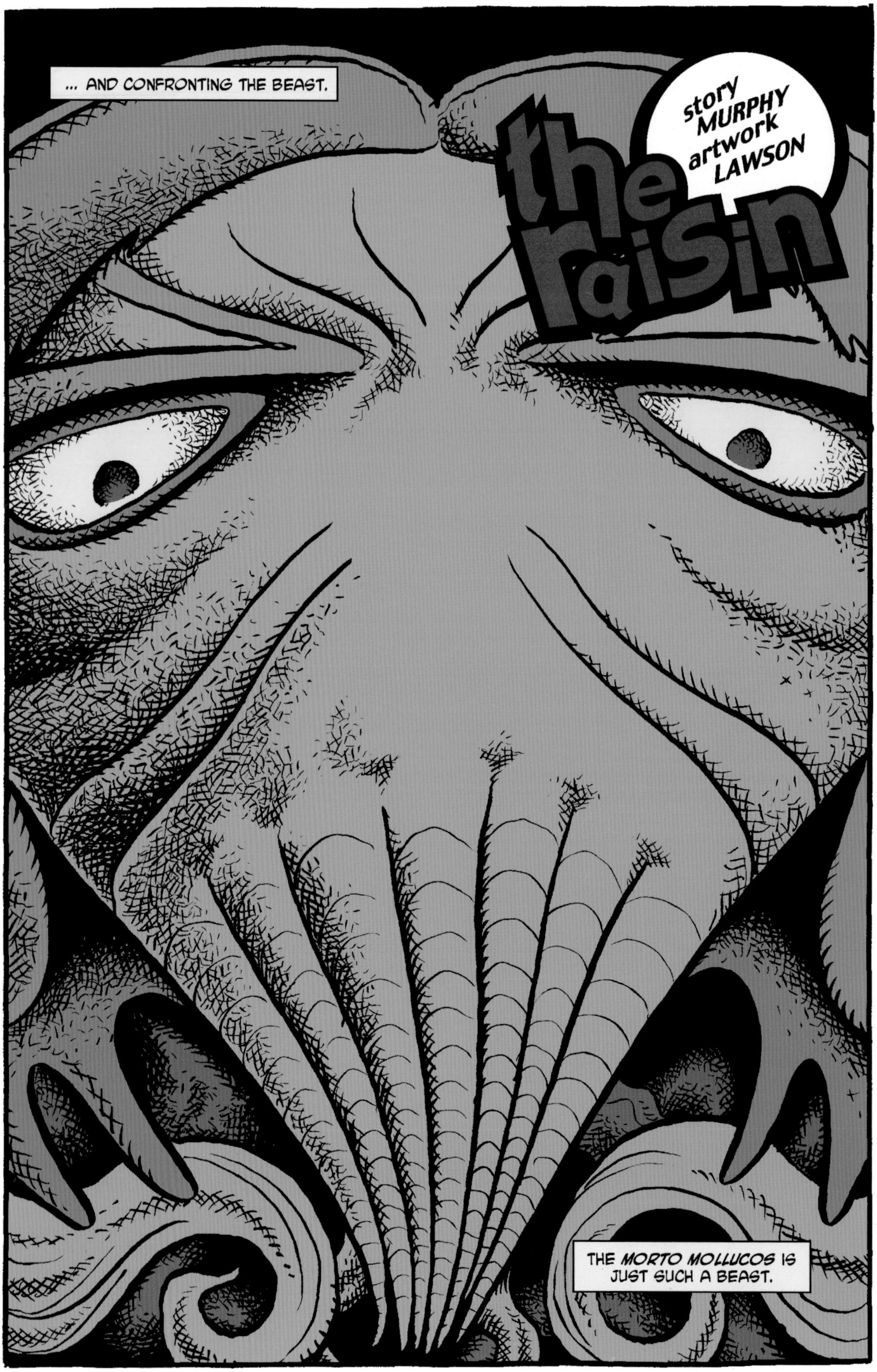

... AND CONFRONTING THE BEAST.
the raisin
story MURPHY artwork LAWSON
THE *MORTO MOLLUCOS* IS JUST SUCH A BEAST.

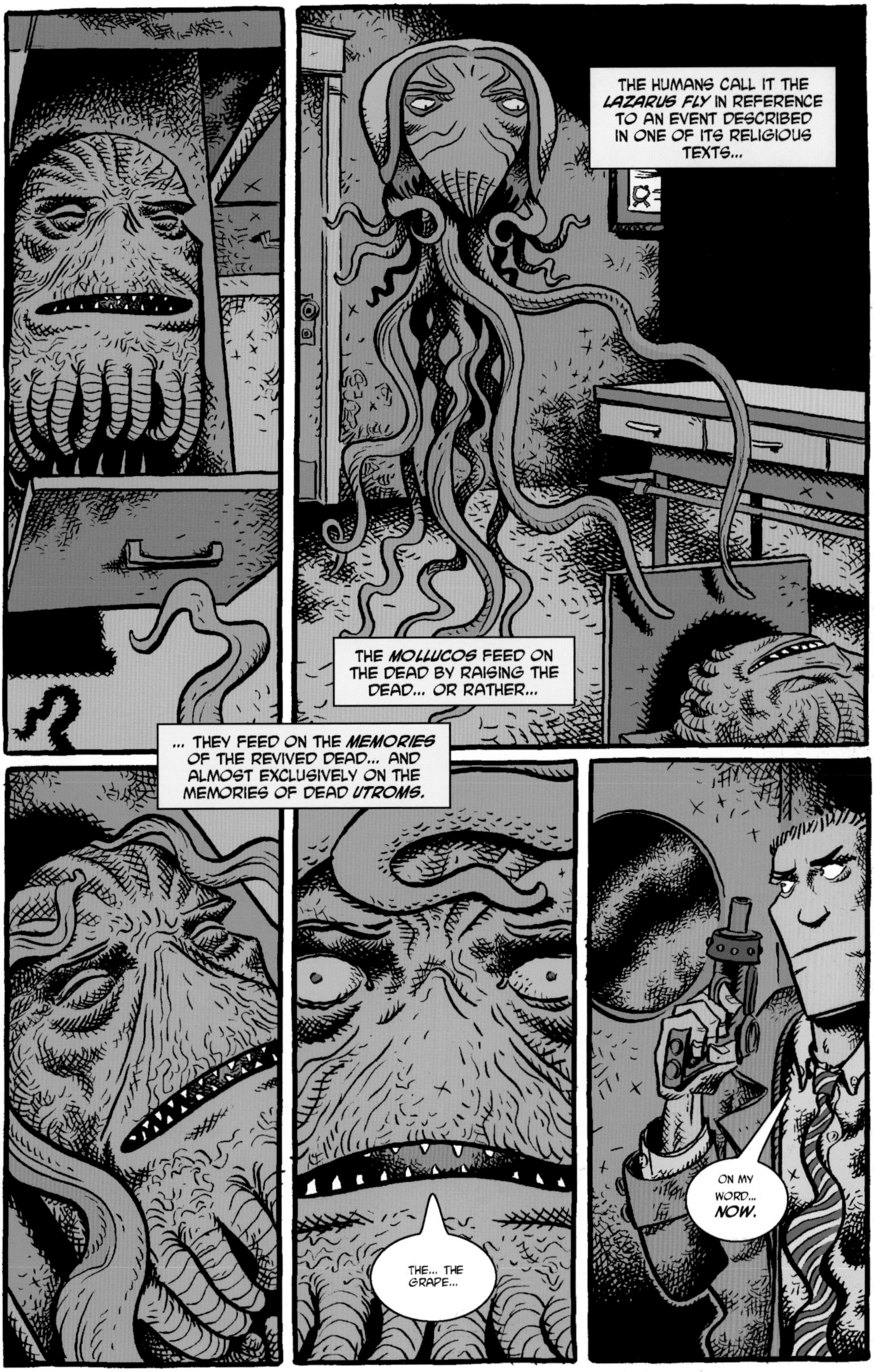
THE HUMANS CALL IT THE LAZARUS FLY IN REFERENCE TO AN EVENT DESCRIBED IN ONE OF ITS RELIGIOUS TEXTS...
THE MOLLUCOS FEED ON THE DEAD BY RAISING THE DEAD... OR RATHER...
... THEY FEED ON THE MEMORIES OF THE REVIVED DEAD... AND ALMOST EXCLUSIVELY ON THE MEMORIES OF DEAD UTROMS.
THE... THE GRAPE...
ON MY WORD... NOW.

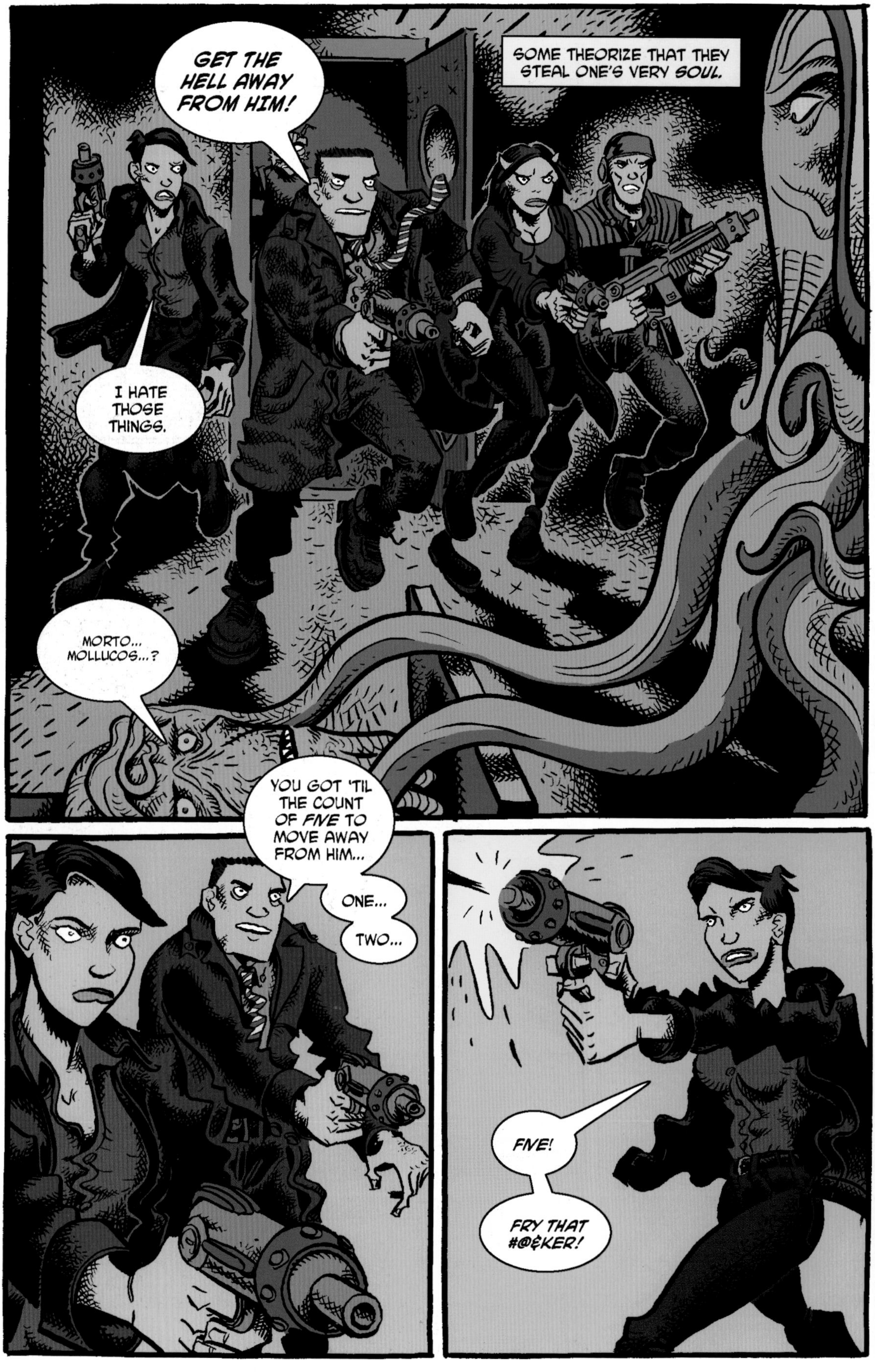
GET THE HELL AWAY FROM HIM!
SOME THEORIZE THAT THEY STEAL ONE'S VERY SOUL.
I HATE THOSE THINGS.
MORTO... MOLLUCOS...?
YOU GOT 'TIL THE COUNT OF FIVE TO MOVE AWAY FROM HIM...
ONE...
TWO...
FIVE!
FRY THAT #@&KER!

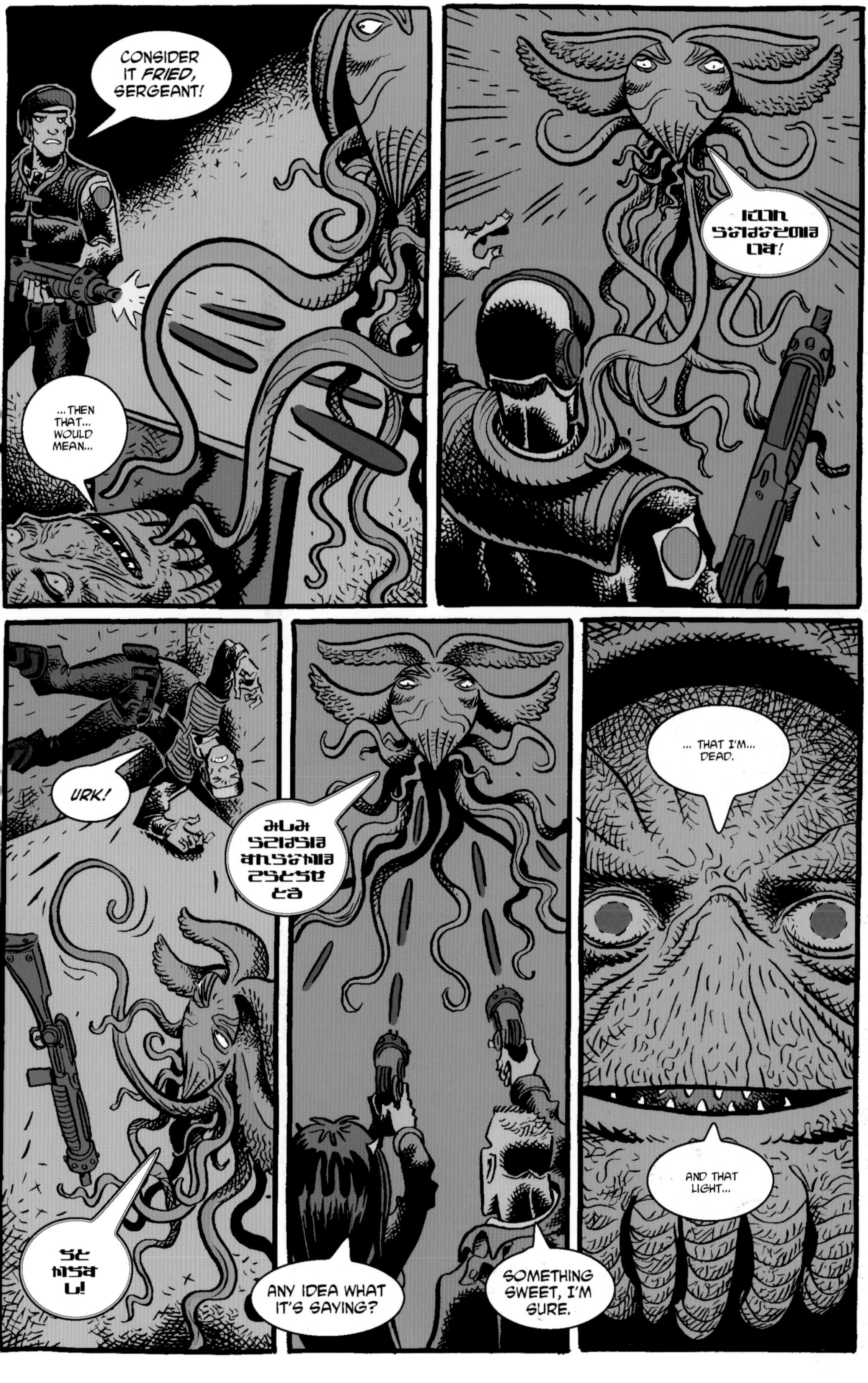
CONSIDER IT *FRIED*, SERGEANT!
...THEN THAT... WOULD MEAN...
URK!
ANY IDEA WHAT IT'S SAYING?
SOMETHING SWEET, I'M SURE.
... THAT I'M... DEAD.
AND THAT LIGHT...

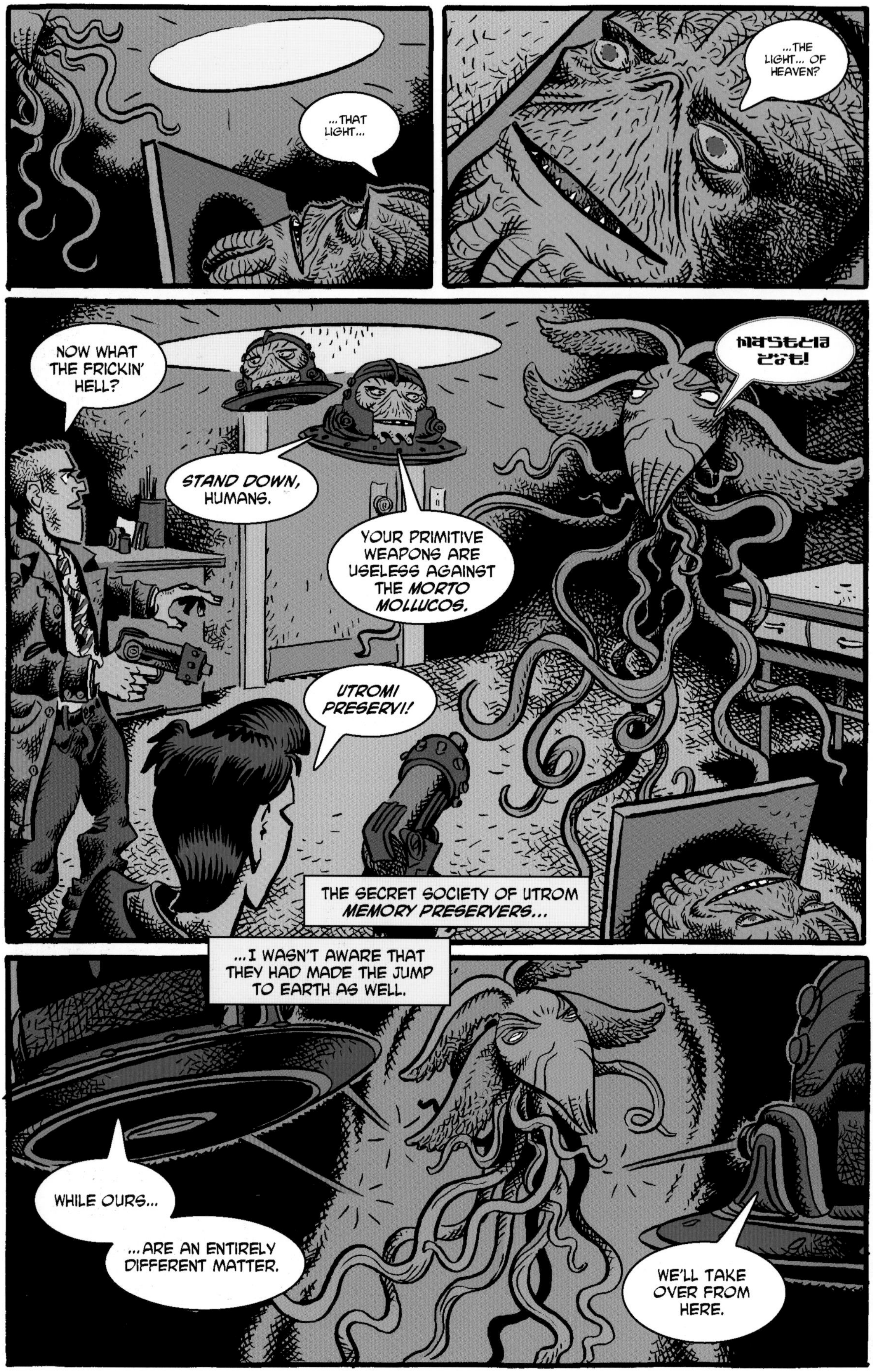
...THAT LIGHT...
...THE LIGHT... OF HEAVEN?
NOW WHAT THE FRICKIN' HELL?
STAND DOWN, HUMANS.
YOUR PRIMITIVE WEAPONS ARE USELESS AGAINST THE MORTO MOLLUCOS.
かすらもとは どなも!
UTROMI PRESERVI!
THE SECRET SOCIETY OF UTROM MEMORY PRESERVERS...
...I WASN'T AWARE THAT THEY HAD MADE THE JUMP TO EARTH AS WELL.
WHILE OURS...
...ARE AN ENTIRELY DIFFERENT MATTER.
WE'LL TAKE OVER FROM HERE.

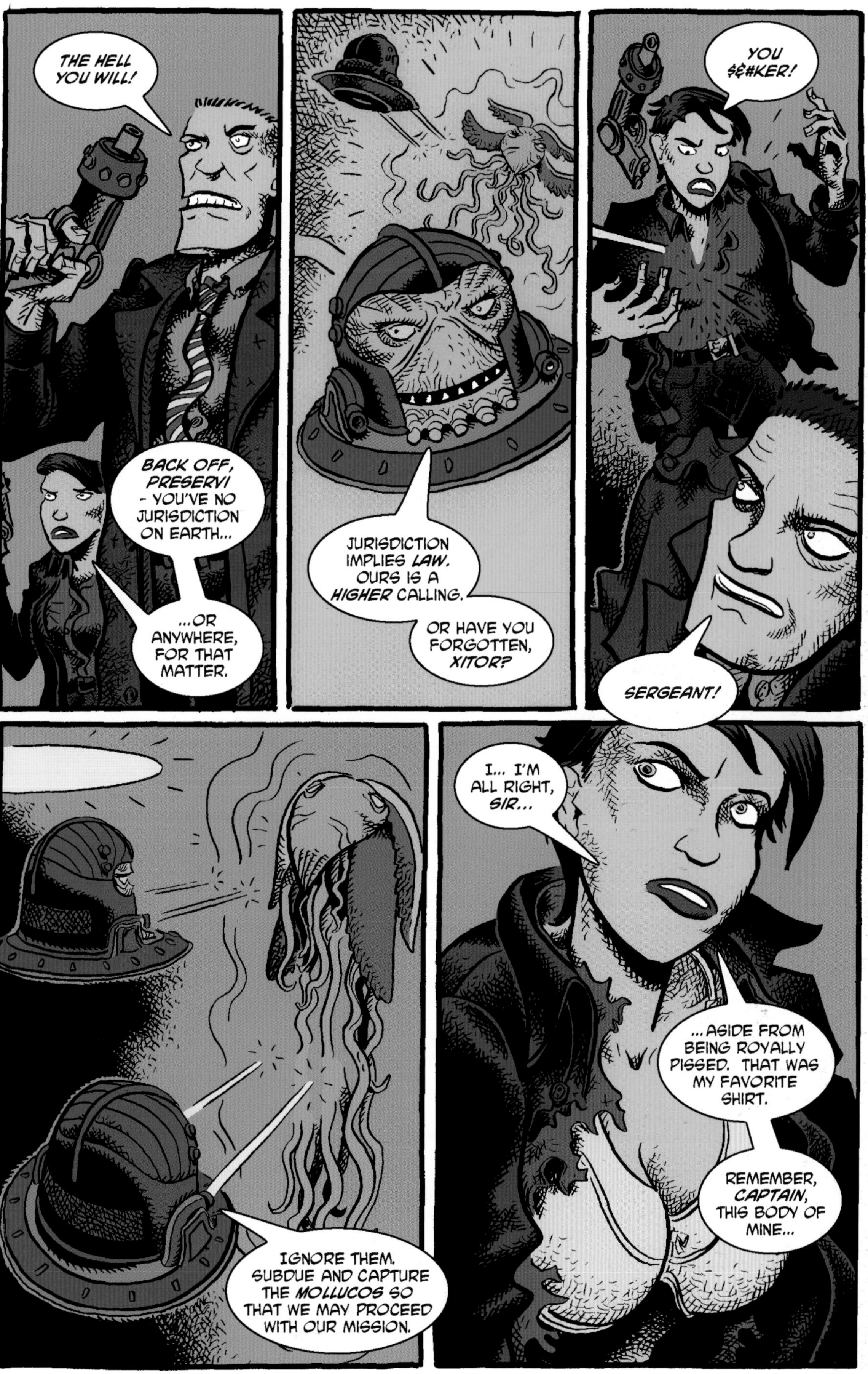
THE HELL YOU WILL!
BACK OFF, PRESERV! - YOU'VE NO JURISDICTION ON EARTH...
...OR ANYWHERE, FOR THAT MATTER.
JURISDICTION IMPLIES LAW. OURS IS A HIGHER CALLING.
OR HAVE YOU FORGOTTEN, XITOR?
YOU $&#KER!
SERGEANT!
I... I'M ALL RIGHT, SIR...
...ASIDE FROM BEING ROYALLY PISSED. THAT WAS MY FAVORITE SHIRT.
REMEMBER, CAPTAIN, THIS BODY OF MINE...
IGNORE THEM. SUBDUE AND CAPTURE THE MOLLUCOS SO THAT WE MAY PROCEED WITH OUR MISSION.

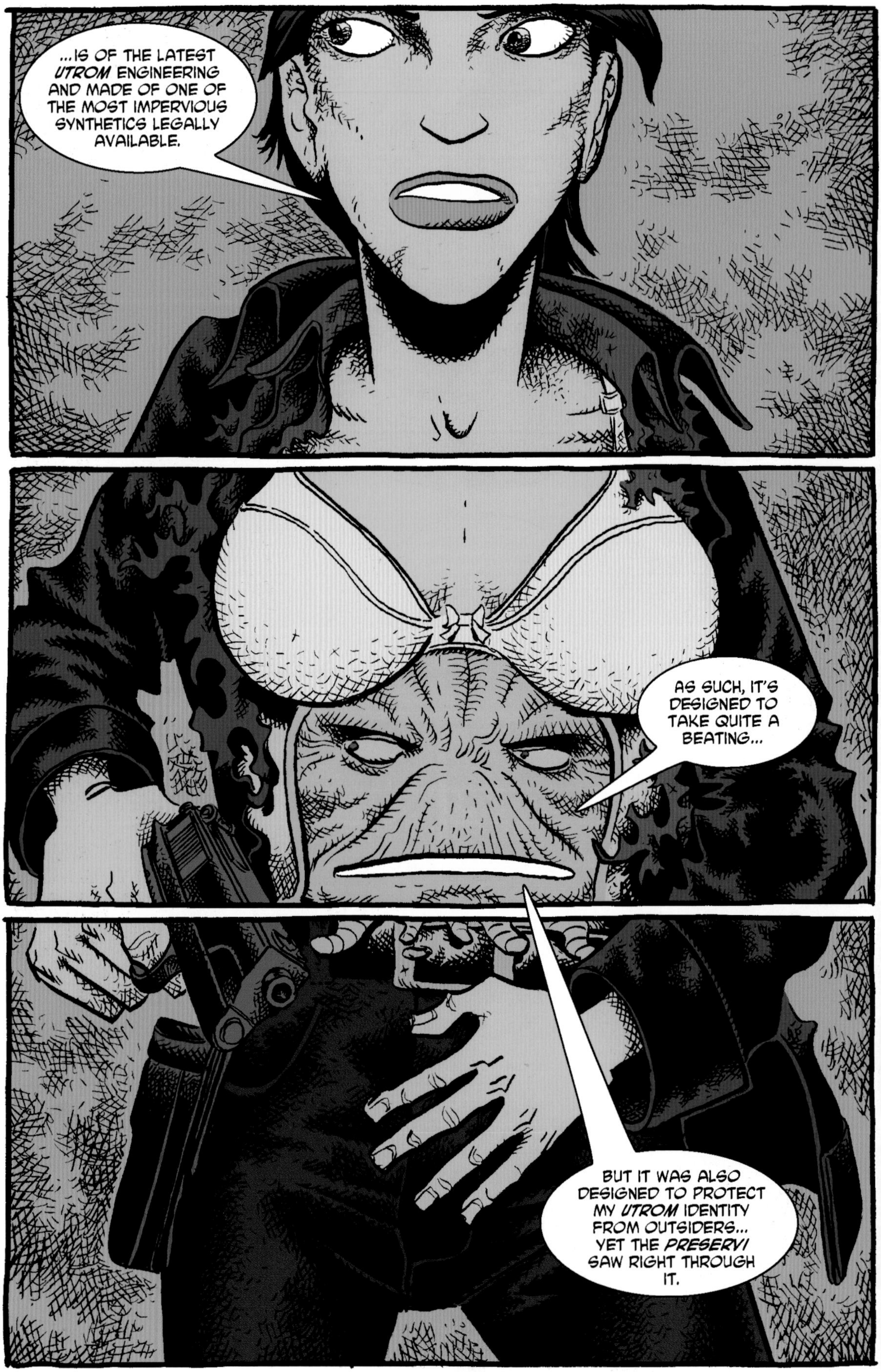
...IS OF THE LATEST *UTROM* ENGINEERING AND MADE OF ONE OF THE MOST IMPERVIOUS SYNTHETICS LEGALLY AVAILABLE.
AS SUCH, IT'S DESIGNED TO TAKE QUITE A BEATING...
BUT IT WAS ALSO DESIGNED TO PROTECT MY *UTROM* IDENTITY FROM OUTSIDERS... YET THE *PRESERVI* SAW RIGHT THROUGH IT.

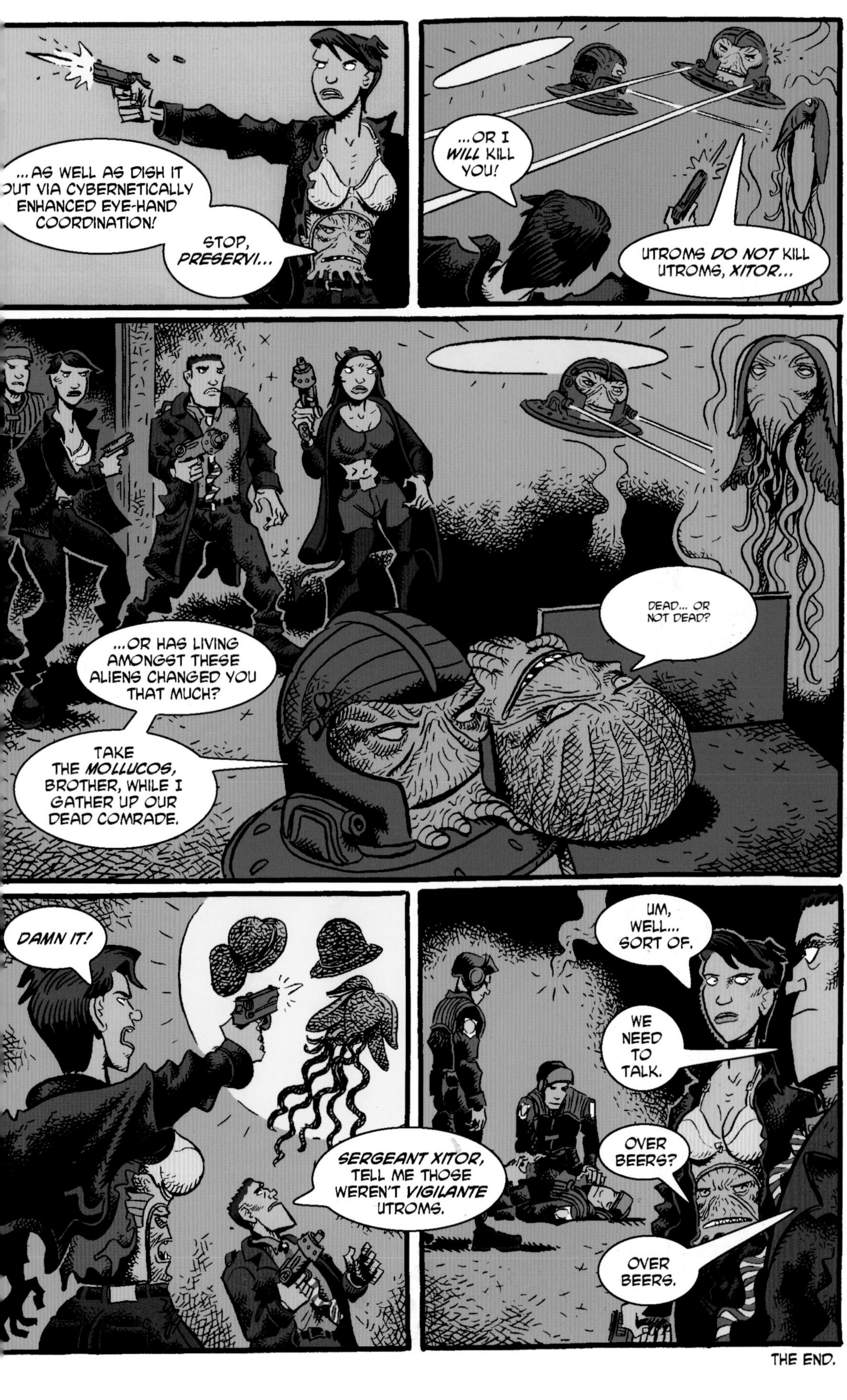

...AS WELL AS DISH IT OUT VIA CYBERNETICALLY ENHANCED EYE-HAND COORDINATION!
STOP, PRESERVI...
...OR I WILL KILL YOU!
UTROMS DO NOT KILL UTROMS, XITOR...
DEAD... OR NOT DEAD?
...OR HAS LIVING AMONGST THESE ALIENS CHANGED YOU THAT MUCH?
TAKE THE MOLLUCOS, BROTHER, WHILE I GATHER UP OUR DEAD COMRADE.
DAMN IT!
SERGEANT XITOR, TELL ME THOSE WEREN'T VIGILANTE UTROMS.
UM, WELL... SORT OF.
WE NEED TO TALK.
OVER BEERS?
OVER BEERS.

THE END.

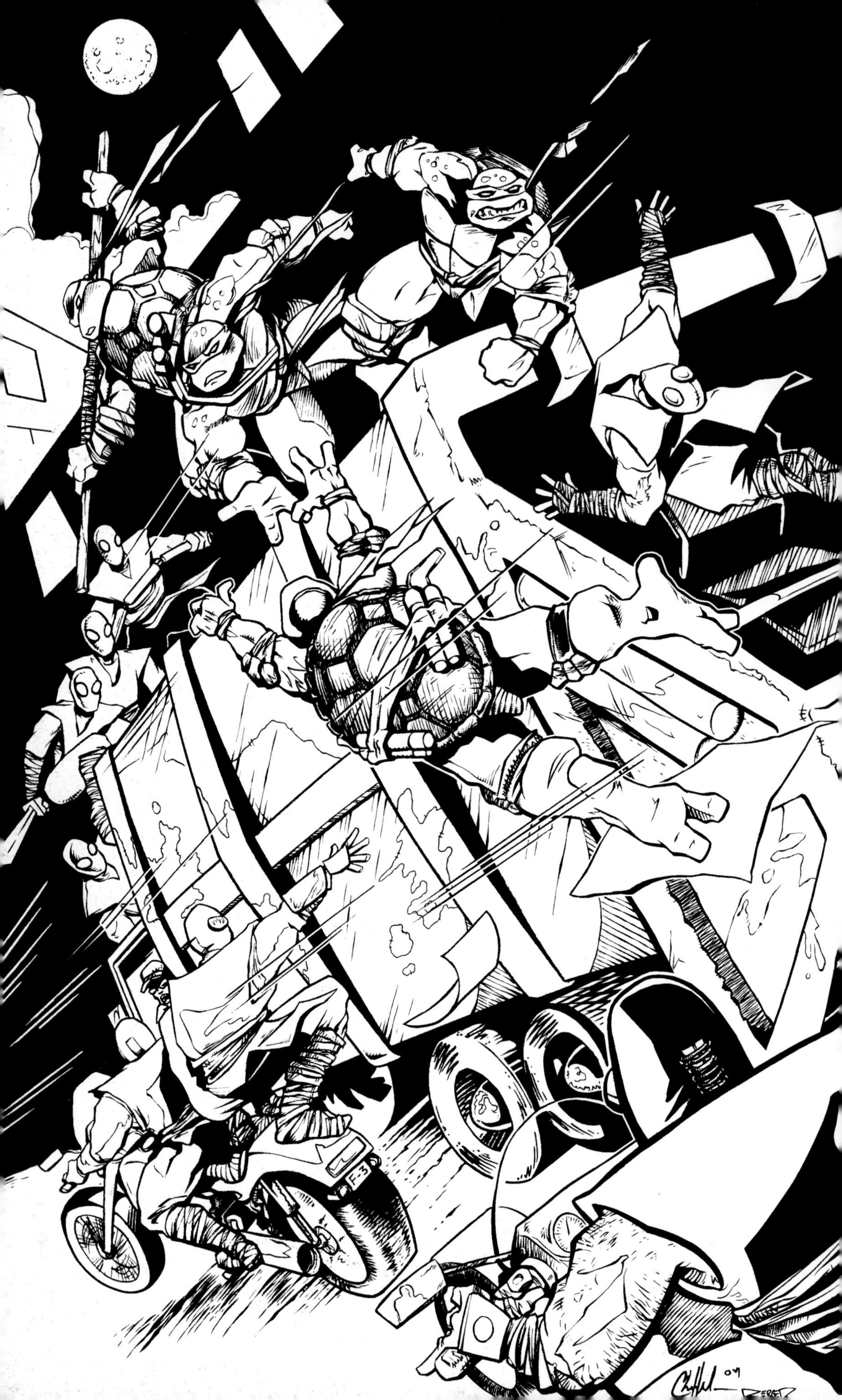

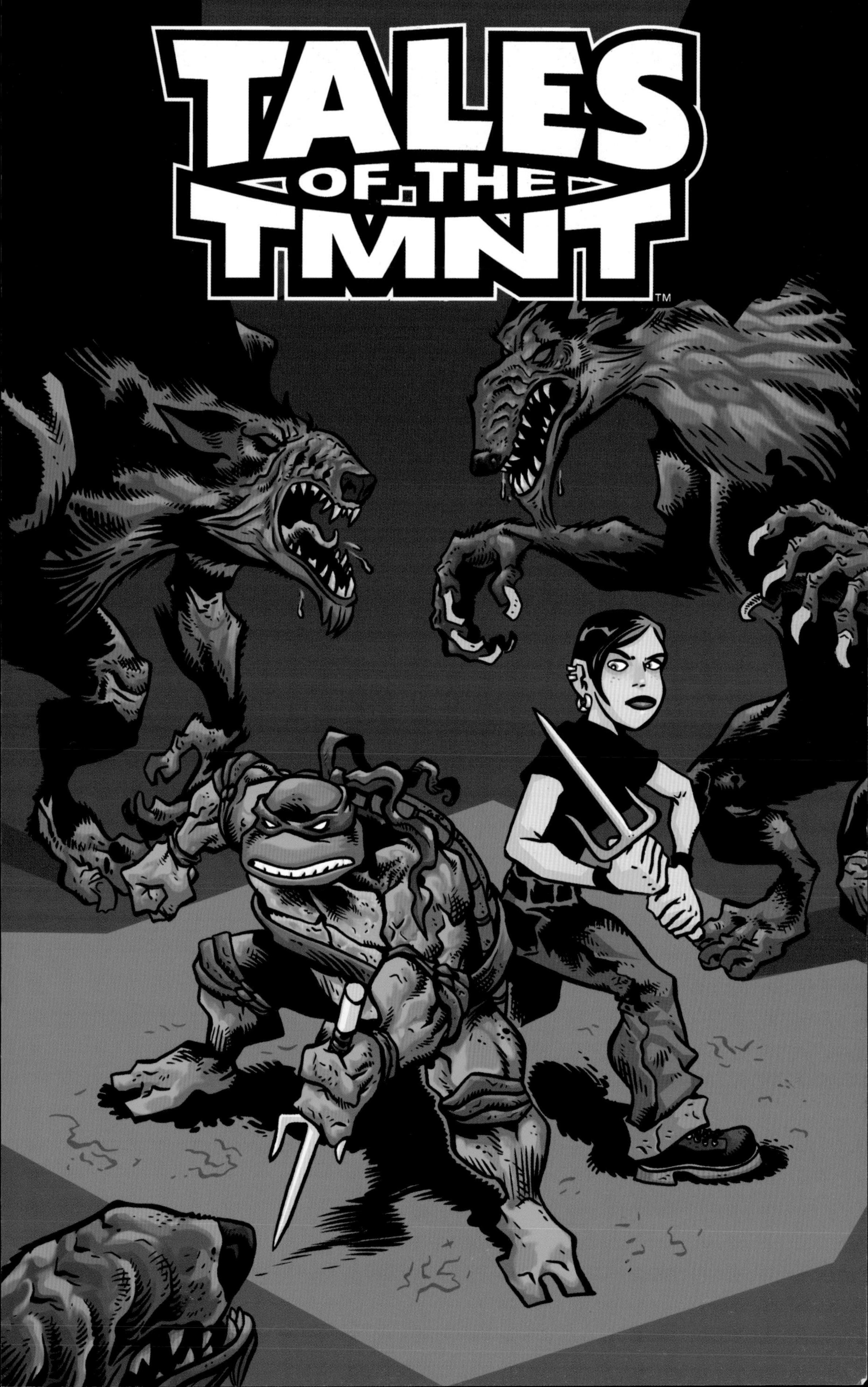
TALES OF THE TMNT™

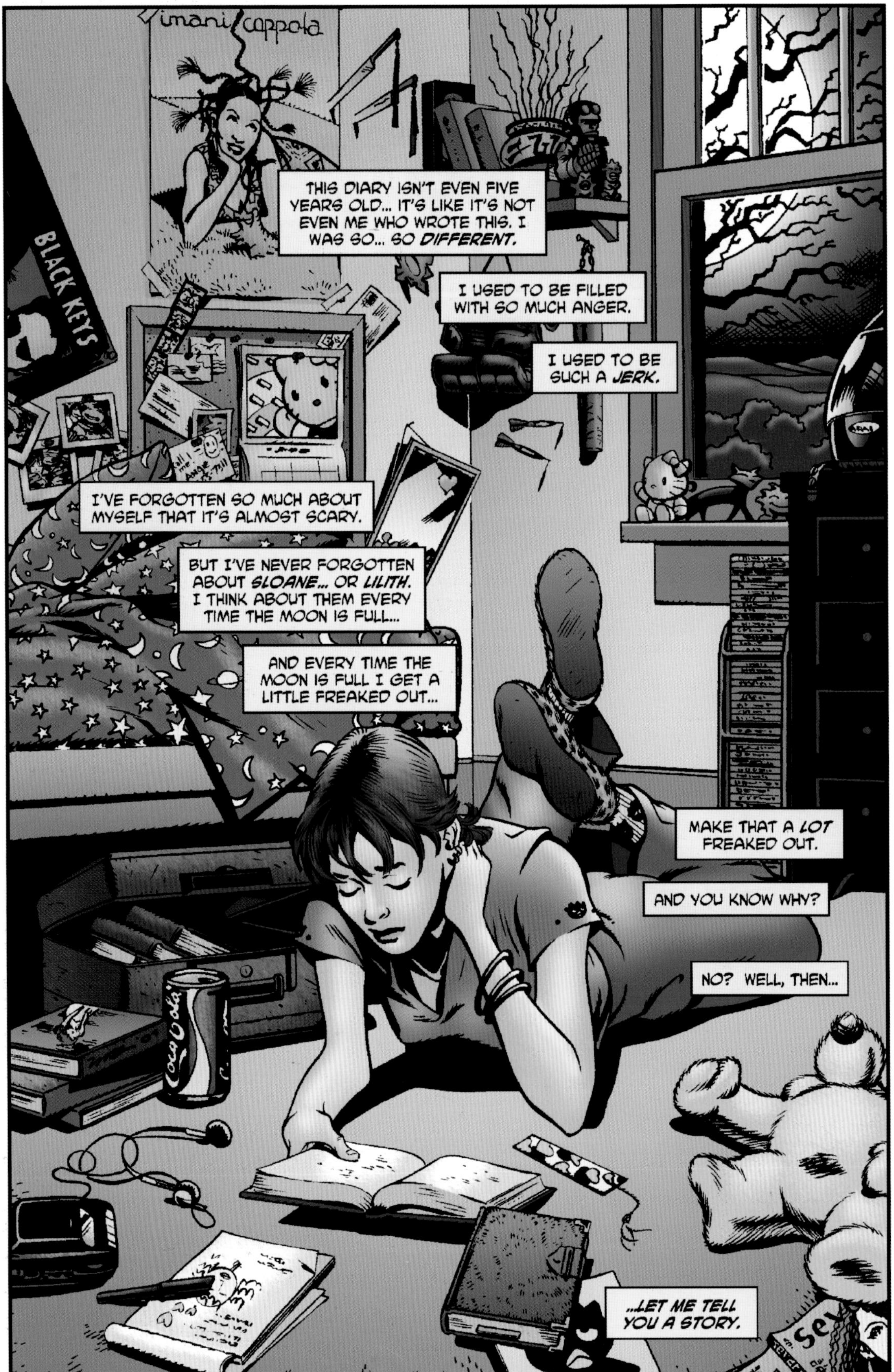
imani coppola
BLACK KEYS
THIS DIARY ISN'T EVEN FIVE YEARS OLD... IT'S LIKE IT'S NOT EVEN ME WHO WROTE THIS. I WAS SO... SO *DIFFERENT.*
I USED TO BE FILLED WITH SO MUCH ANGER.
I USED TO BE SUCH A *JERK.*
I'VE FORGOTTEN SO MUCH ABOUT MYSELF THAT IT'S ALMOST SCARY.
BUT I'VE NEVER FORGOTTEN ABOUT *SLOANE... OR LILITH.* I THINK ABOUT THEM EVERY TIME THE MOON IS FULL...
AND EVERY TIME THE MOON IS FULL I GET A LITTLE FREAKED OUT...
MAKE THAT A *LOT* FREAKED OUT.
AND YOU KNOW WHY?
NO? WELL, THEN...
...LET ME TELL YOU A STORY.

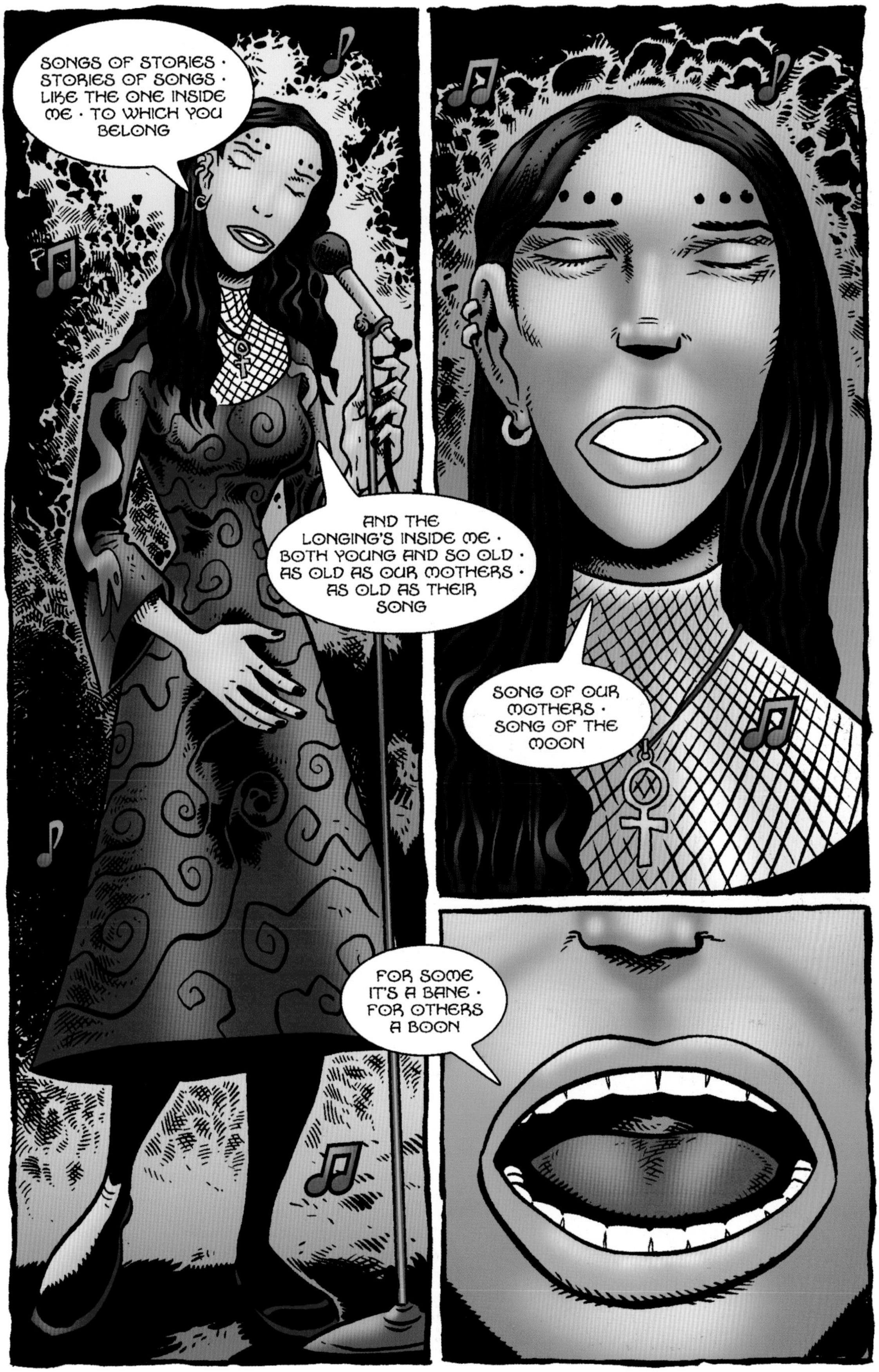
SONGS OF STORIES · STORIES OF SONGS · LIKE THE ONE INSIDE ME · TO WHICH YOU BELONG
AND THE LONGING'S INSIDE ME · BOTH YOUNG AND SO OLD · AS OLD AS OUR MOTHERS · AS OLD AS THEIR SONG
SONG OF OUR MOTHERS · SONG OF THE MOON
FOR SOME IT'S A BANE · FOR OTHERS A BOON

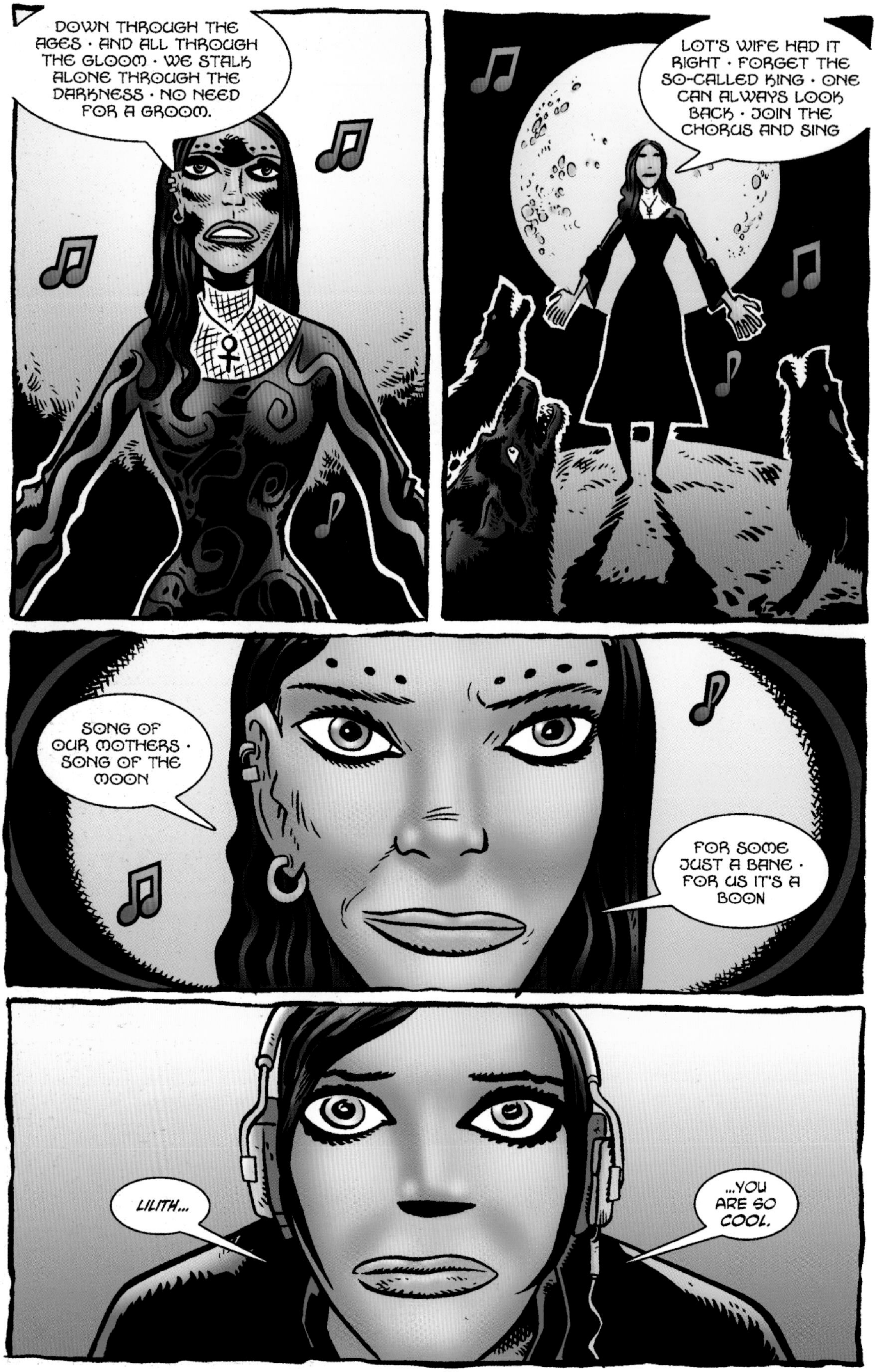
DOWN THROUGH THE AGES · AND ALL THROUGH THE GLOOM · WE STALK ALONE THROUGH THE DARKNESS · NO NEED FOR A GROOM.
LOT'S WIFE HAD IT RIGHT · FORGET THE SO-CALLED KING · ONE CAN ALWAYS LOOK BACK · JOIN THE CHORUS AND SING
SONG OF OUR MOTHERS · SONG OF THE MOON
FOR SOME JUST A BANE · FOR US IT'S A BOON
LILITH...
...YOU ARE SO COOL.

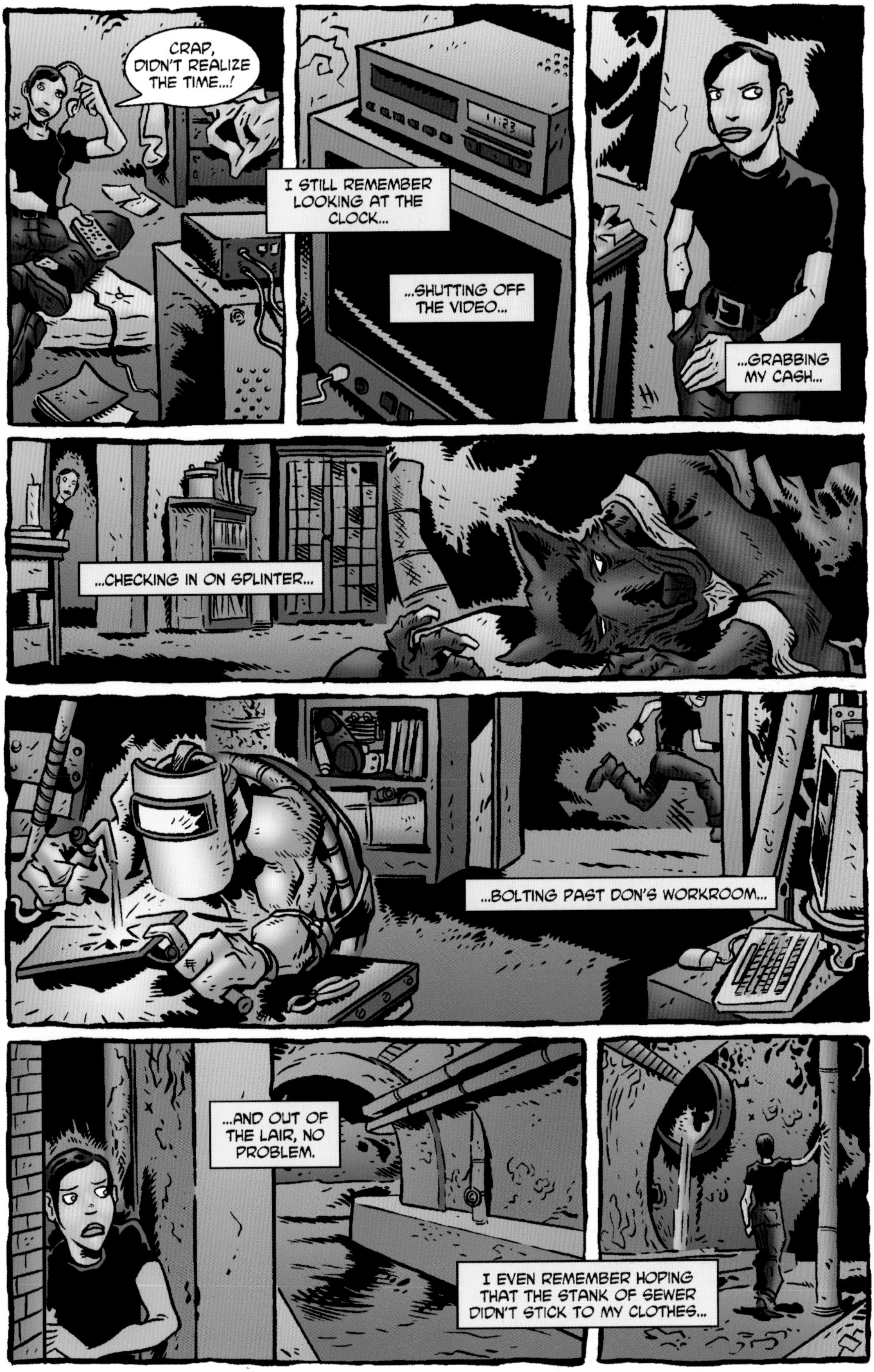
CRAP, DIDN'T REALIZE THE TIME...!
I STILL REMEMBER LOOKING AT THE CLOCK...
...SHUTTING OFF THE VIDEO...
...GRABBING MY CASH...
...CHECKING IN ON SPLINTER...
...BOLTING PAST DON'S WORKROOM...
...AND OUT OF THE LAIR, NO PROBLEM.
I EVEN REMEMBER HOPING THAT THE STANK OF SEWER DIDN'T STICK TO MY CLOTHES...

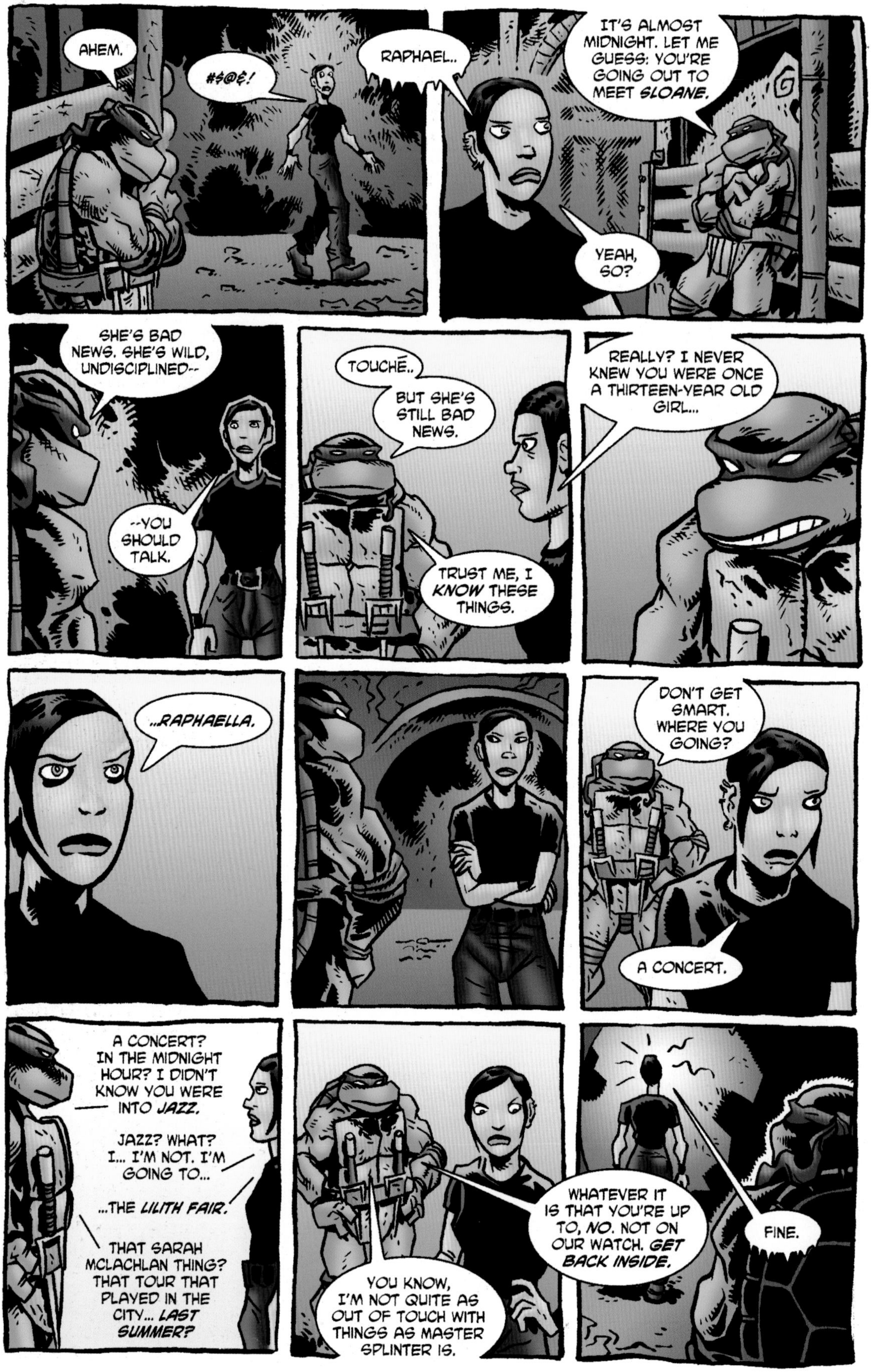
AHEM.
#$@&!
RAPHAEL..
IT'S ALMOST MIDNIGHT. LET ME GUESS: YOU'RE GOING OUT TO MEET SLOANE.
YEAH, SO?
SHE'S BAD NEWS. SHE'S WILD, UNDISCIPLINED--
--YOU SHOULD TALK.
TOUCHÉ..
BUT SHE'S STILL BAD NEWS.
TRUST ME, I KNOW THESE THINGS.
REALLY? I NEVER KNEW YOU WERE ONCE A THIRTEEN-YEAR OLD GIRL...
...RAPHAELLA.
DON'T GET SMART. WHERE YOU GOING?
A CONCERT.
A CONCERT? IN THE MIDNIGHT HOUR? I DIDN'T KNOW YOU WERE INTO JAZZ.
JAZZ? WHAT? I... I'M NOT. I'M GOING TO...
...THE LILITH FAIR.
THAT SARAH MCLACHLAN THING? THAT TOUR THAT PLAYED IN THE CITY... LAST SUMMER?
YOU KNOW, I'M NOT QUITE AS OUT OF TOUCH WITH THINGS AS MASTER SPLINTER IS.
WHATEVER IT IS THAT YOU'RE UP TO, NO. NOT ON OUR WATCH. GET BACK INSIDE.
FINE.

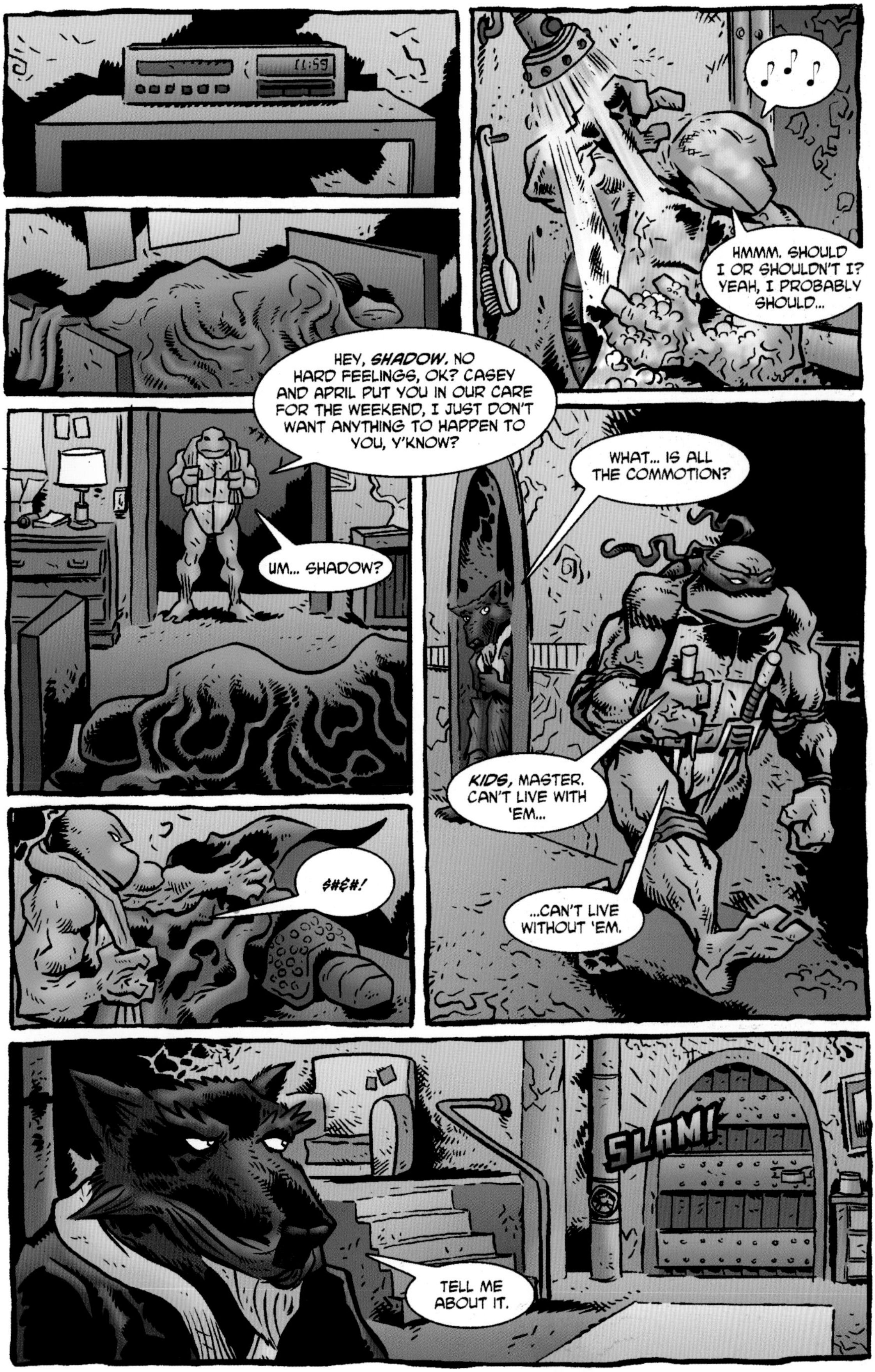
11:59
♪♪♪
HMMM. SHOULD I OR SHOULDN'T I? YEAH, I PROBABLY SHOULD...
HEY, SHADOW. NO HARD FEELINGS, OK? CASEY AND APRIL PUT YOU IN OUR CARE FOR THE WEEKEND, I JUST DON'T WANT ANYTHING TO HAPPEN TO YOU, Y'KNOW?
UM... SHADOW?
$#&#!
WHAT... IS ALL THE COMMOTION?
KIDS, MASTER. CAN'T LIVE WITH 'EM...
...CAN'T LIVE WITHOUT 'EM.
SLAM!
TELL ME ABOUT IT.

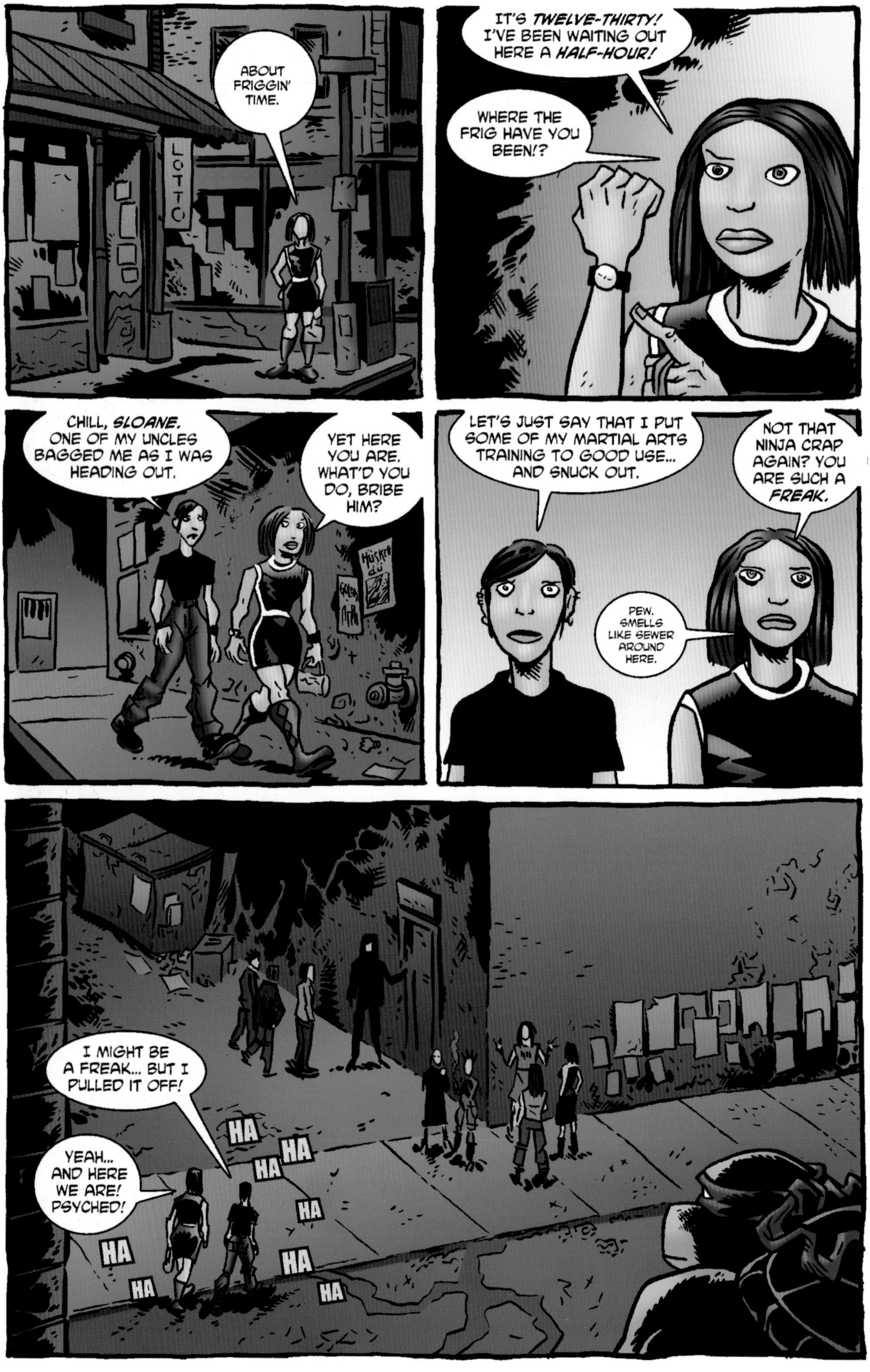
ABOUT FRIGGIN' TIME.
IT'S TWELVE-THIRTY! I'VE BEEN WAITING OUT HERE A HALF-HOUR!
WHERE THE FRIG HAVE YOU BEEN!?
CHILL, SLOANE. ONE OF MY UNCLES BAGGED ME AS I WAS HEADING OUT.
YET HERE YOU ARE. WHAT'D YOU DO, BRIBE HIM?
LET'S JUST SAY THAT I PUT SOME OF MY MARTIAL ARTS TRAINING TO GOOD USE... AND SNUCK OUT.
NOT THAT NINJA CRAP AGAIN? YOU ARE SUCH A FREAK.
PEW. SMELLS LIKE SEWER AROUND HERE.
I MIGHT BE A FREAK... BUT I PULLED IT OFF!
YEAH... AND HERE WE ARE! PSYCHED!
HA HA HA HA HA HA HA HA

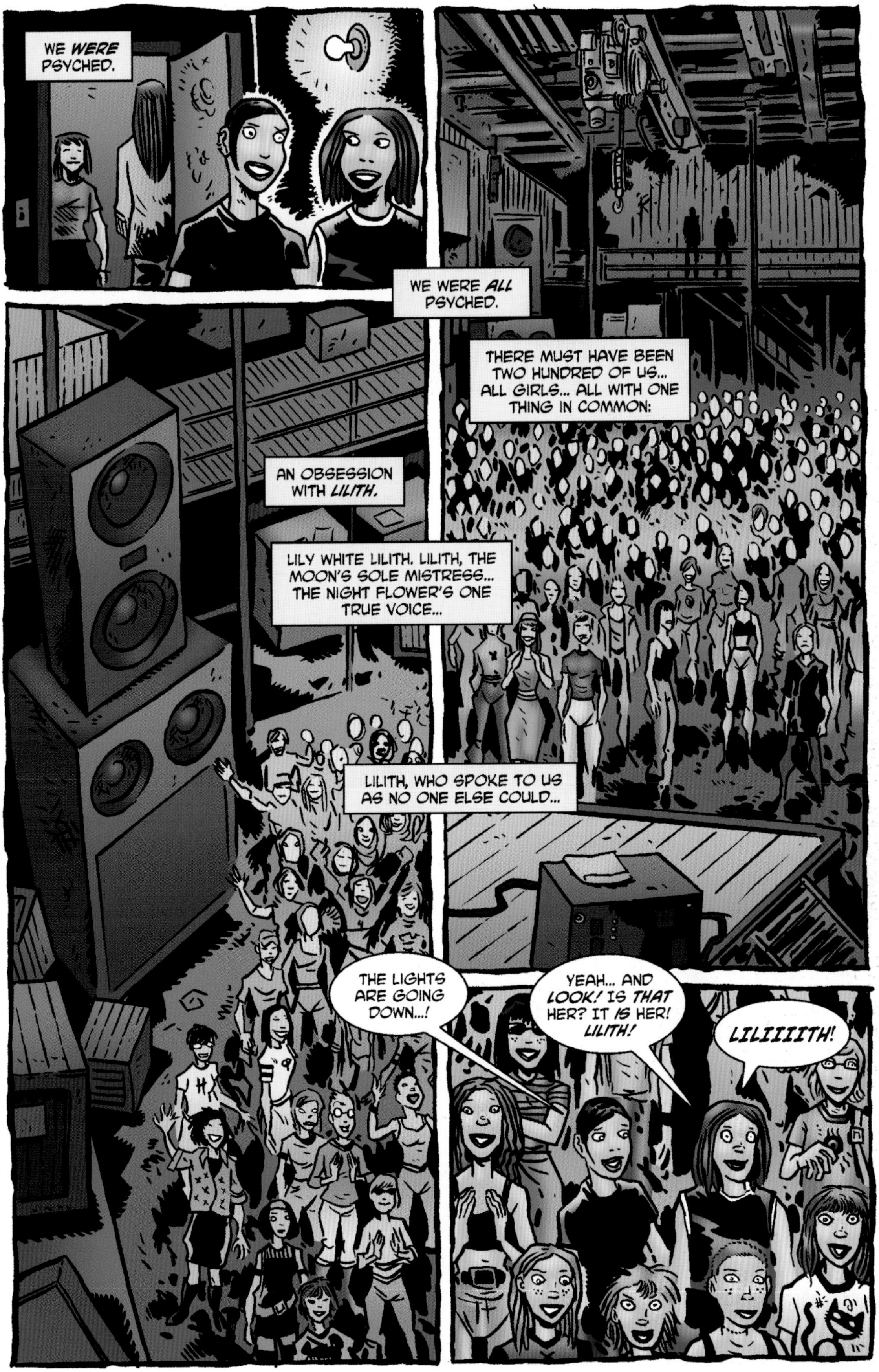
WE *WERE* PSYCHED.
WE WERE *ALL* PSYCHED.
THERE MUST HAVE BEEN TWO HUNDRED OF US... ALL GIRLS... ALL WITH ONE THING IN COMMON:
AN OBSESSION WITH *LILITH.*
LILY WHITE LILITH. LILITH, THE MOON'S SOLE MISTRESS... THE NIGHT FLOWER'S ONE TRUE VOICE...
LILITH, WHO SPOKE TO US AS NO ONE ELSE COULD...
THE LIGHTS ARE GOING DOWN...!
YEAH... AND *LOOK!* IS *THAT* HER? IT *IS* HER! *LILITH!*
LILIIIITH!

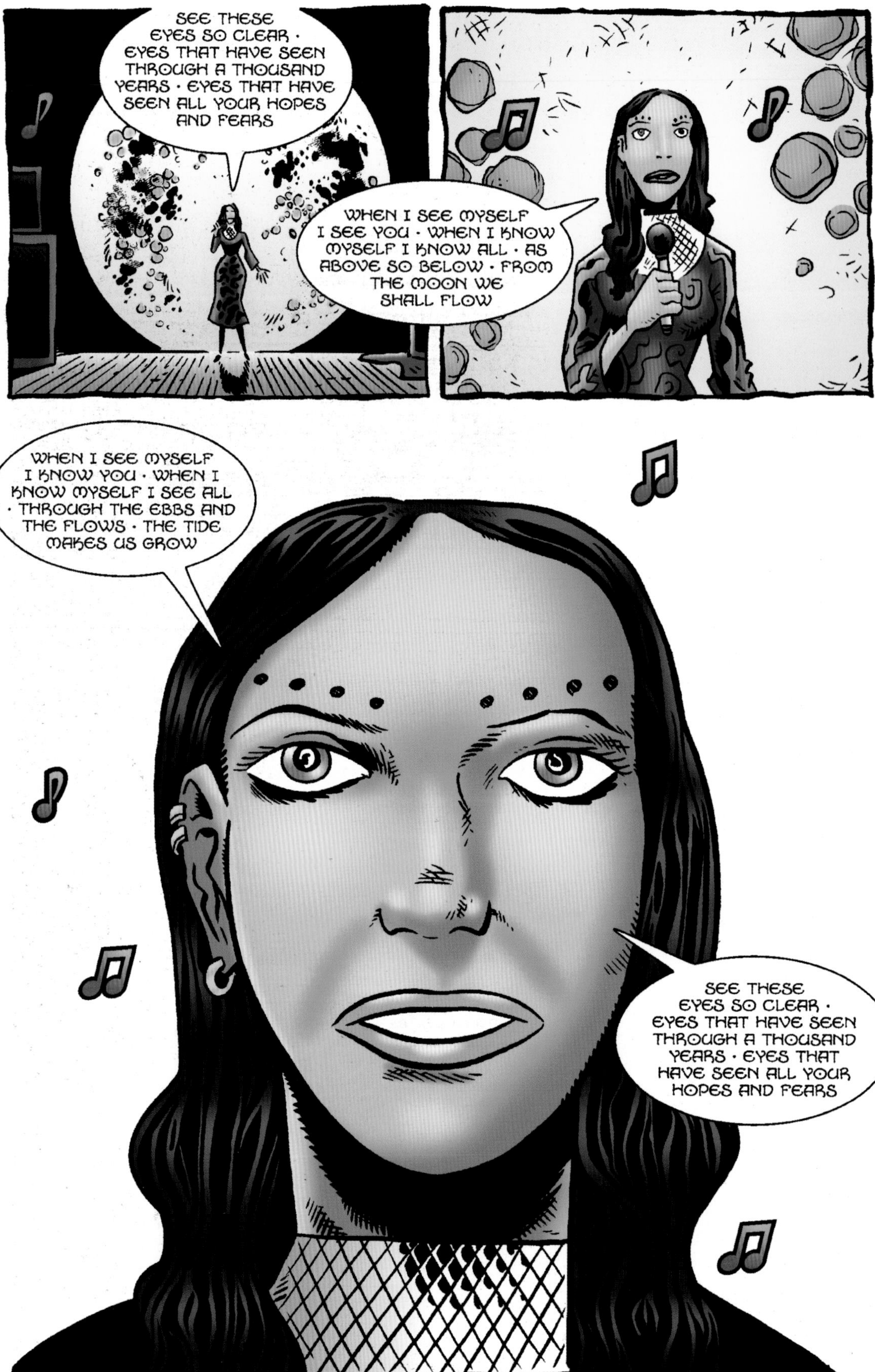
SEE THESE EYES SO CLEAR · EYES THAT HAVE SEEN THROUGH A THOUSAND YEARS · EYES THAT HAVE SEEN ALL YOUR HOPES AND FEARS
WHEN I SEE MYSELF I SEE YOU · WHEN I KNOW MYSELF I KNOW ALL · AS ABOVE SO BELOW · FROM THE MOON WE SHALL FLOW
WHEN I SEE MYSELF I KNOW YOU · WHEN I KNOW MYSELF I SEE ALL · THROUGH THE EBBS AND THE FLOWS · THE TIDE MAKES US GROW
SEE THESE EYES SO CLEAR · EYES THAT HAVE SEEN THROUGH A THOUSAND YEARS · EYES THAT HAVE SEEN ALL YOUR HOPES AND FEARS

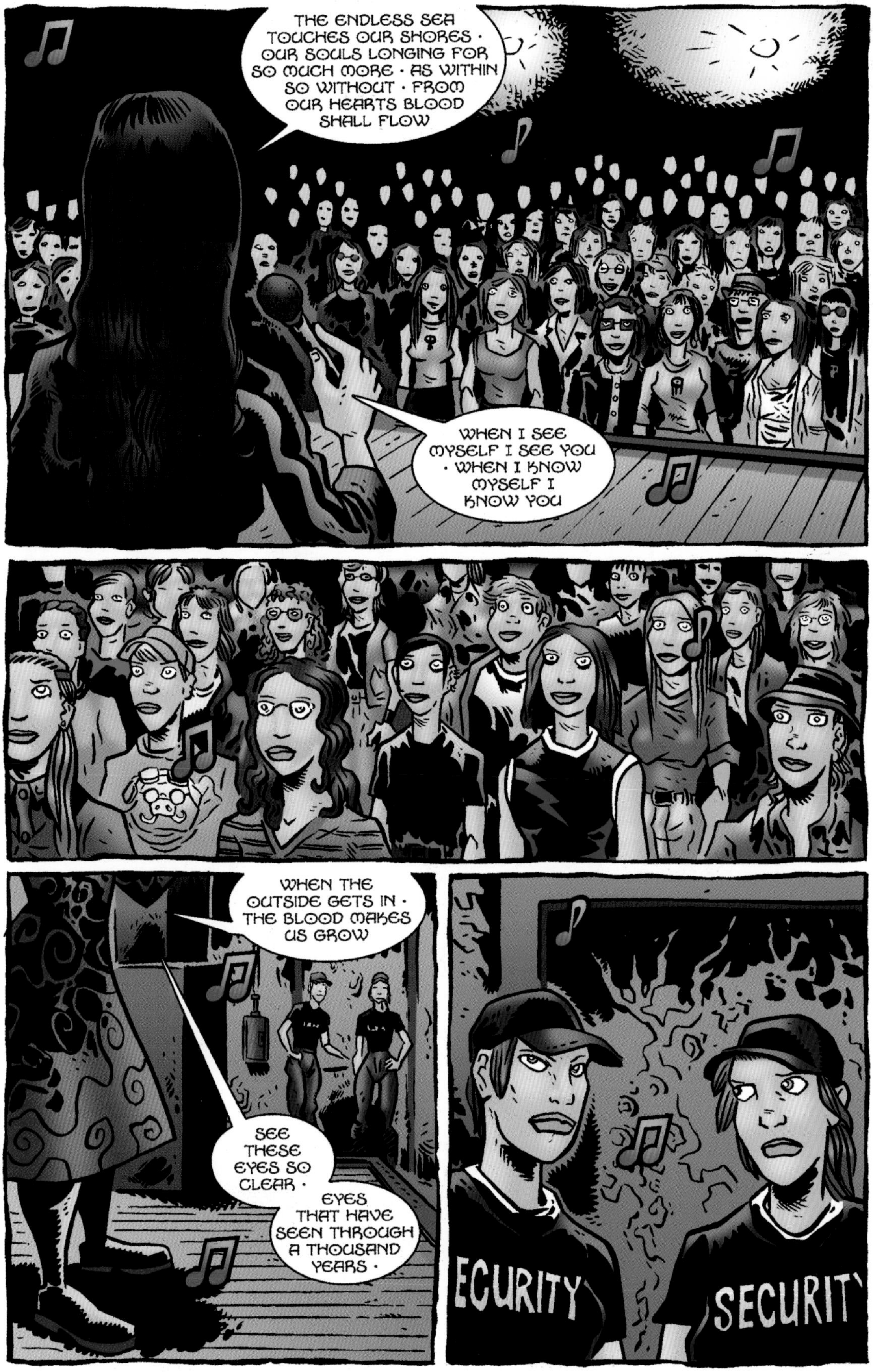
THE ENDLESS SEA TOUCHES OUR SHORES · OUR SOULS LONGING FOR SO MUCH MORE · AS WITHIN SO WITHOUT · FROM OUR HEARTS BLOOD SHALL FLOW
WHEN I SEE MYSELF I SEE YOU · WHEN I KNOW MYSELF I KNOW YOU
WHEN THE OUTSIDE GETS IN · THE BLOOD MAKES US GROW
SEE THESE EYES SO CLEAR ·
EYES THAT HAVE SEEN THROUGH A THOUSAND YEARS ·
ECURITY
SECURITY

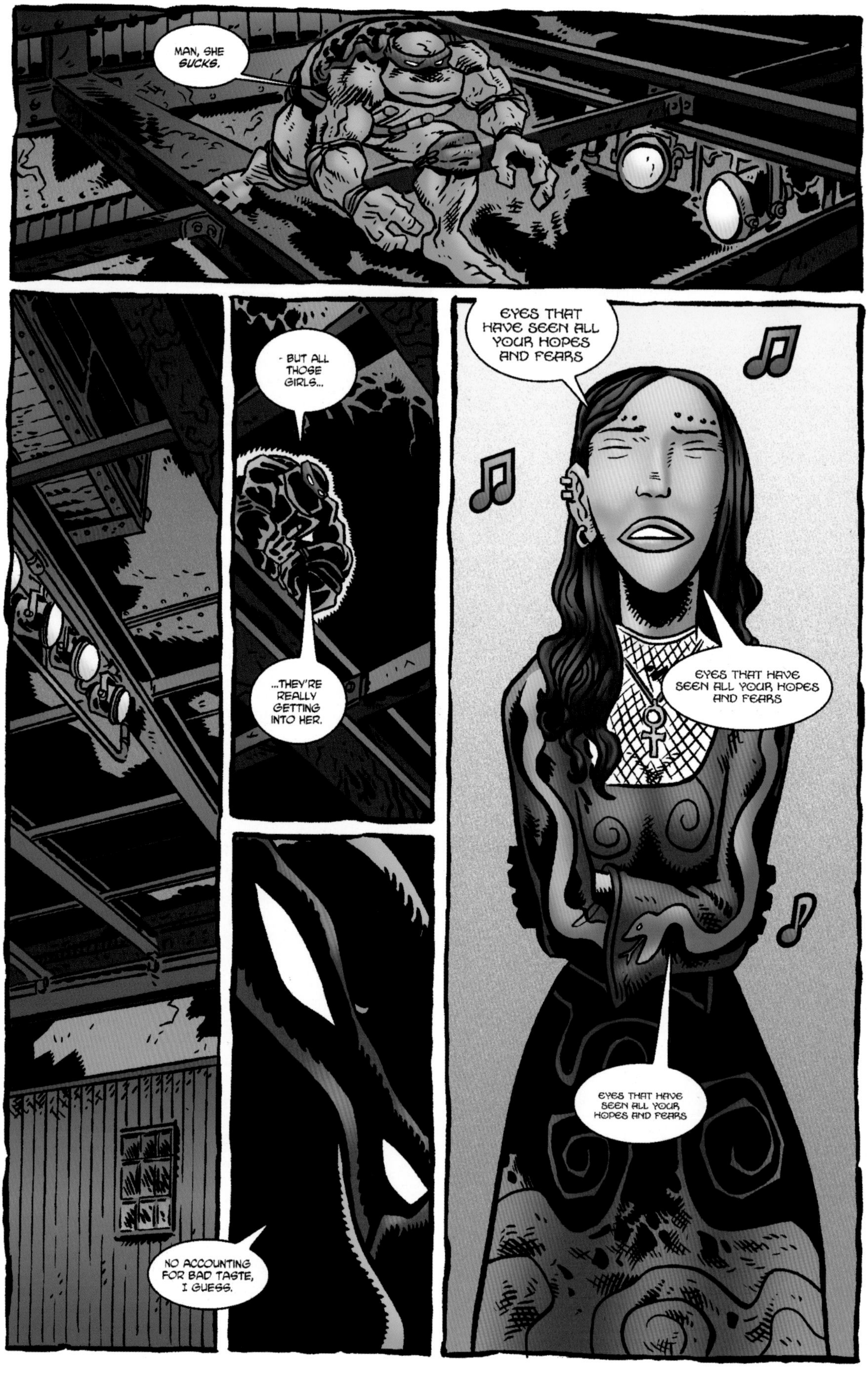
MAN, SHE SUCKS.
- BUT ALL THOSE GIRLS...
...THEY'RE REALLY GETTING INTO HER.
NO ACCOUNTING FOR BAD TASTE, I GUESS.
EYES THAT HAVE SEEN ALL YOUR HOPES AND FEARS
EYES THAT HAVE SEEN ALL YOUR HOPES AND FEARS
EYES THAT HAVE SEEN ALL YOUR HOPES AND FEARS

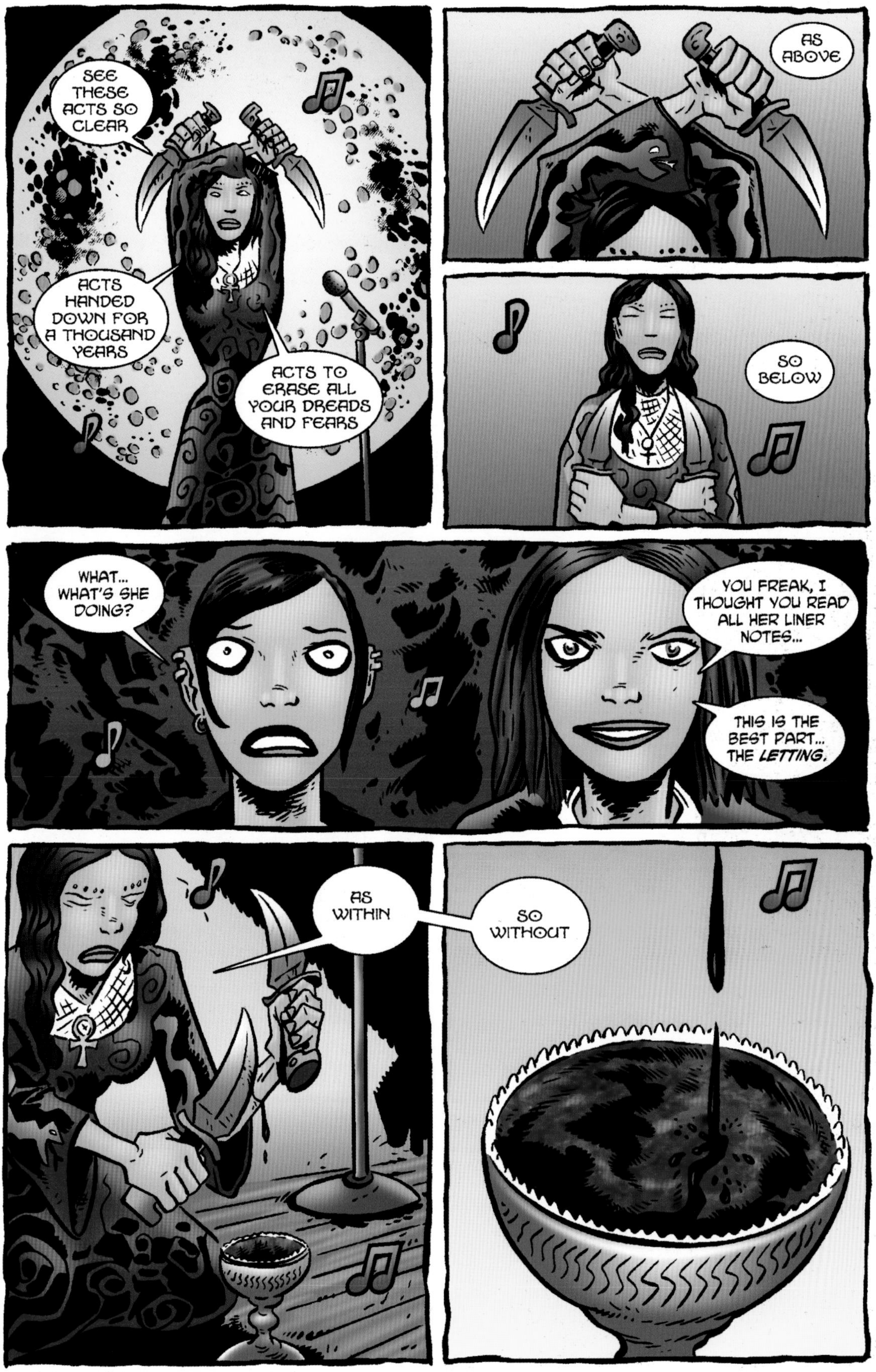
SEE THESE ACTS SO CLEAR
ACTS HANDED DOWN FOR A THOUSAND YEARS
ACTS TO ERASE ALL YOUR DREADS AND FEARS
AS ABOVE
SO BELOW
WHAT... WHAT'S SHE DOING?
YOU FREAK, I THOUGHT YOU READ ALL HER LINER NOTES...
THIS IS THE BEST PART... THE *LETTING.*
AS WITHIN
SO WITHOUT

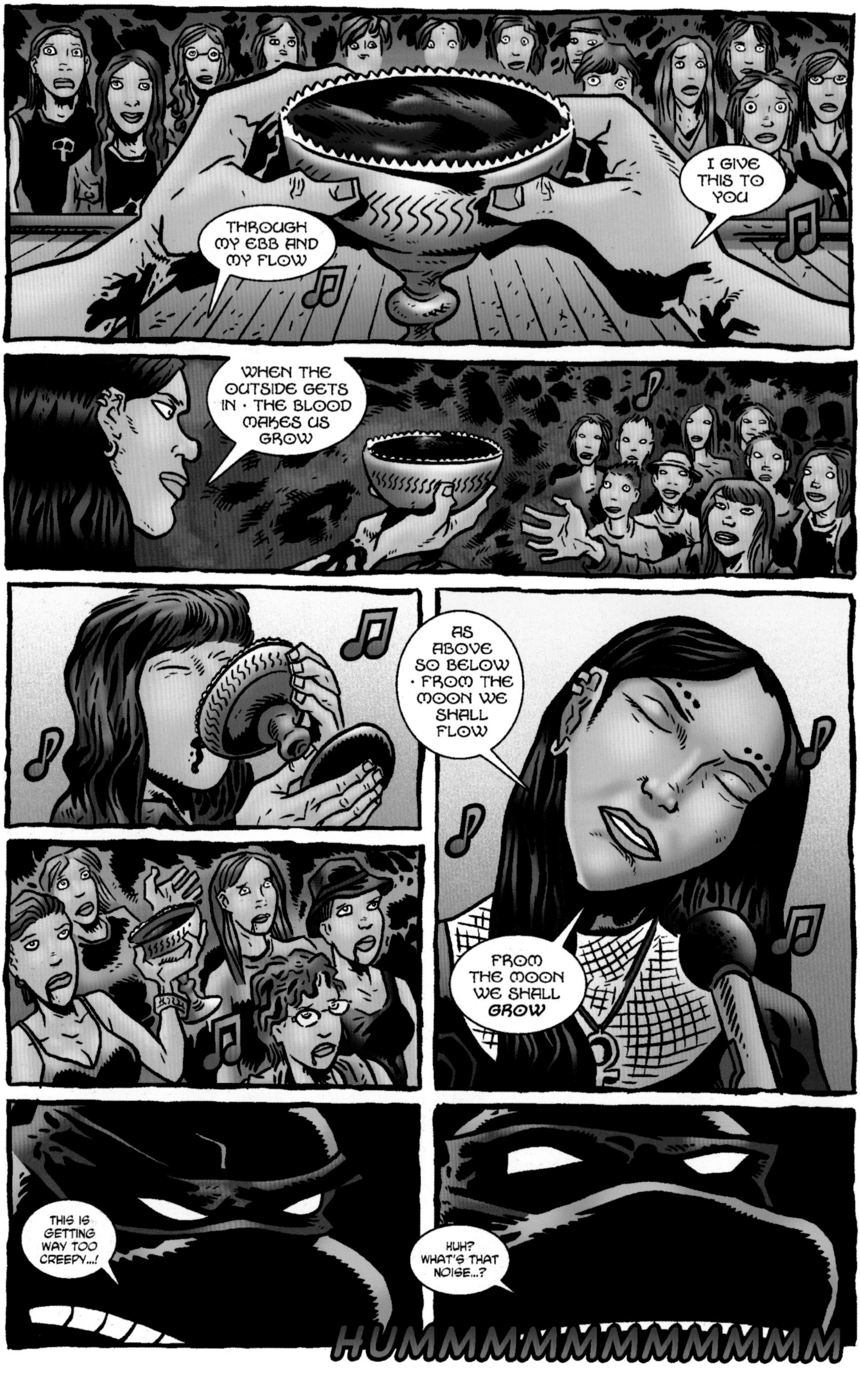
THROUGH MY EBB AND MY FLOW
I GIVE THIS TO YOU
WHEN THE OUTSIDE GETS IN · THE BLOOD MAKES US GROW
AS ABOVE SO BELOW · FROM THE MOON WE SHALL FLOW
FROM THE MOON WE SHALL *GROW*
THIS IS GETTING WAY TOO CREEPY...!
HUH? WHAT'S THAT NOISE...?
HUMMMMMMMMMMMMMM

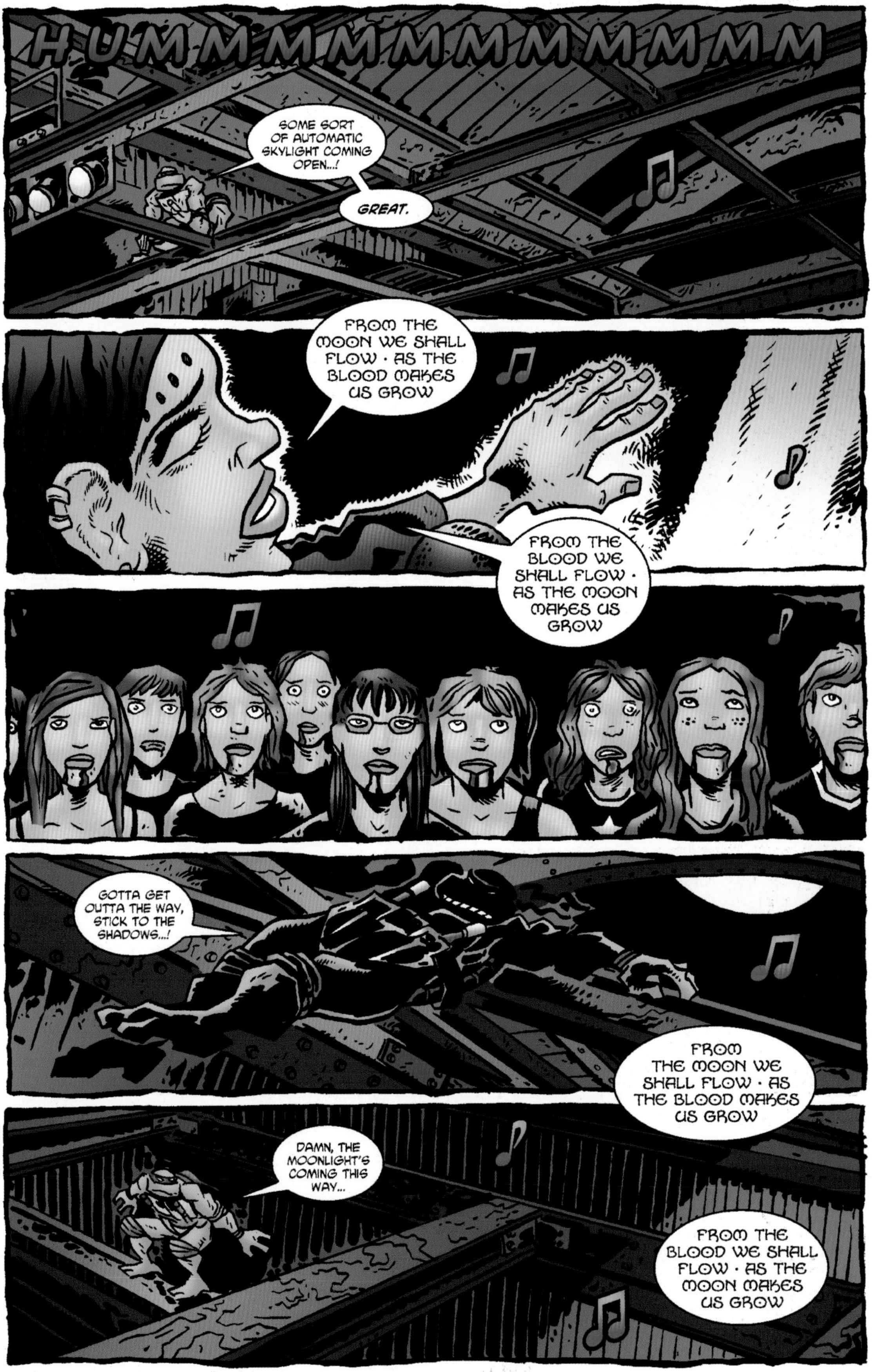
HUMMMMMMMMMMMMM
SOME SORT OF AUTOMATIC SKYLIGHT COMING OPEN...!
GREAT.
FROM THE MOON WE SHALL FLOW · AS THE BLOOD MAKES US GROW
FROM THE BLOOD WE SHALL FLOW · AS THE MOON MAKES US GROW
GOTTA GET OUTTA THE WAY, STICK TO THE SHADOWS...!
FROM THE MOON WE SHALL FLOW · AS THE BLOOD MAKES US GROW
DAMN, THE MOONLIGHT'S COMING THIS WAY...
FROM THE BLOOD WE SHALL FLOW · AS THE MOON MAKES US GROW

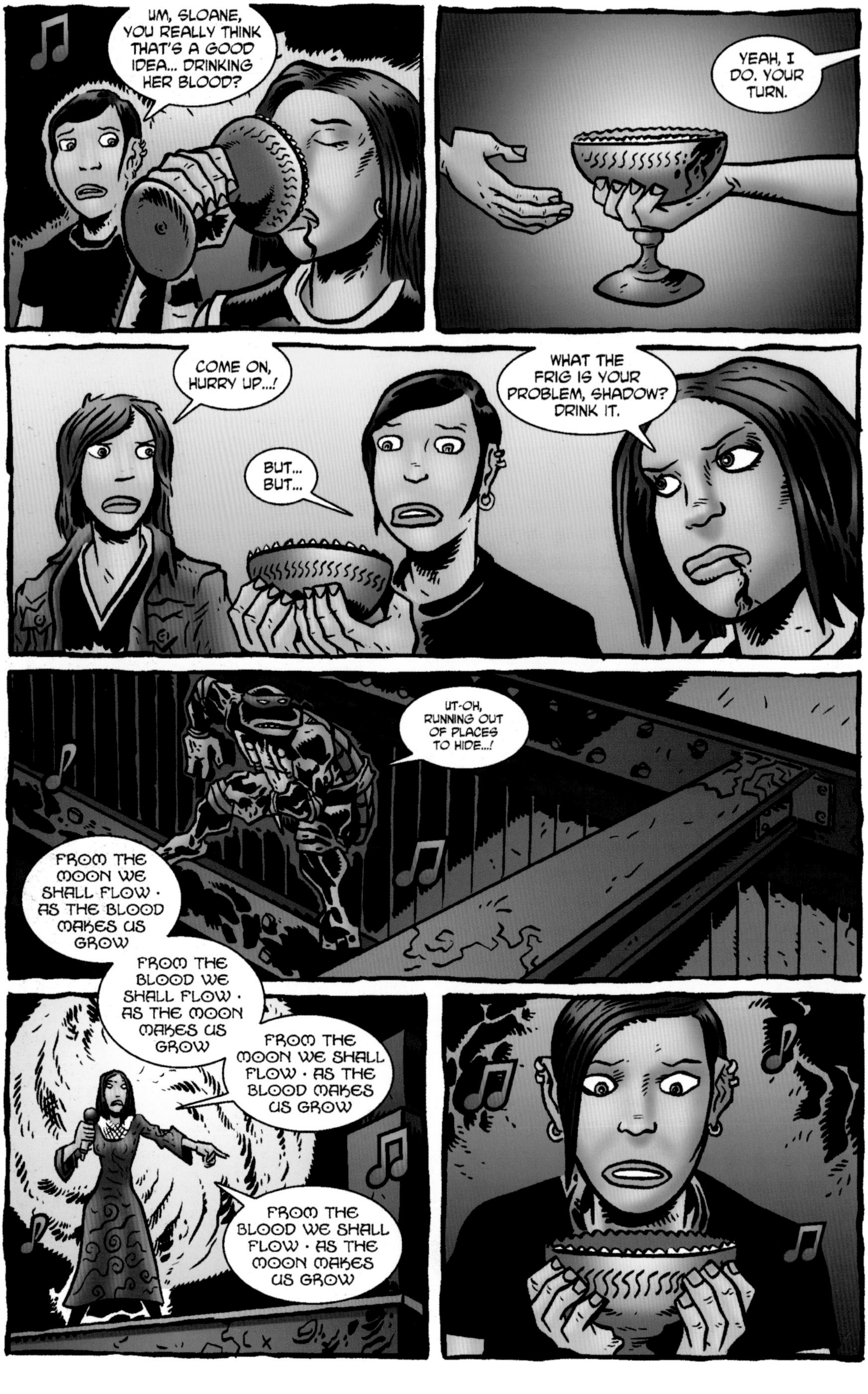
UM, SLOANE, YOU REALLY THINK THAT'S A GOOD IDEA... DRINKING HER BLOOD?
YEAH, I DO. YOUR TURN.
COME ON, HURRY UP...!
BUT... BUT...
WHAT THE FRIG IS YOUR PROBLEM, SHADOW? DRINK IT.
UT-OH, RUNNING OUT OF PLACES TO HIDE...!
FROM THE MOON WE SHALL FLOW · AS THE BLOOD MAKES US GROW
FROM THE BLOOD WE SHALL FLOW · AS THE MOON MAKES US GROW
FROM THE MOON WE SHALL FLOW · AS THE BLOOD MAKES US GROW
FROM THE BLOOD WE SHALL FLOW · AS THE MOON MAKES US GROW

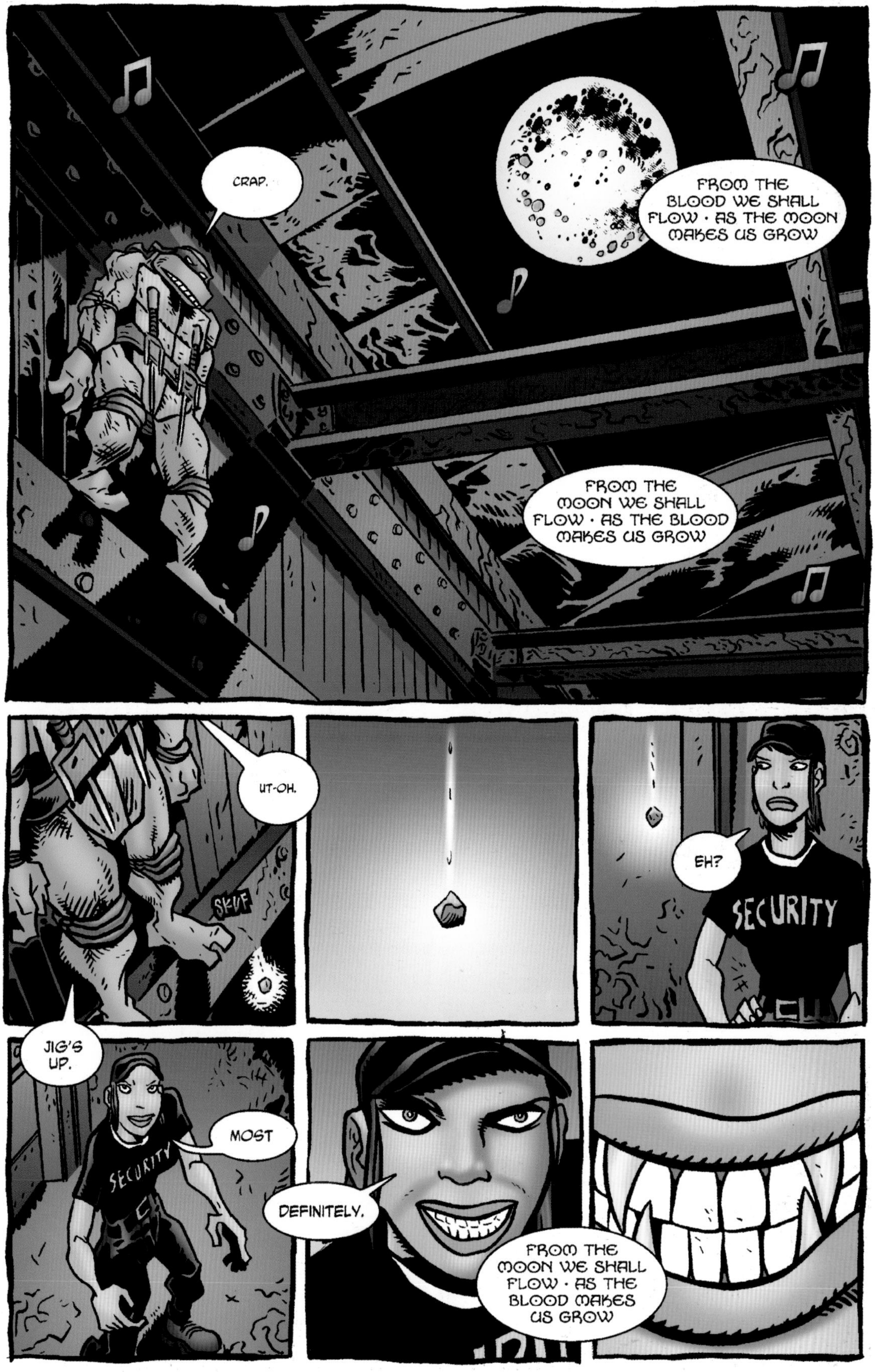
CRAP.
FROM THE BLOOD WE SHALL FLOW · AS THE MOON MAKES US GROW
FROM THE MOON WE SHALL FLOW · AS THE BLOOD MAKES US GROW
UT-OH.
SKUF
EH?
SECURITY
JIG'S UP.
MOST
SECURITY
DEFINITELY.
FROM THE MOON WE SHALL FLOW · AS THE BLOOD MAKES US GROW

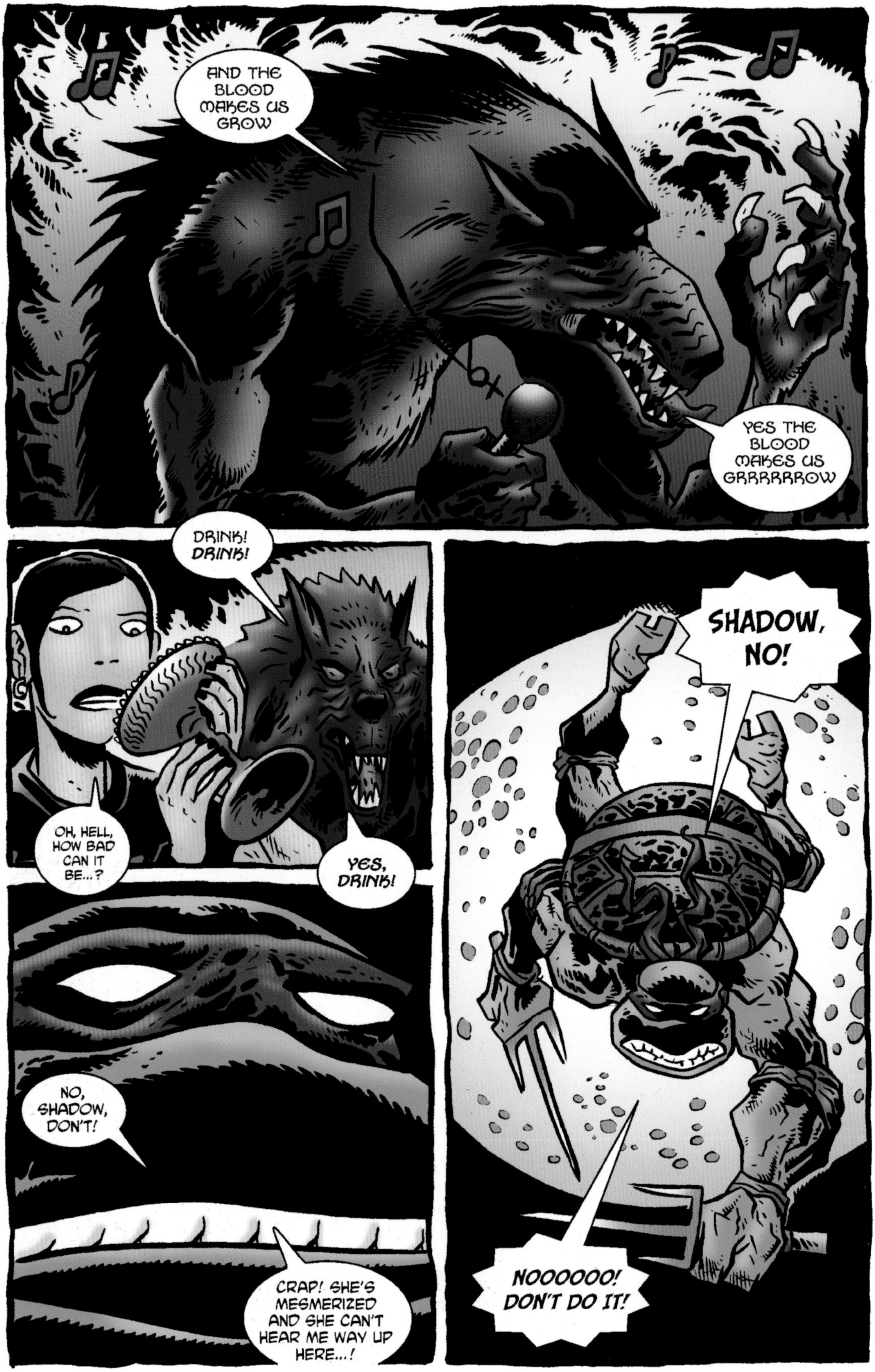
AND THE BLOOD MAKES US GROW
YES THE BLOOD MAKES US GRRRRRROW
DRINK! DRINK!
OH, HELL, HOW BAD CAN IT BE...?
YES, DRINK!
NO, SHADOW, DON'T!
CRAP! SHE'S MESMERIZED AND SHE CAN'T HEAR ME WAY UP HERE...!
SHADOW, NO!
NOOOOOO! DON'T DO IT!

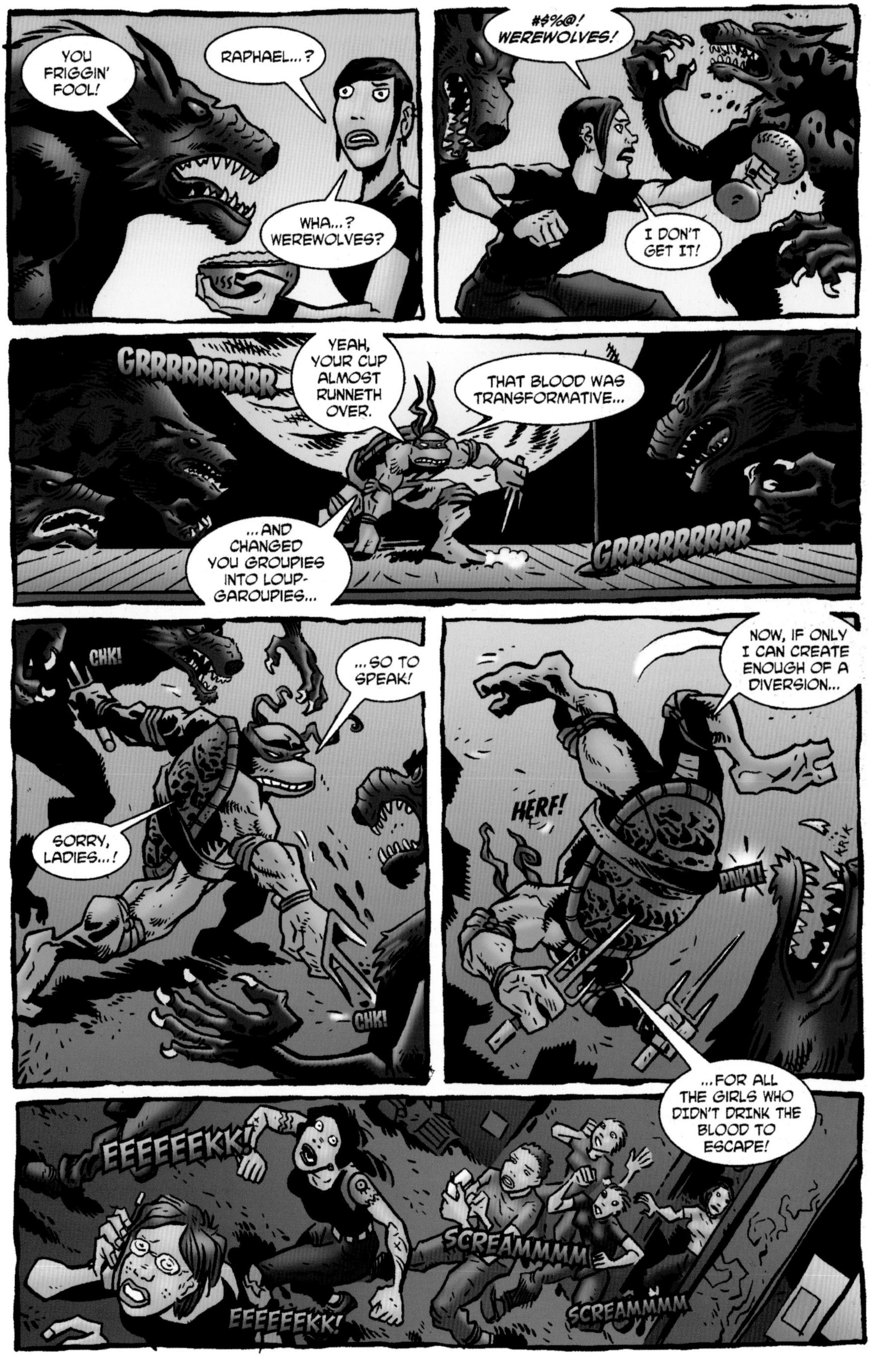
YOU FRIGGIN' FOOL!
RAPHAEL...?
WHA...? WEREWOLVES?
#$%@! WEREWOLVES!
I DON'T GET IT!
GRRRRRRRRRR
YEAH, YOUR CUP ALMOST RUNNETH OVER.
THAT BLOOD WAS TRANSFORMATIVE...
...AND CHANGED YOU GROUPIES INTO LOUP-GAROUPIES...
GRRRRRRRRR
CHK!
...SO TO SPEAK!
SORRY, LADIES...!
CHK!
NOW, IF ONLY I CAN CREATE ENOUGH OF A DIVERSION...
HERF!
KRIK
PNKT!
...FOR ALL THE GIRLS WHO DIDN'T DRINK THE BLOOD TO ESCAPE!
EEEEEEKK!
SCREAMMMMM
EEEEEEKK!
SCREAMMMM

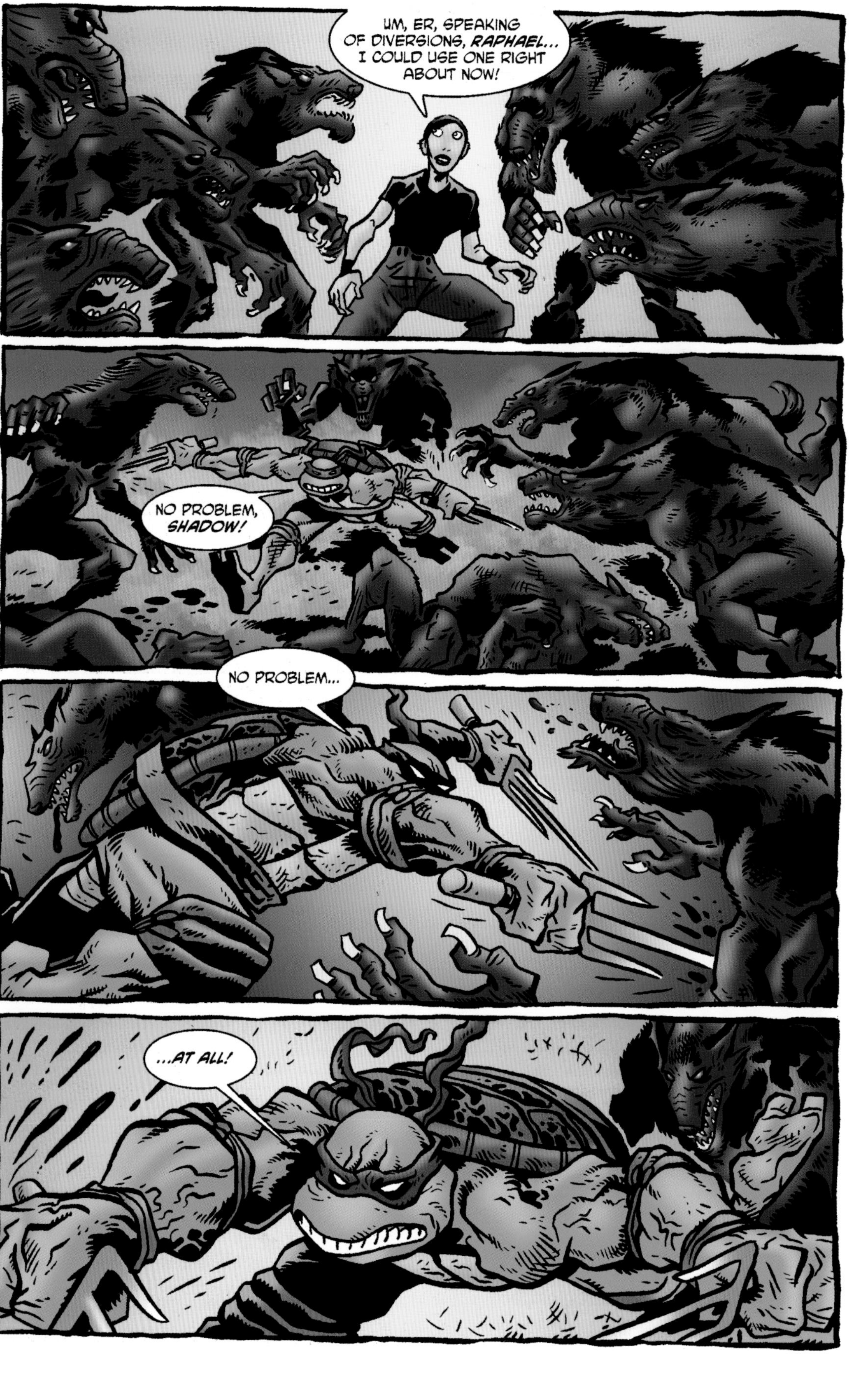
UM, ER, SPEAKING OF DIVERSIONS, *RAPHAEL*... I COULD USE ONE RIGHT ABOUT NOW!
NO PROBLEM, *SHADOW!*
NO PROBLEM...
...AT ALL!

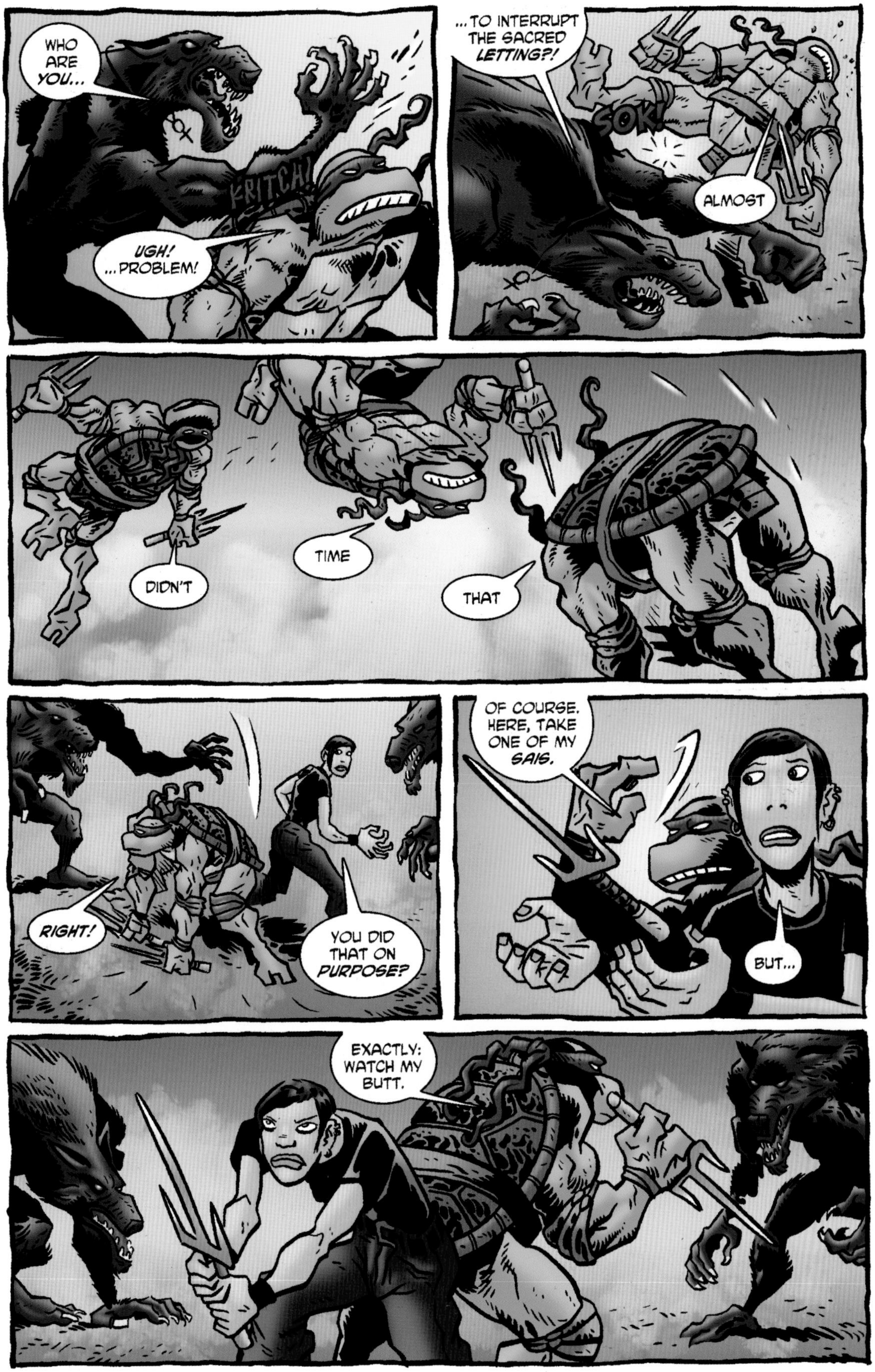
WHO ARE YOU...
KRITCH!
UGH! ...PROBLEM!
...TO INTERRUPT THE SACRED LETTING?!
SOK!
ALMOST
DIDN'T
TIME
THAT
RIGHT!
YOU DID THAT ON PURPOSE?
OF COURSE. HERE, TAKE ONE OF MY SAIS.
BUT...
EXACTLY: WATCH MY BUTT.

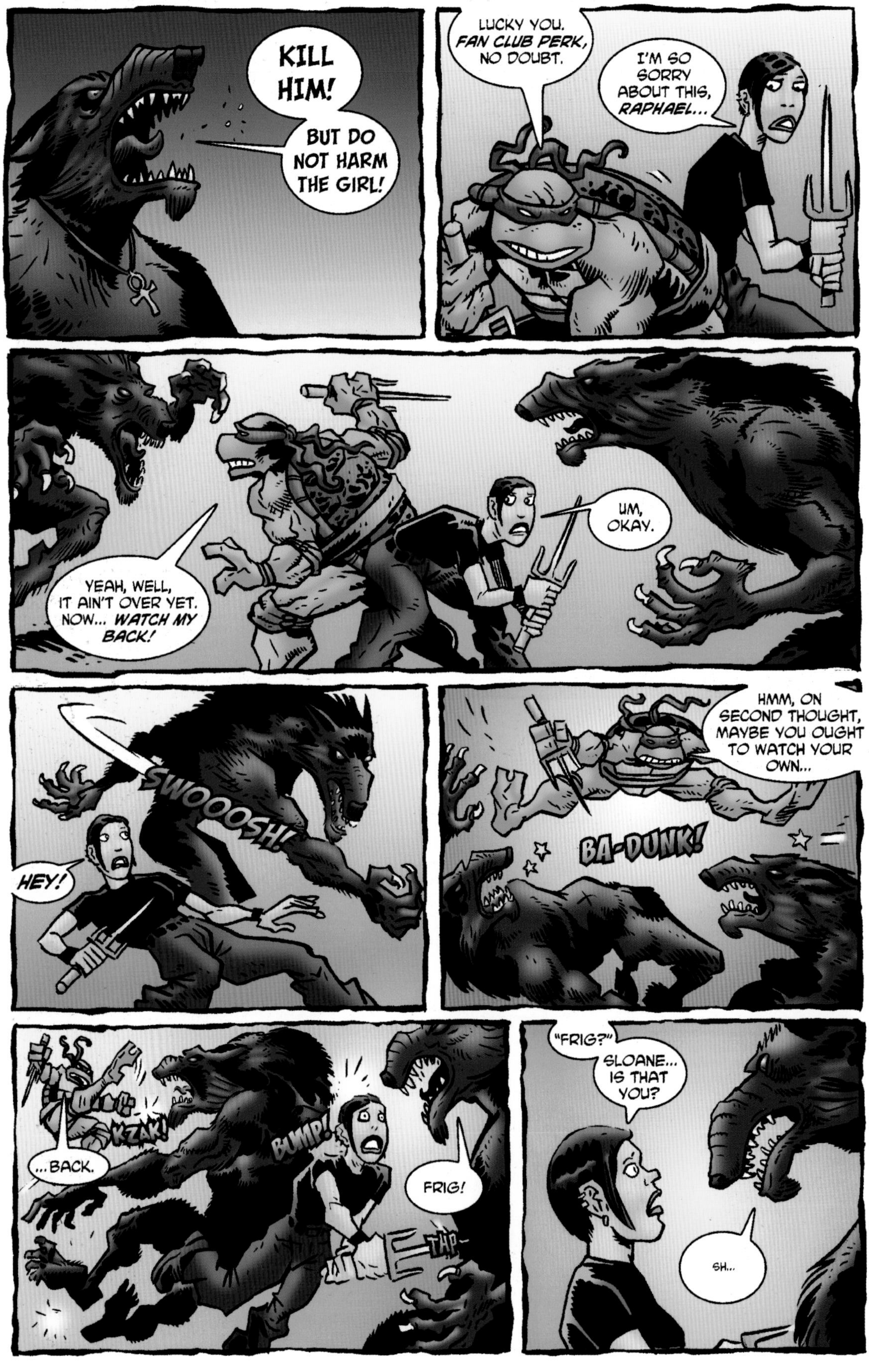
KILL HIM!
BUT DO NOT HARM THE GIRL!
LUCKY YOU. *FAN CLUB PERK,* NO DOUBT.
I'M SO SORRY ABOUT THIS, *RAPHAEL...*
YEAH, WELL, IT AIN'T OVER YET. NOW... *WATCH MY BACK!*
UM, OKAY.
SWOOOSH!
HEY!
HMM, ON SECOND THOUGHT, MAYBE YOU OUGHT TO WATCH YOUR OWN...
BA-DUNK!
KZAK!
...BACK.
BUMP!
FRIG!
TAP
"FRIG?"
SLOANE... IS THAT YOU?
SH...

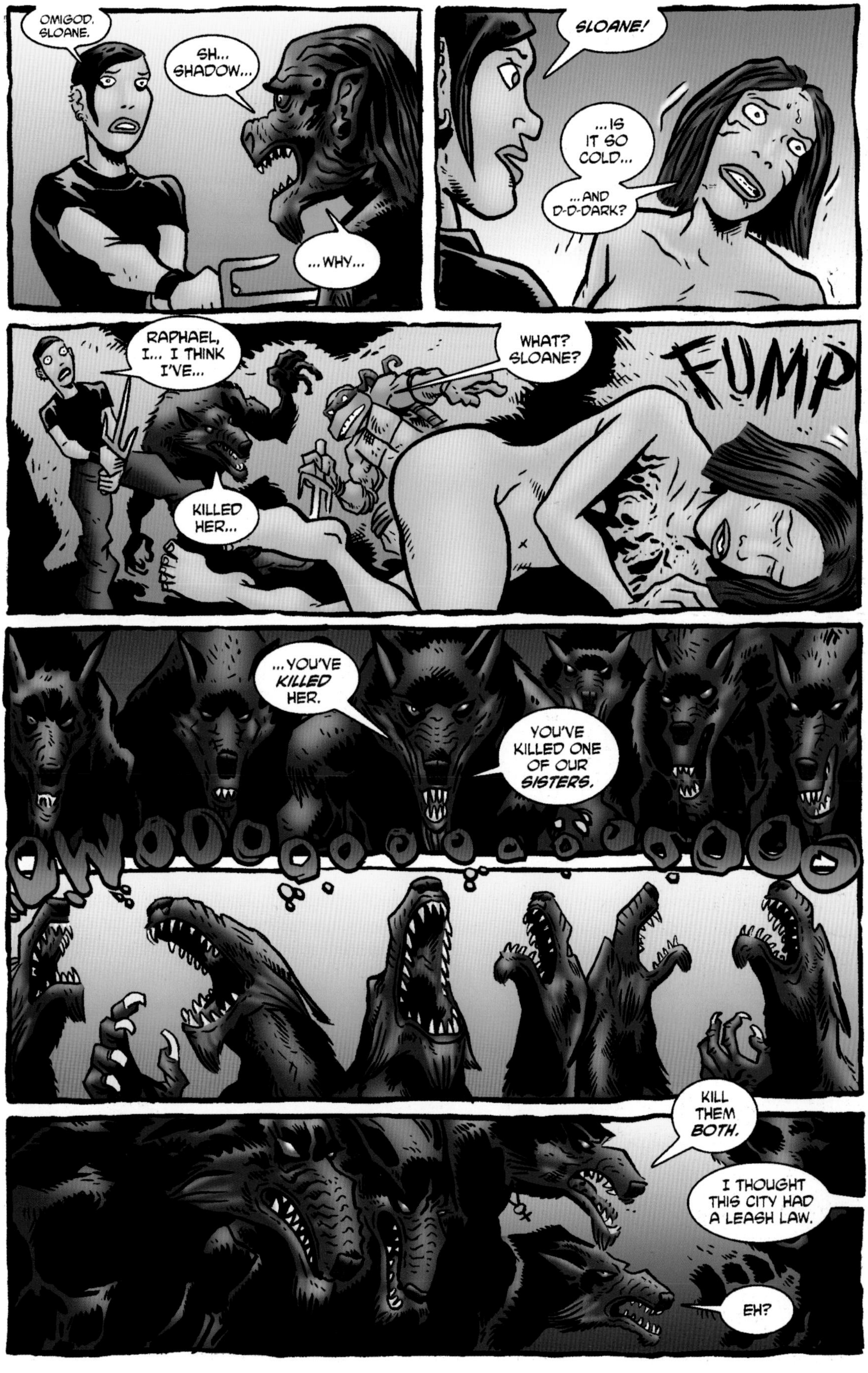
OMIGOD. SLOANE.
SH... SHADOW...
...WHY...
SLOANE!
...IS IT SO COLD...
...AND D-D-DARK?
RAPHAEL, I... I THINK I'VE...
KILLED HER...
WHAT? SLOANE?
FUMP
...YOU'VE KILLED HER.
YOU'VE KILLED ONE OF OUR SISTERS.
KILL THEM BOTH.
I THOUGHT THIS CITY HAD A LEASH LAW.
EH?

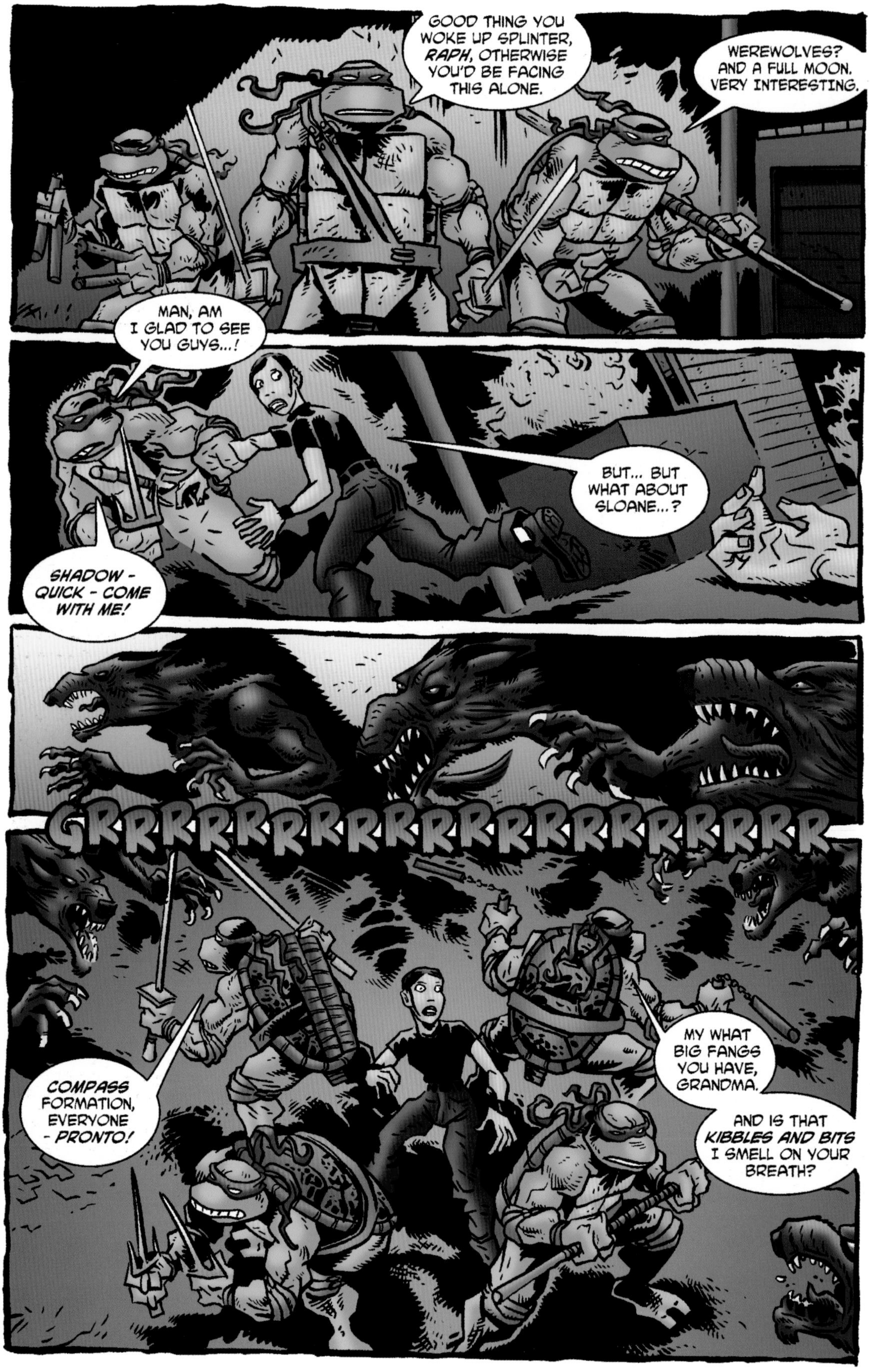
GOOD THING YOU WOKE UP SPLINTER, RAPH, OTHERWISE YOU'D BE FACING THIS ALONE.
WEREWOLVES? AND A FULL MOON. VERY INTERESTING.
MAN, AM I GLAD TO SEE YOU GUYS...!
BUT... BUT WHAT ABOUT SLOANE...?
SHADOW - QUICK - COME WITH ME!
GRRRRRRRRRRRRRRRRRRRR
COMPASS FORMATION, EVERYONE - PRONTO!
MY WHAT BIG FANGS YOU HAVE, GRANDMA.
AND IS THAT KIBBLES AND BITS I SMELL ON YOUR BREATH?

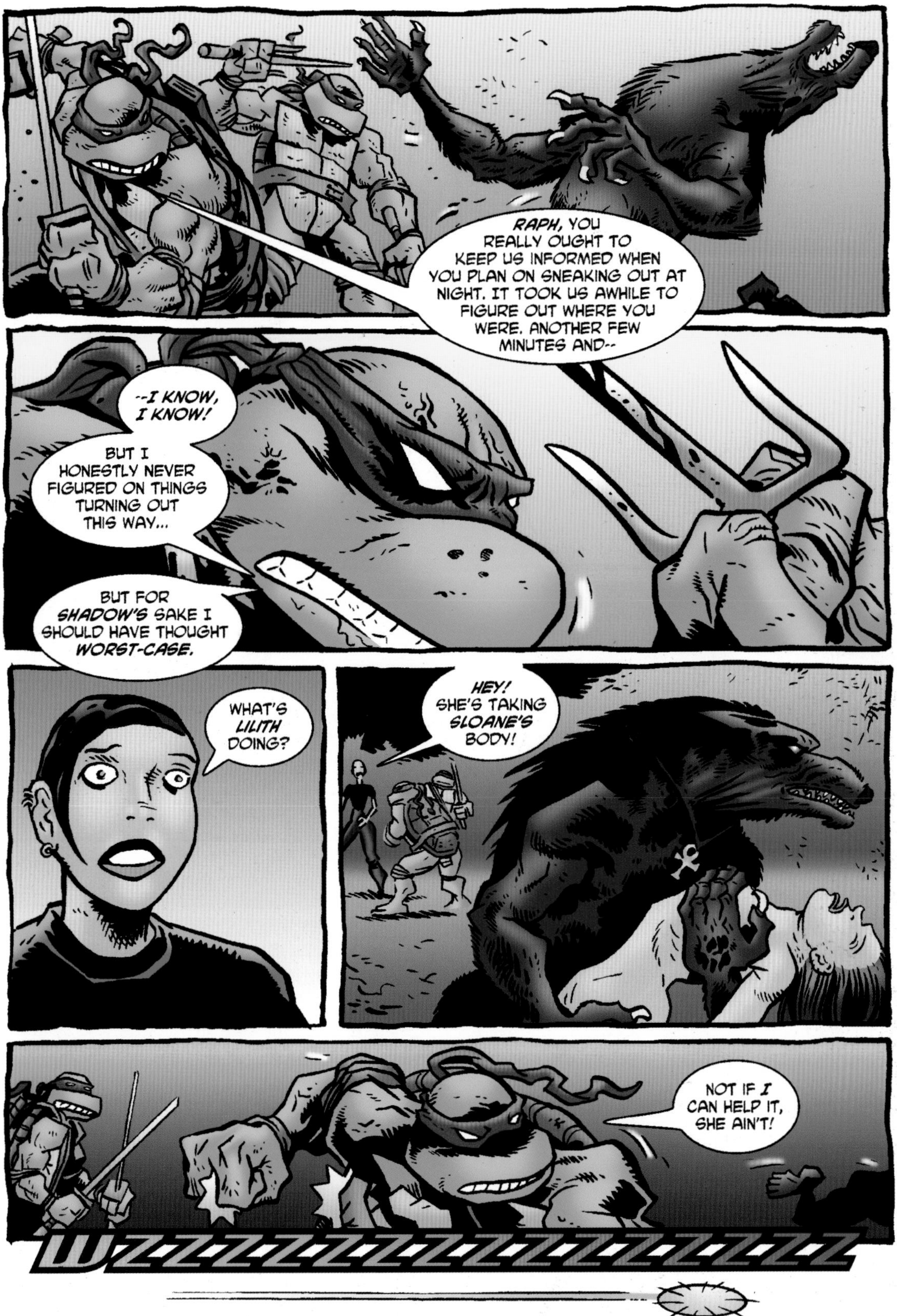
RAPH, YOU REALLY OUGHT TO KEEP US INFORMED WHEN YOU PLAN ON SNEAKING OUT AT NIGHT. IT TOOK US AWHILE TO FIGURE OUT WHERE YOU WERE. ANOTHER FEW MINUTES AND--
--I KNOW, I KNOW!
BUT I HONESTLY NEVER FIGURED ON THINGS TURNING OUT THIS WAY...
BUT FOR SHADOW'S SAKE I SHOULD HAVE THOUGHT WORST-CASE.
WHAT'S LILITH DOING?
HEY! SHE'S TAKING SLOANE'S BODY!
NOT IF I CAN HELP IT, SHE AIN'T!
WZZZZZZZZZZZZZZZZZZZZ

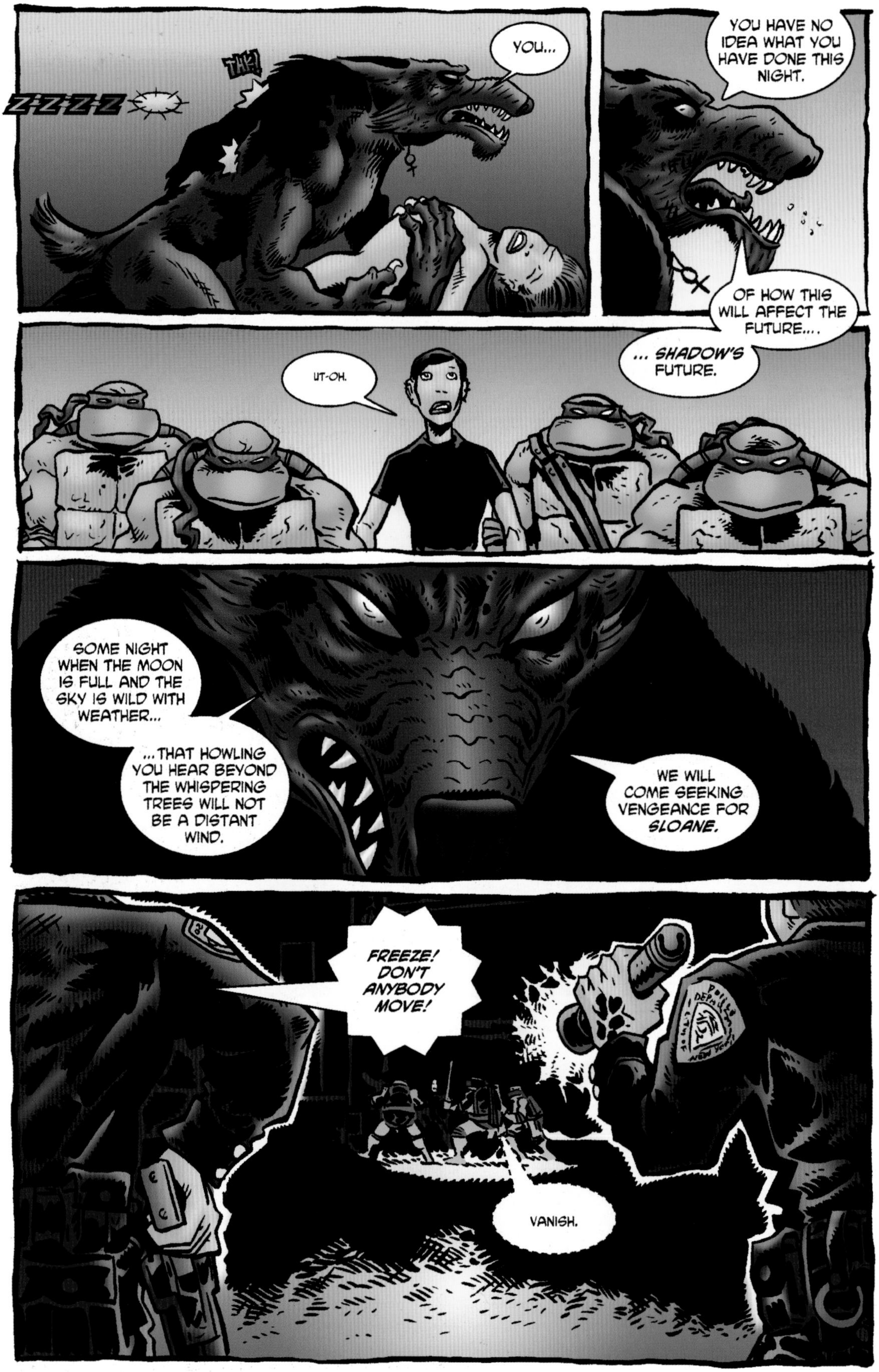
Z-Z-Z-Z
THK!
YOU...
YOU HAVE NO IDEA WHAT YOU HAVE DONE THIS NIGHT.
OF HOW THIS WILL AFFECT THE FUTURE....
... SHADOW'S FUTURE.
UT-OH.
SOME NIGHT WHEN THE MOON IS FULL AND THE SKY IS WILD WITH WEATHER...
...THAT HOWLING YOU HEAR BEYOND THE WHISPERING TREES WILL NOT BE A DISTANT WIND.
WE WILL COME SEEKING VENGEANCE FOR SLOANE.
FREEZE! DON'T ANYBODY MOVE!
VANISH.

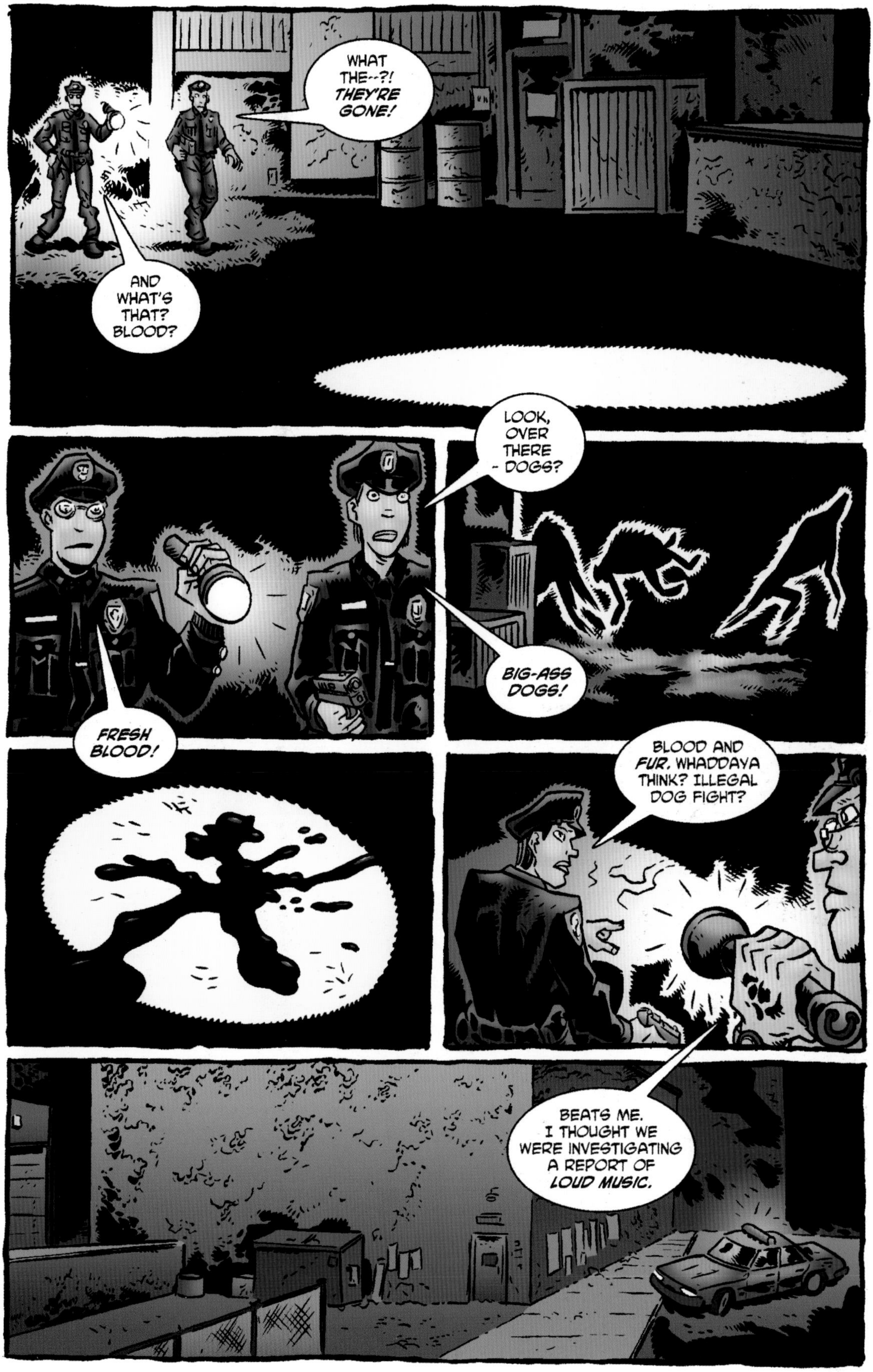
WHAT THE--?! THEY'RE GONE!
AND WHAT'S THAT? BLOOD?
LOOK, OVER THERE - DOGS?
BIG-ASS DOGS!
FRESH BLOOD!
BLOOD AND FUR. WHADDAYA THINK? ILLEGAL DOG FIGHT?
BEATS ME. I THOUGHT WE WERE INVESTIGATING A REPORT OF LOUD MUSIC.

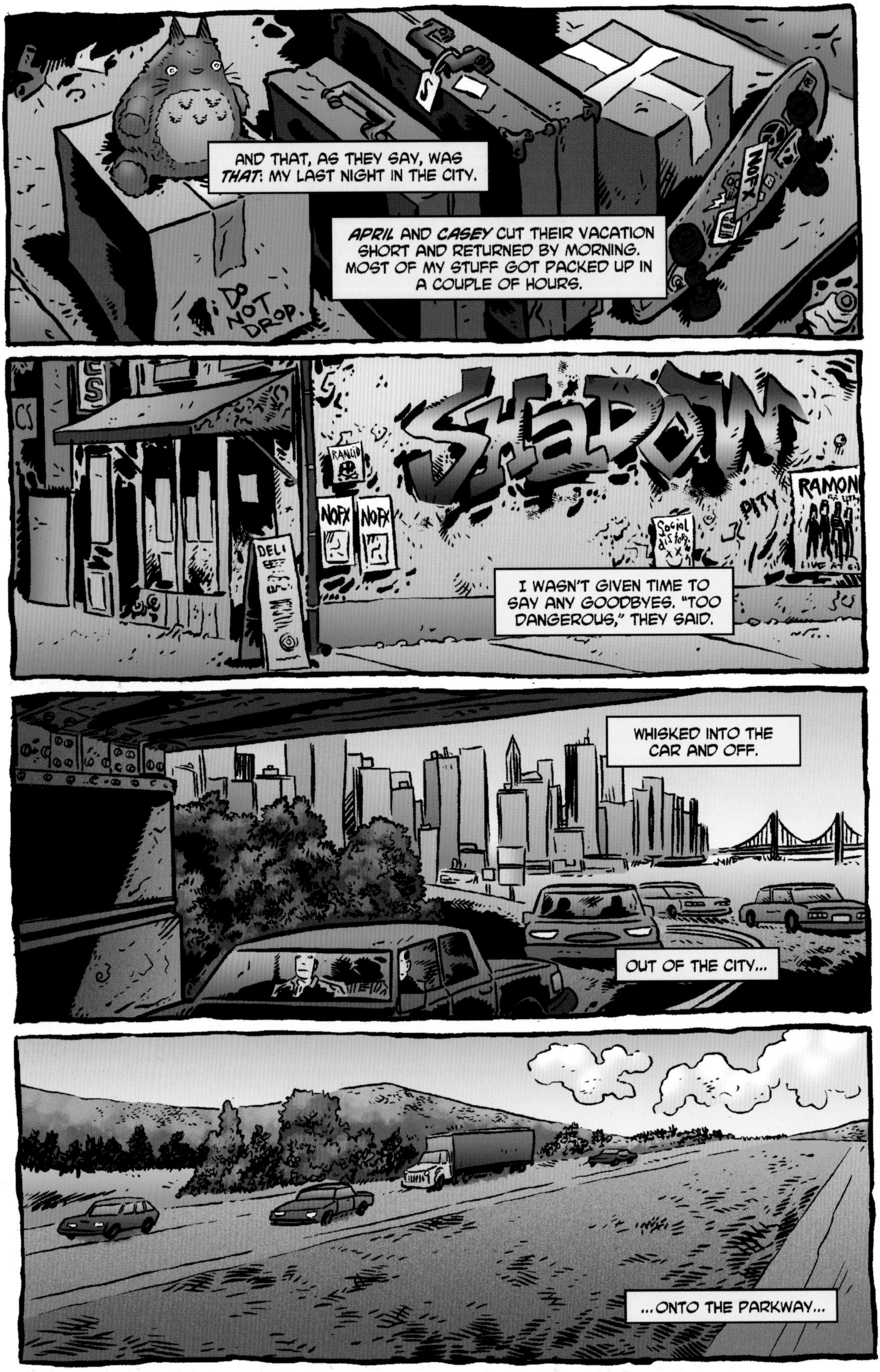
AND THAT, AS THEY SAY, WAS *THAT*: MY LAST NIGHT IN THE CITY.
APRIL AND *CASEY* CUT THEIR VACATION SHORT AND RETURNED BY MORNING. MOST OF MY STUFF GOT PACKED UP IN A COUPLE OF HOURS.
DO NOT DROP.
NOFX
NOFX
NOFX
DELI
RAMON
I WASN'T GIVEN TIME TO SAY ANY GOODBYES. "TOO DANGEROUS," THEY SAID.
WHISKED INTO THE CAR AND OFF.
OUT OF THE CITY...
...ONTO THE PARKWAY...

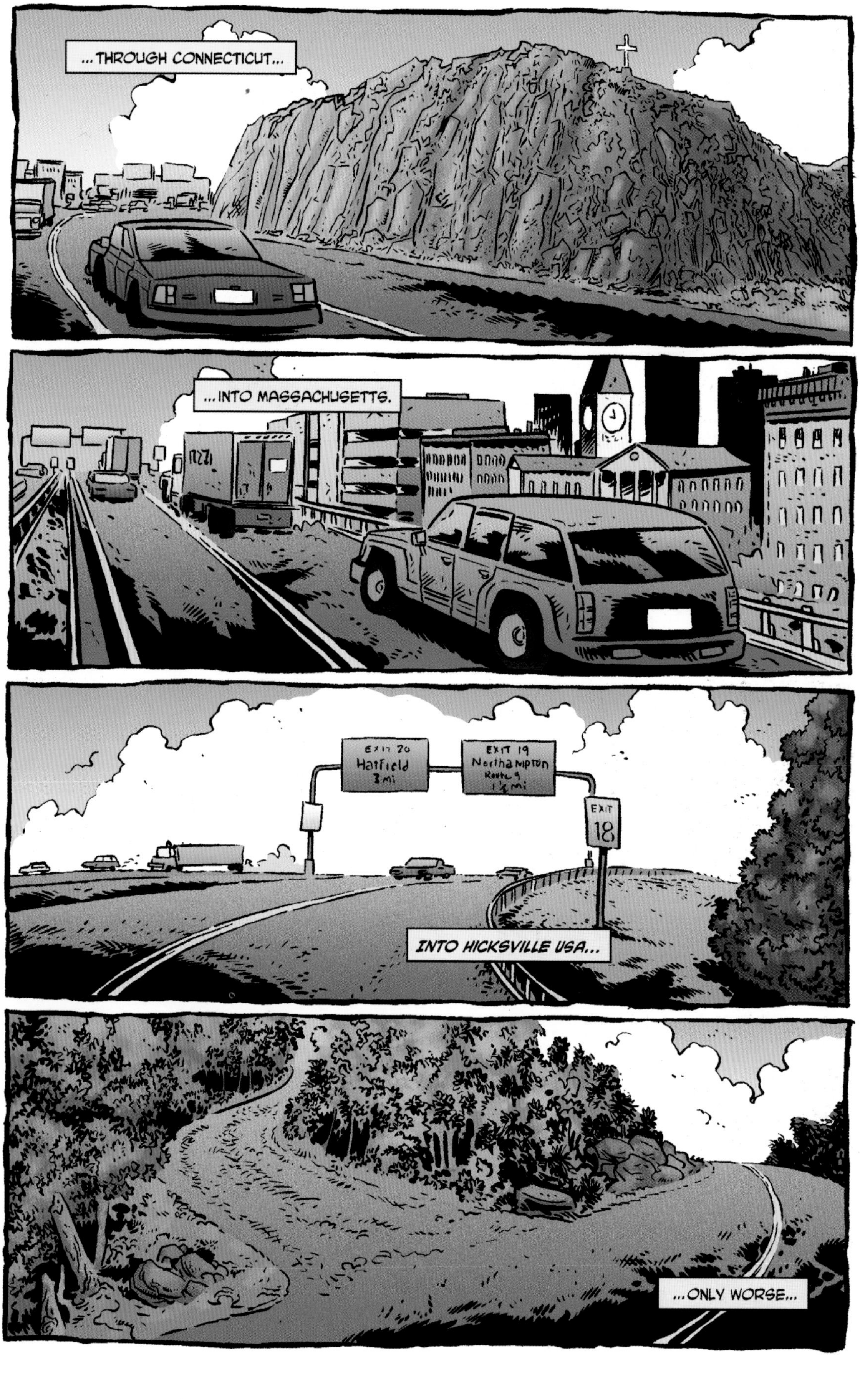
...THROUGH CONNECTICUT...
...INTO MASSACHUSETTS.
EXIT 20 Hatfield 3 mi
EXIT 19 Northampton Route 9
EXIT 18
INTO HICKSVILLE USA...
...ONLY WORSE...

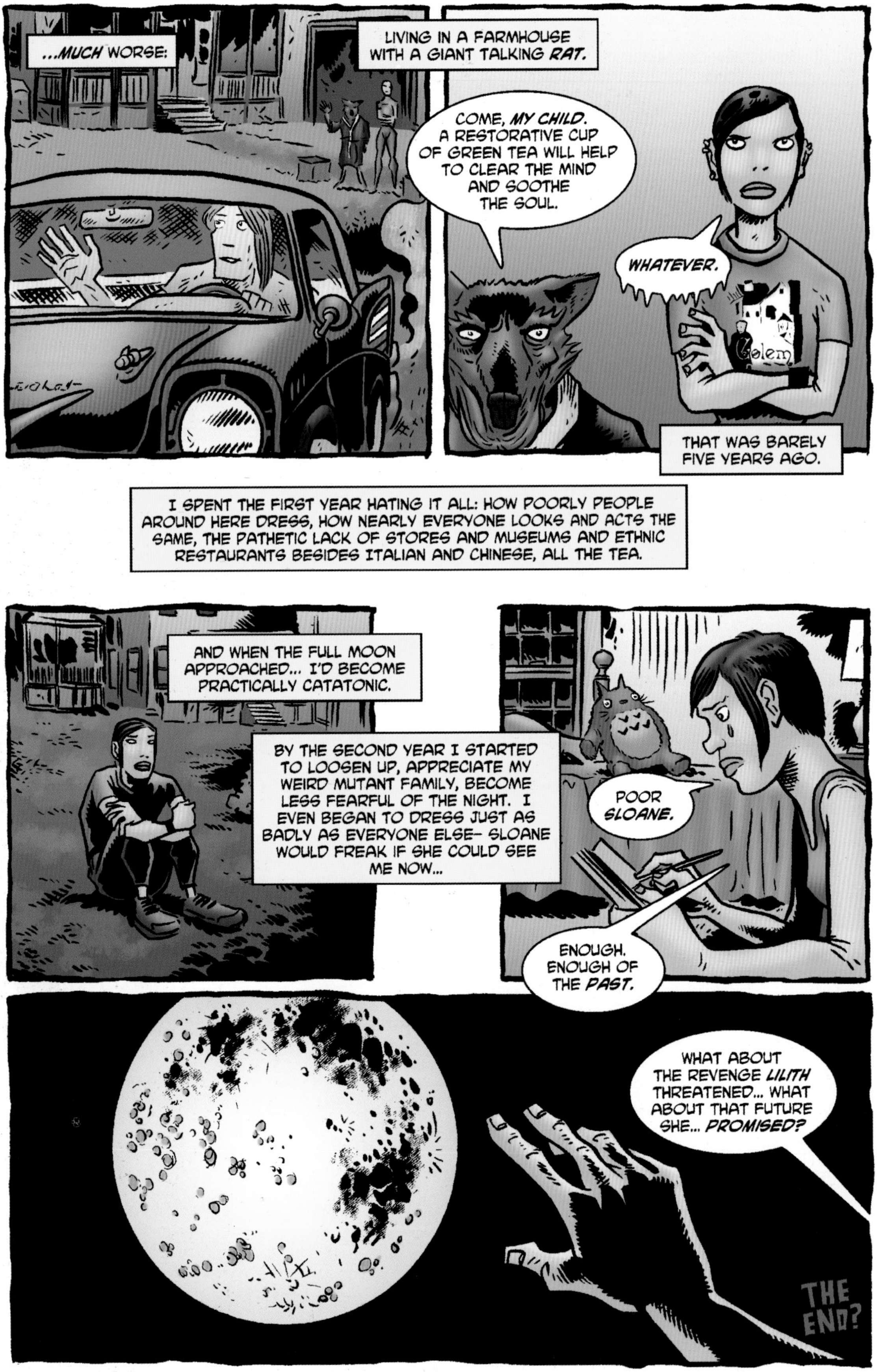

...MUCH WORSE:
LIVING IN A FARMHOUSE WITH A GIANT TALKING RAT.
COME, MY CHILD. A RESTORATIVE CUP OF GREEN TEA WILL HELP TO CLEAR THE MIND AND SOOTHE THE SOUL.
WHATEVER.
Golem
THAT WAS BARELY FIVE YEARS AGO.
I SPENT THE FIRST YEAR HATING IT ALL: HOW POORLY PEOPLE AROUND HERE DRESS, HOW NEARLY EVERYONE LOOKS AND ACTS THE SAME, THE PATHETIC LACK OF STORES AND MUSEUMS AND ETHNIC RESTAURANTS BESIDES ITALIAN AND CHINESE, ALL THE TEA.
AND WHEN THE FULL MOON APPROACHED... I'D BECOME PRACTICALLY CATATONIC.
BY THE SECOND YEAR I STARTED TO LOOSEN UP, APPRECIATE MY WEIRD MUTANT FAMILY, BECOME LESS FEARFUL OF THE NIGHT. I EVEN BEGAN TO DRESS JUST AS BADLY AS EVERYONE ELSE- SLOANE WOULD FREAK IF SHE COULD SEE ME NOW...
POOR SLOANE.
ENOUGH. ENOUGH OF THE PAST.
WHAT ABOUT THE REVENGE LILITH THREATENED... WHAT ABOUT THAT FUTURE SHE... PROMISED?
THE END?

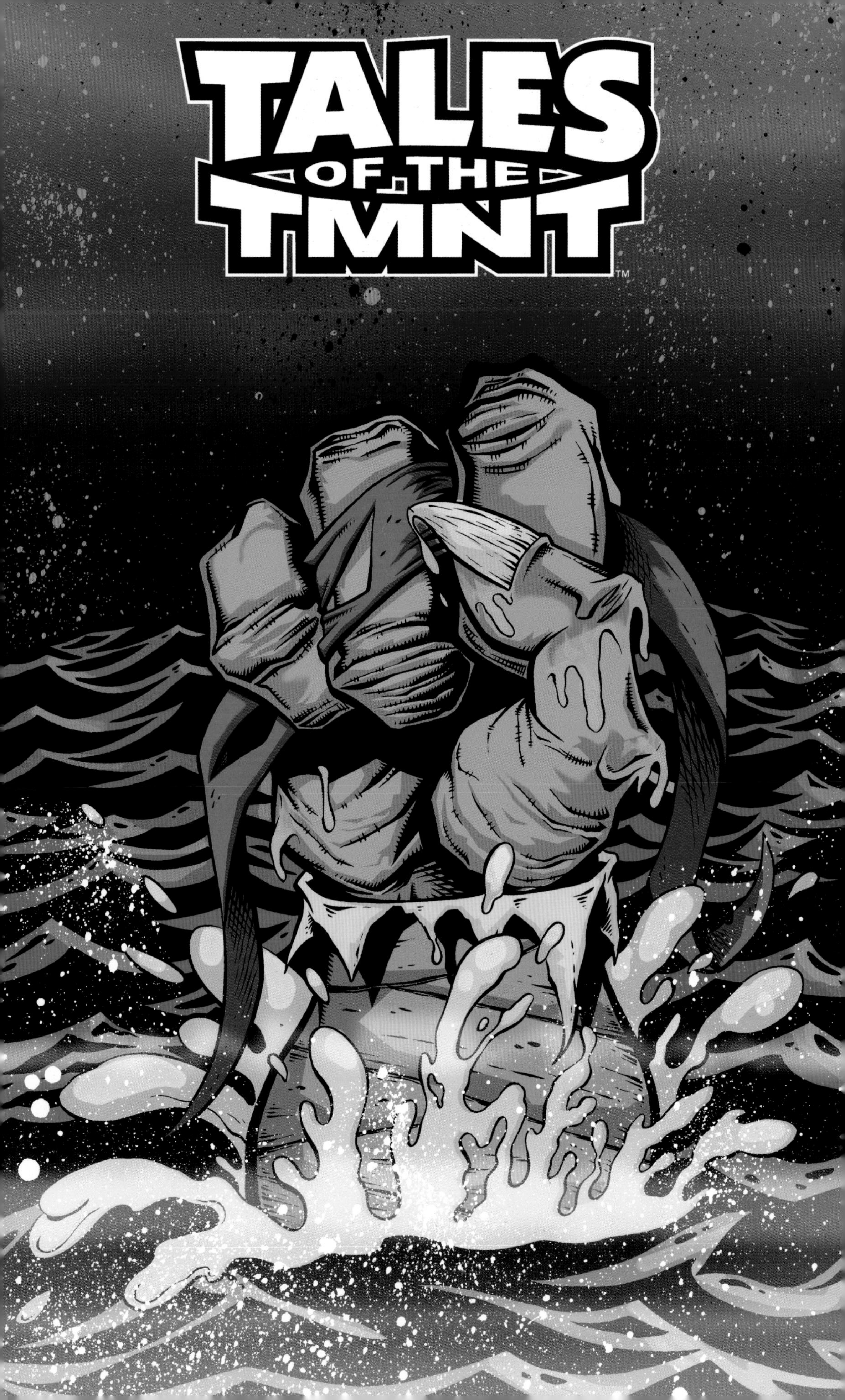
TALES
OF THE
TMNT™

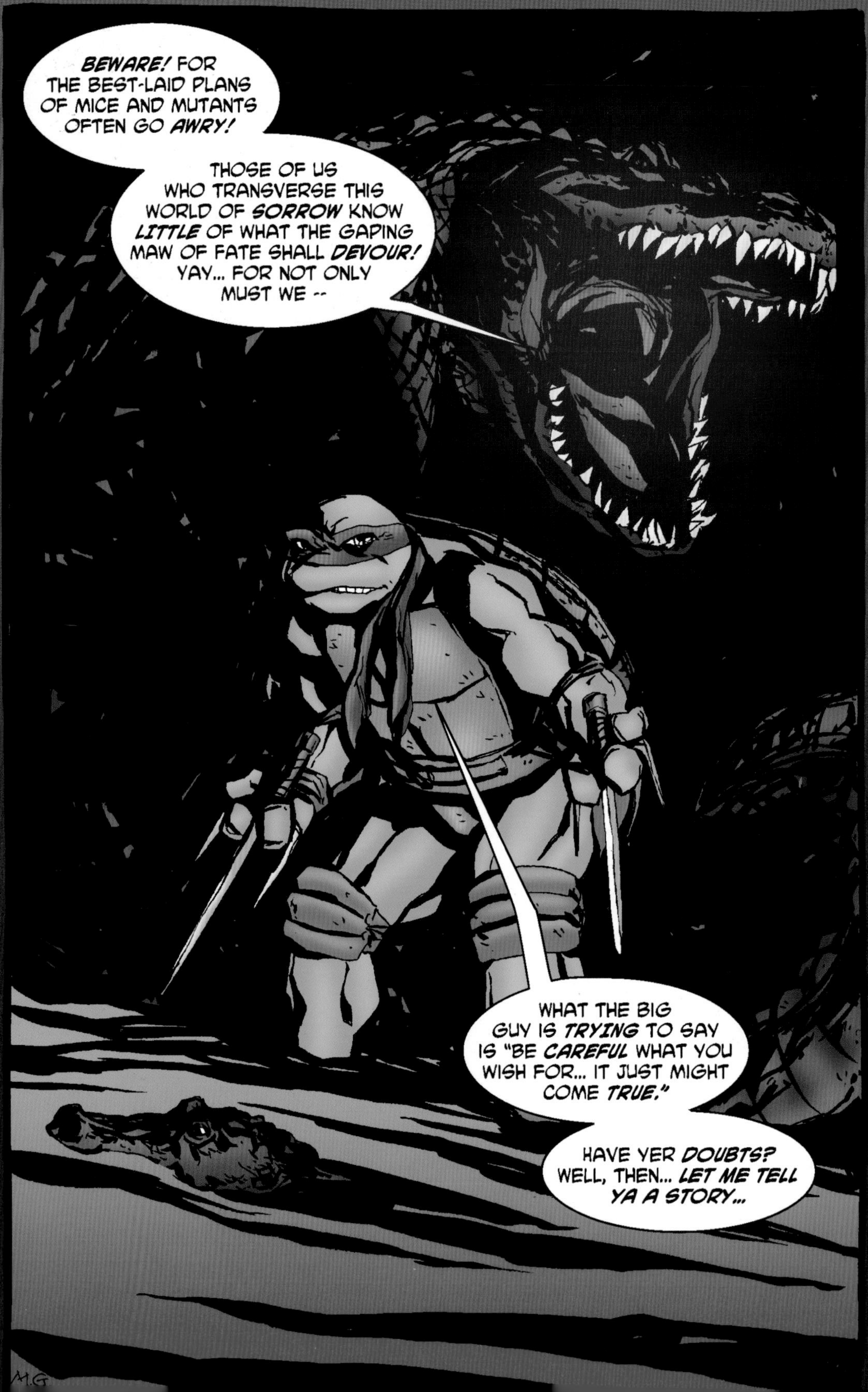

BEWARE! FOR THE BEST-LAID PLANS OF MICE AND MUTANTS OFTEN GO AWRY!
THOSE OF US WHO TRANSVERSE THIS WORLD OF SORROW KNOW LITTLE OF WHAT THE GAPING MAW OF FATE SHALL DEVOUR! YAY... FOR NOT ONLY MUST WE --
WHAT THE BIG GUY IS TRYING TO SAY IS "BE CAREFUL WHAT YOU WISH FOR... IT JUST MIGHT COME TRUE."
HAVE YER DOUBTS? WELL, THEN... LET ME TELL YA A STORY...
M.G

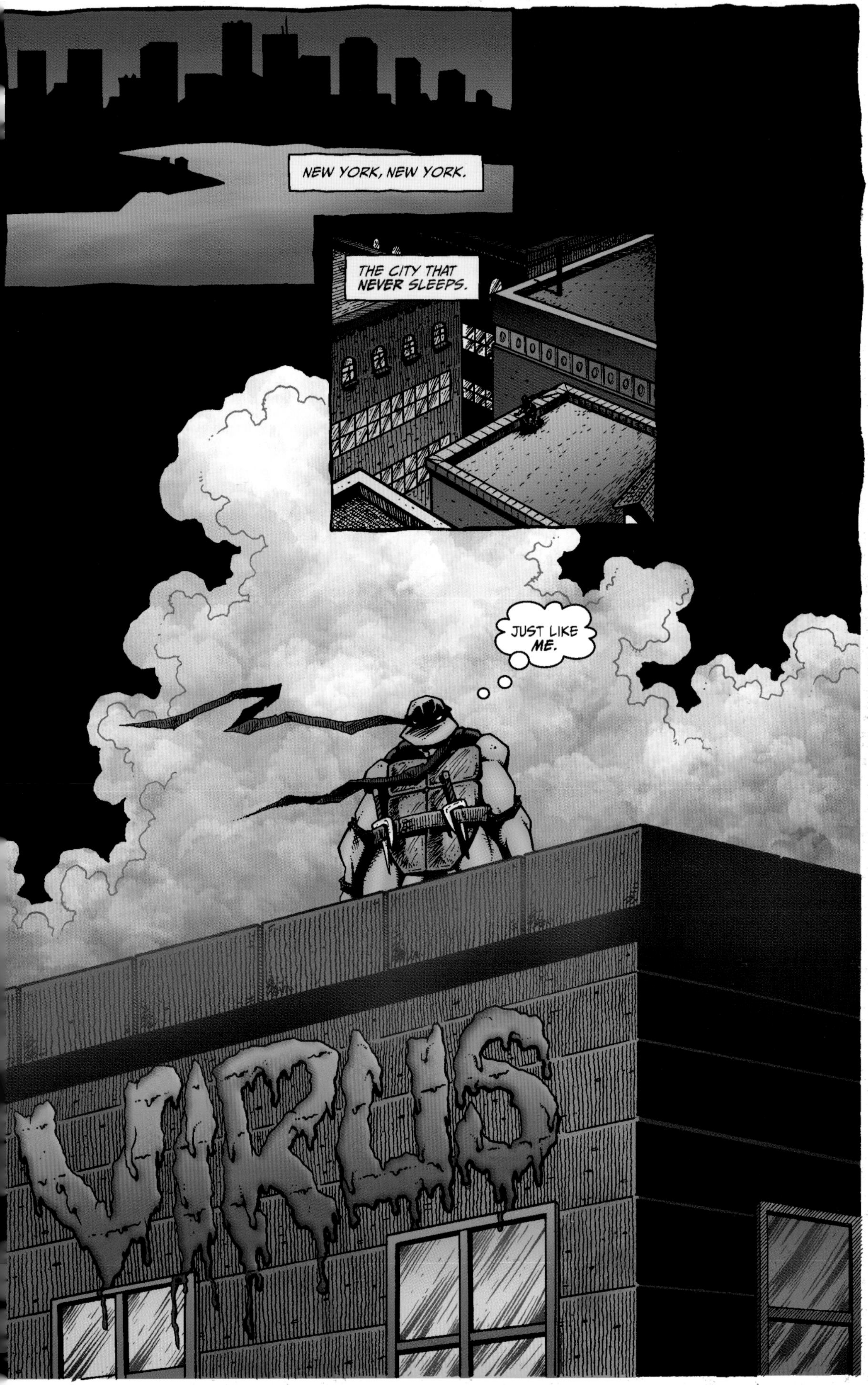
NEW YORK, NEW YORK.
THE CITY THAT NEVER SLEEPS.
JUST LIKE ME.
VIRUS

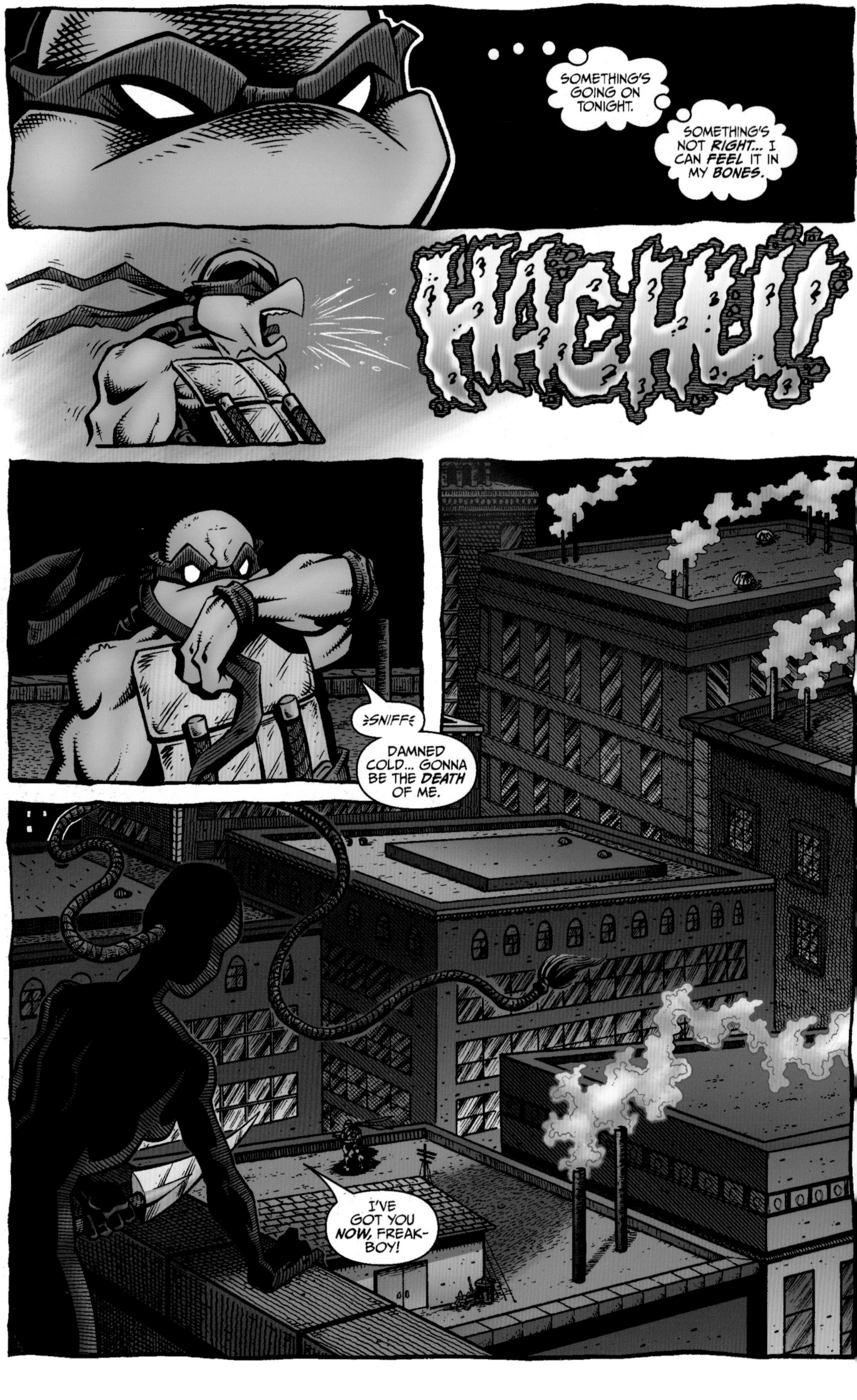
. . .
SOMETHING'S GOING ON TONIGHT.
SOMETHING'S NOT *RIGHT*... I CAN *FEEL* IT IN MY *BONES*.
HACHOO!
SNIFF
DAMNED COLD... GONNA BE THE *DEATH* OF ME.
I'VE GOT YOU *NOW*, FREAK-BOY!

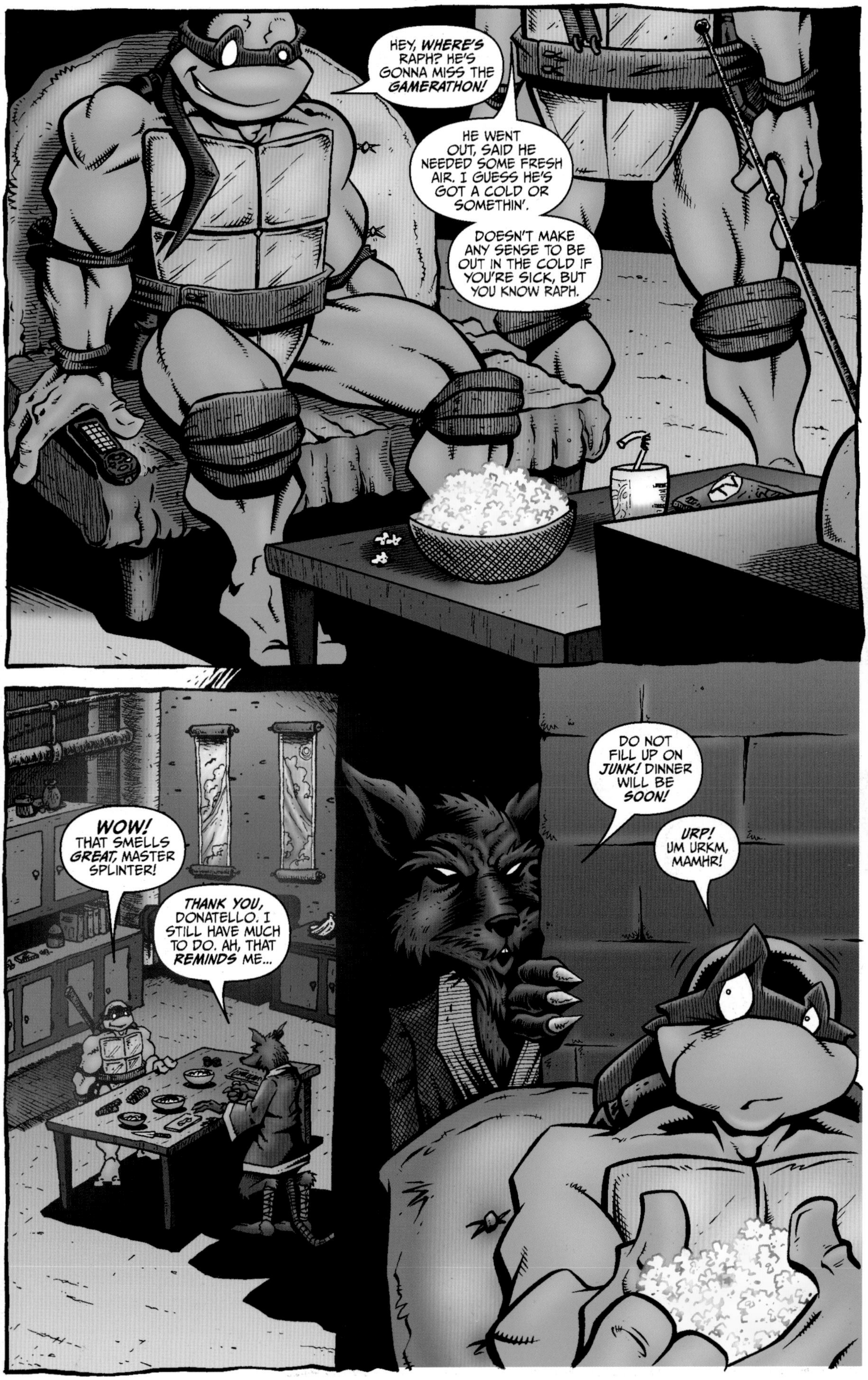
HEY, WHERE'S RAPH? HE'S GONNA MISS THE GAMERATHON!
HE WENT OUT, SAID HE NEEDED SOME FRESH AIR. I GUESS HE'S GOT A COLD OR SOMETHIN'.
DOESN'T MAKE ANY SENSE TO BE OUT IN THE COLD IF YOU'RE SICK, BUT YOU KNOW RAPH.
WOW! THAT SMELLS GREAT, MASTER SPLINTER!
THANK YOU, DONATELLO. I STILL HAVE MUCH TO DO. AH, THAT REMINDS ME...
DO NOT FILL UP ON JUNK! DINNER WILL BE SOON!
URP! UM URKM, MAMHR!

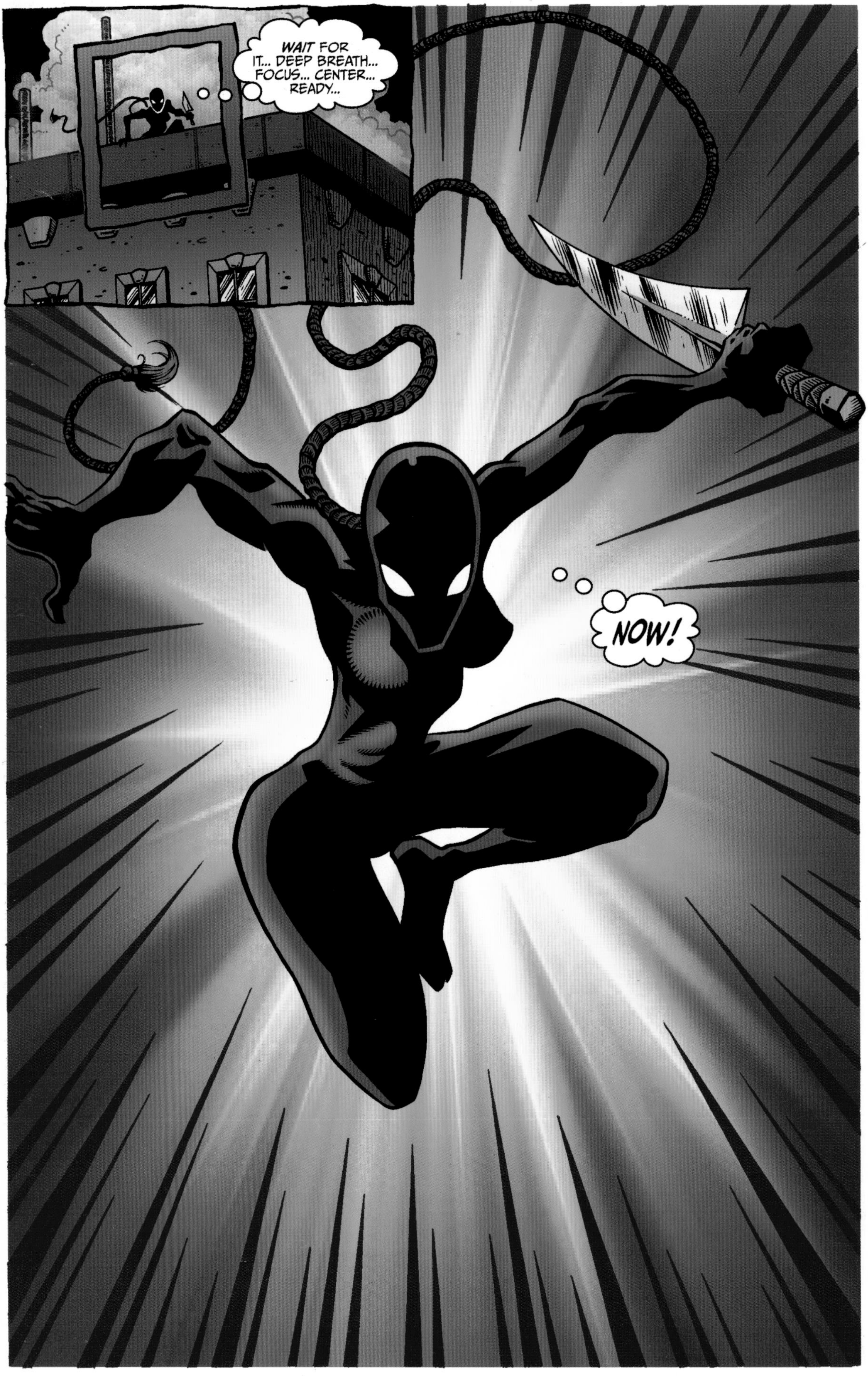
WAIT FOR IT... DEEP BREATH... FOCUS... CENTER... READY...
NOW!

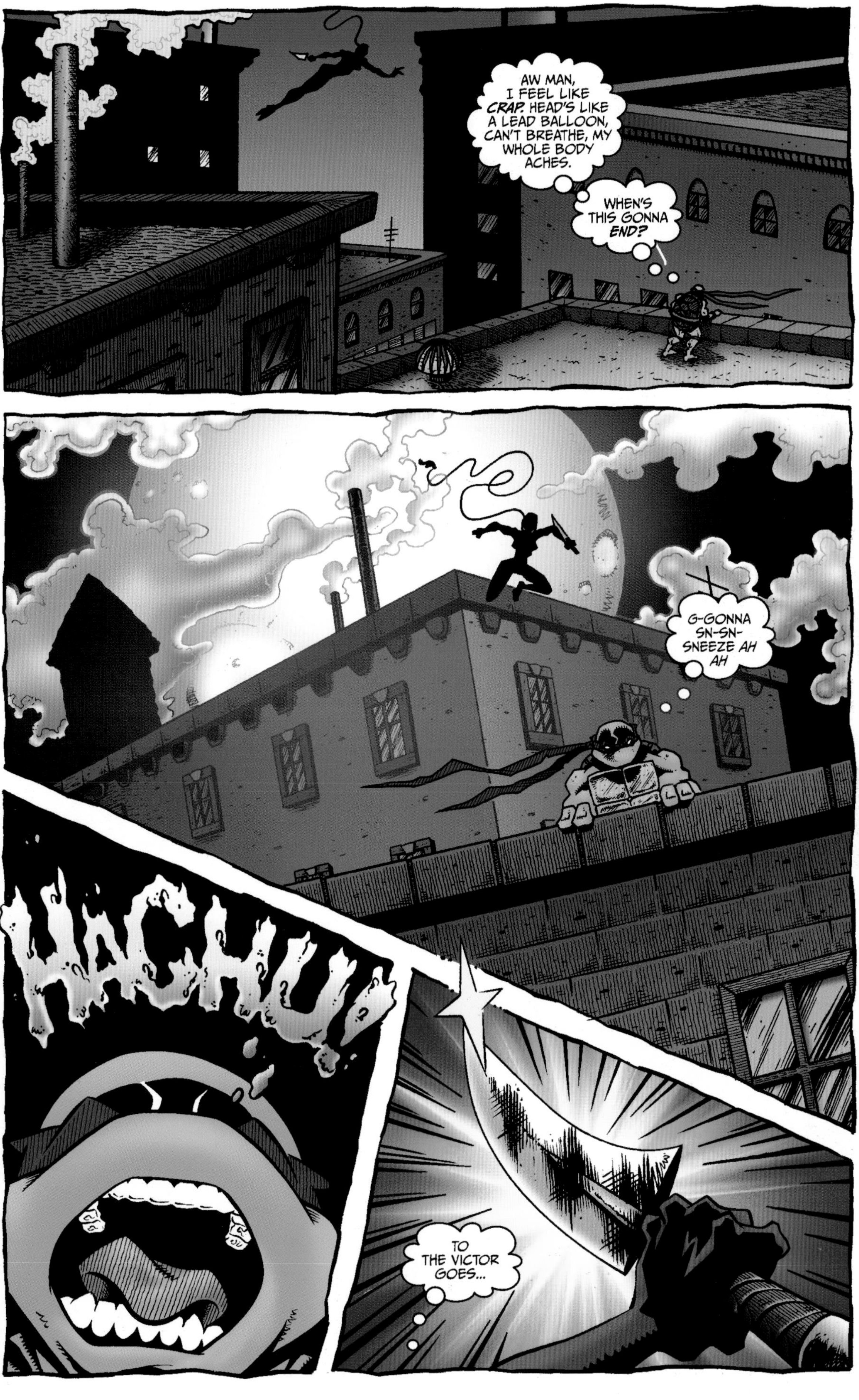
AW MAN, I FEEL LIKE CRAP. HEAD'S LIKE A LEAD BALLOON, CAN'T BREATHE, MY WHOLE BODY ACHES.
WHEN'S THIS GONNA END?
G-GONNA SN-SN-SNEEZE AH AH
HACHU!!
TO THE VICTOR GOES...

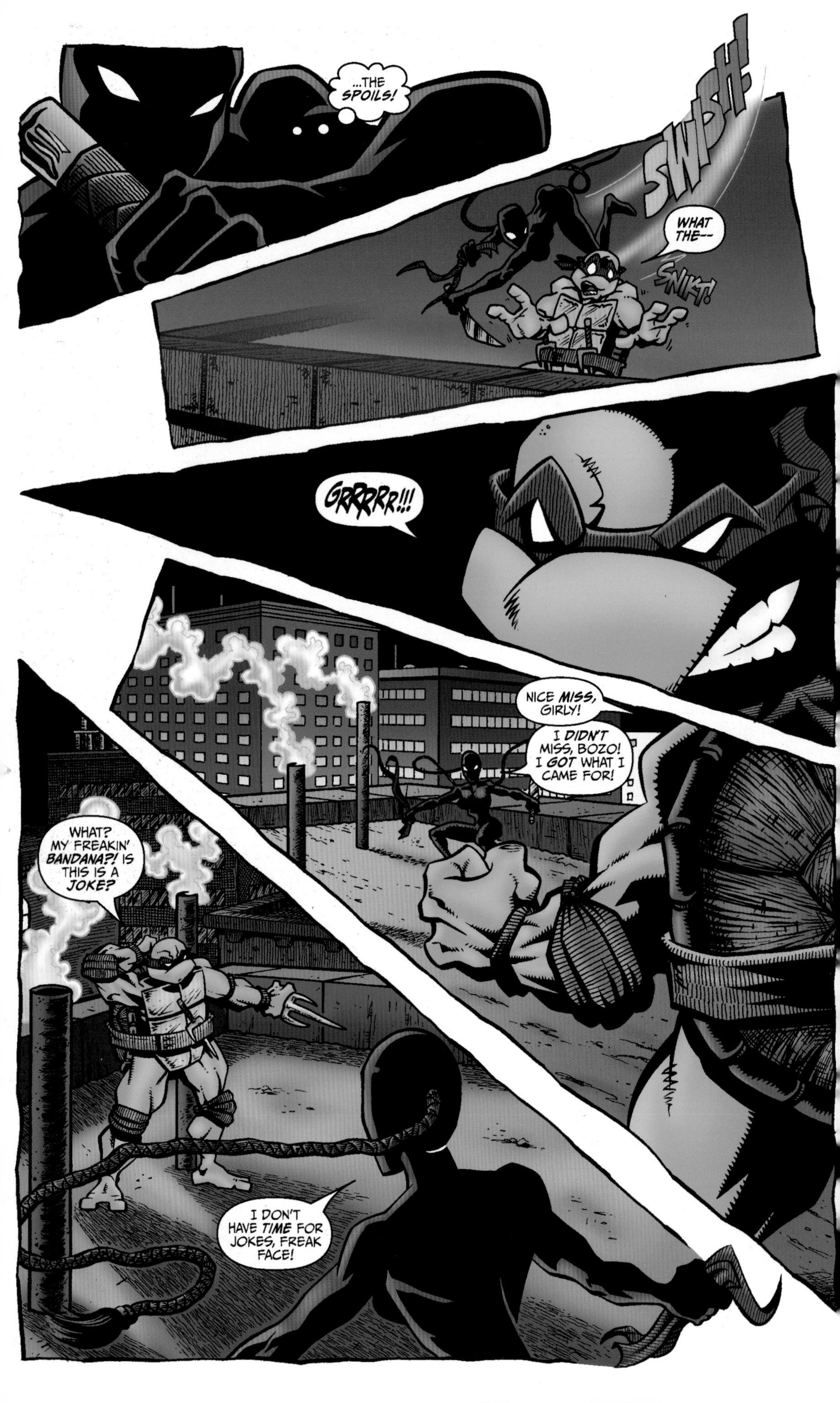
...THE SPOILS!
SWISH!
WHAT THE--
SNIKT!
GRRRRR!!!
NICE MISS, GIRLY!
I DIDN'T MISS, BOZO! I GOT WHAT I CAME FOR!
WHAT? MY FREAKIN' BANDANA?! IS THIS IS A JOKE?
I DON'T HAVE TIME FOR JOKES, FREAK FACE!

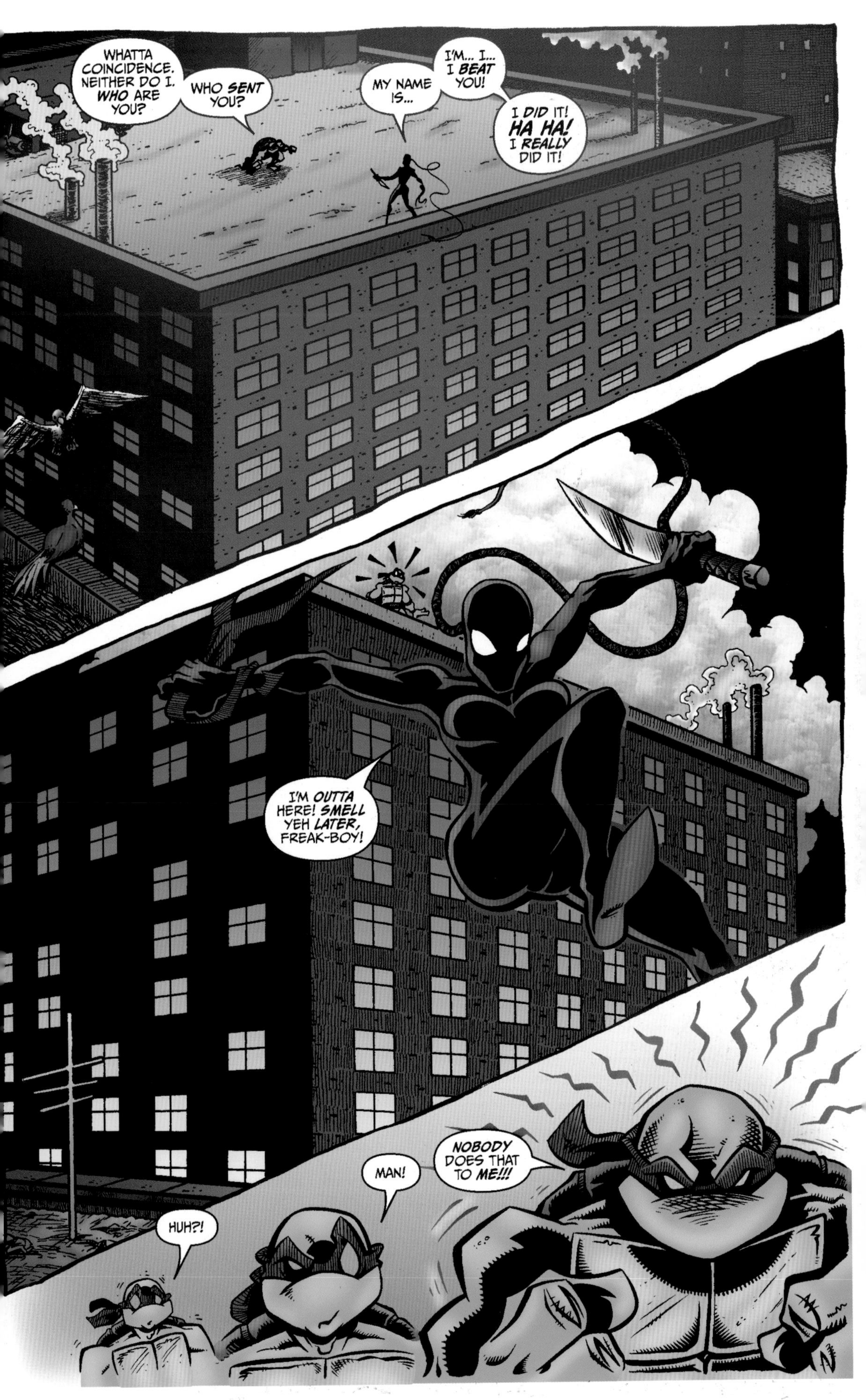
WHATTA COINCIDENCE. NEITHER DO I. WHO ARE YOU?
WHO SENT YOU?
MY NAME IS...
I'M... I... I BEAT YOU!
I DID IT! HA HA! I REALLY DID IT!
I'M OUTTA HERE! SMELL YEH LATER, FREAK-BOY!
HUH?!
MAN!
NOBODY DOES THAT TO ME!!!

THAT'S *ODD...*

I WONDER WHAT'S CAUSING THIS. BETTER CHECK THE DATABASE TO BE SURE.

YES, IT'S *DEFINITELY* AN ANOMALOUS SIGNATURE. NOT IN ANY OF MY OLD CHARTS. *MOST* CURIOUS!

TAP TAPPITY TAK TAK

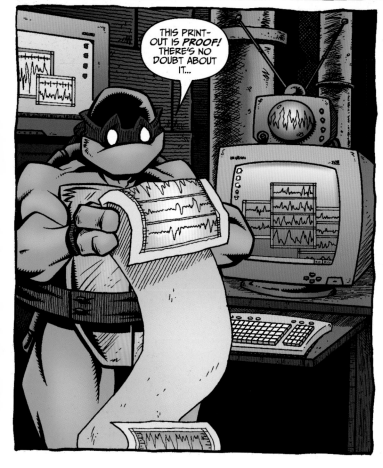

THIS PRINT-OUT IS *PROOF!* THERE'S NO DOUBT ABOUT IT...

SOMETHING'S *NOT* RIGHT! I CAN FEEL IT IN MY BONES!

I'D BETTER TELL THE GUYS!

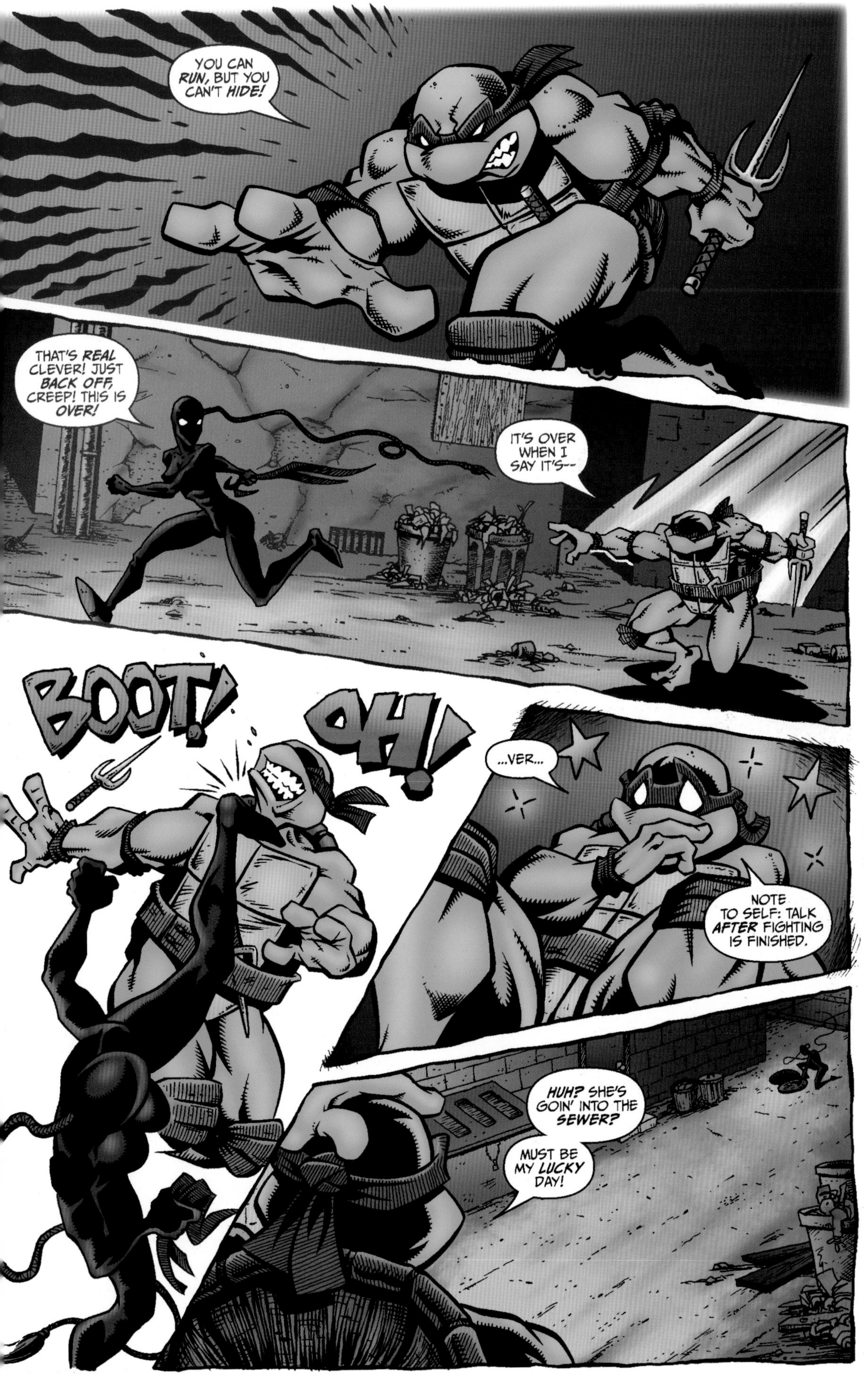
YOU CAN RUN, BUT YOU CAN'T HIDE!
THAT'S REAL CLEVER! JUST BACK OFF, CREEP! THIS IS OVER!
IT'S OVER WHEN I SAY IT'S--
BOOT!
OH!
...VER...
NOTE TO SELF: TALK AFTER FIGHTING IS FINISHED.
HUH? SHE'S GOIN' INTO THE SEWER?
MUST BE MY LUCKY DAY!

AH! IT IS FINISHED!

PREPARING SUSHI IS PAINSTAKING, BUT THE REWARDS ARE GREAT... AS IT IS A WONDROUS DELICACY!

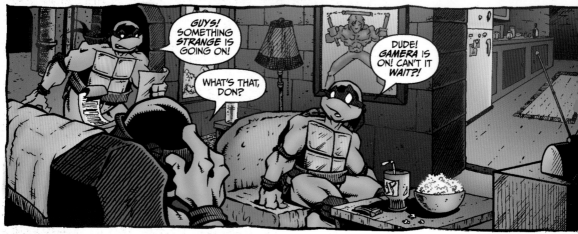

GUYS! SOMETHING STRANGE IS GOING ON!

WHAT'S THAT, DON?

DUDE! GAMERA IS ON! CAN'T IT WAIT?!

UM... I DON'T THINK SO!

WHAT'S THE MATTER?

AN ODD ELECTRO-MAGNETIC SIGNAL IS PERIODICALLY BEING BROADCAST FROM THE DEEP SEWERS. IT'S QUITE STRONG, VERY UNUSUAL AND IT COULD BE DANGEROUS!

HMMM. WE'D BETTER LOOK INTO IT, JUST TO BE SAFE.

BUT NOW I'LL NEVER KNOW IF GAMERA SAVES THE UNIVERSE!

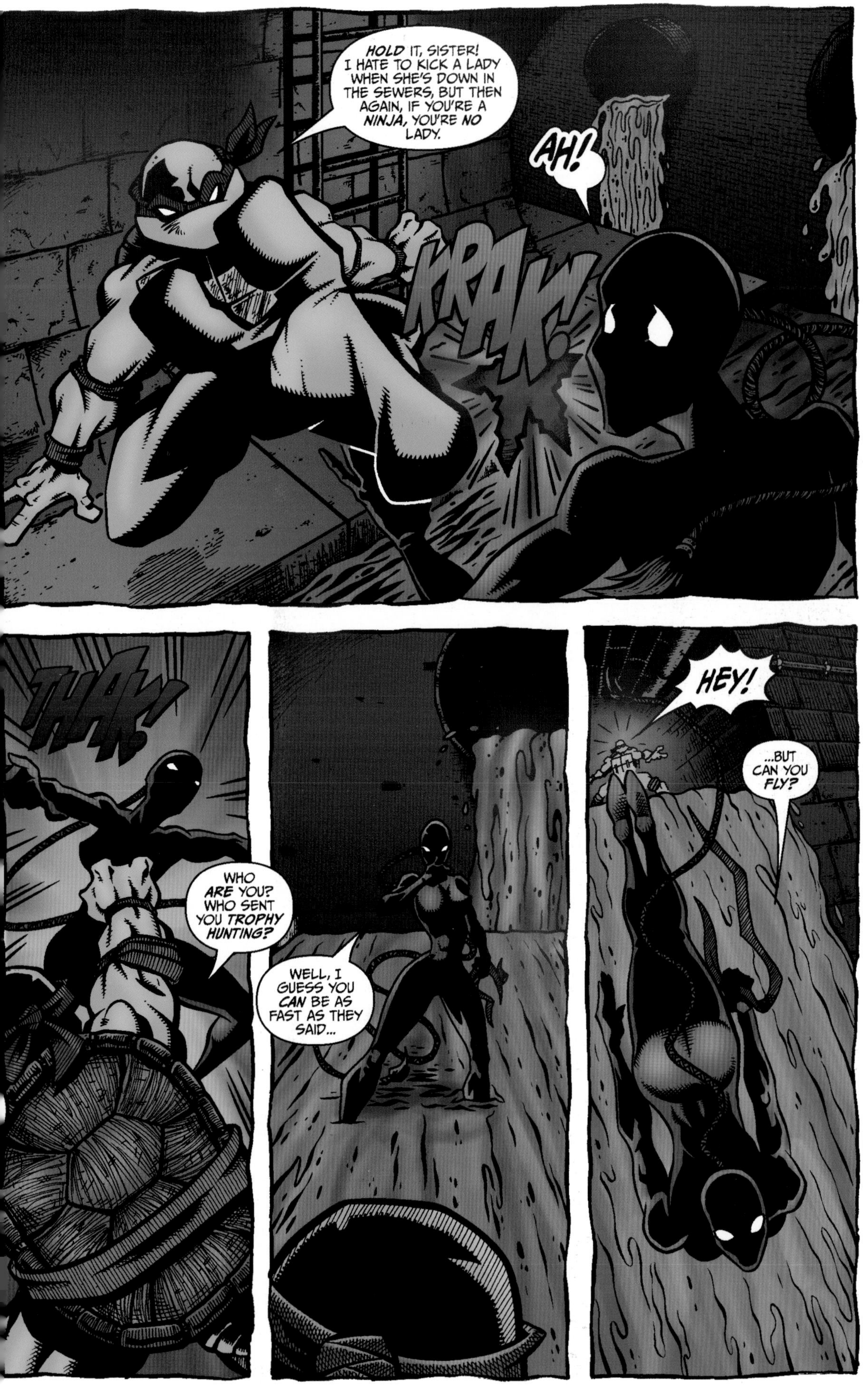
HOLD IT, SISTER! I HATE TO KICK A LADY WHEN SHE'S DOWN IN THE SEWERS, BUT THEN AGAIN, IF YOU'RE A NINJA, YOU'RE NO LADY.
AH!
KRAK!
THAK!
WHO ARE YOU? WHO SENT YOU TROPHY HUNTING?
WELL, I GUESS YOU CAN BE AS FAST AS THEY SAID...
HEY!
...BUT CAN YOU FLY?

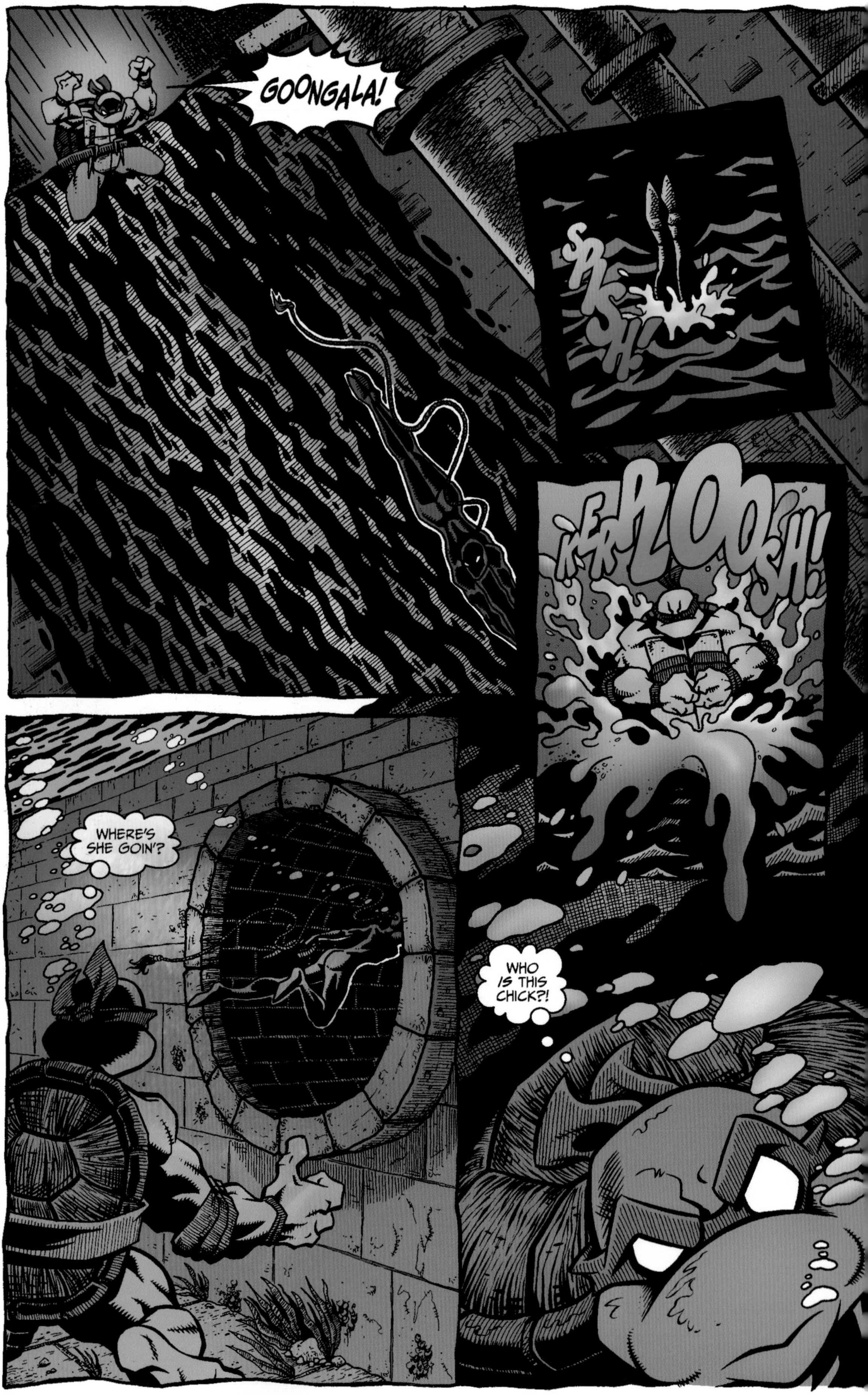
GOONGALA!
SPLOOSH!
KERPLOOSH!
WHERE'S SHE GOIN'?
WHO IS THIS CHICK?!

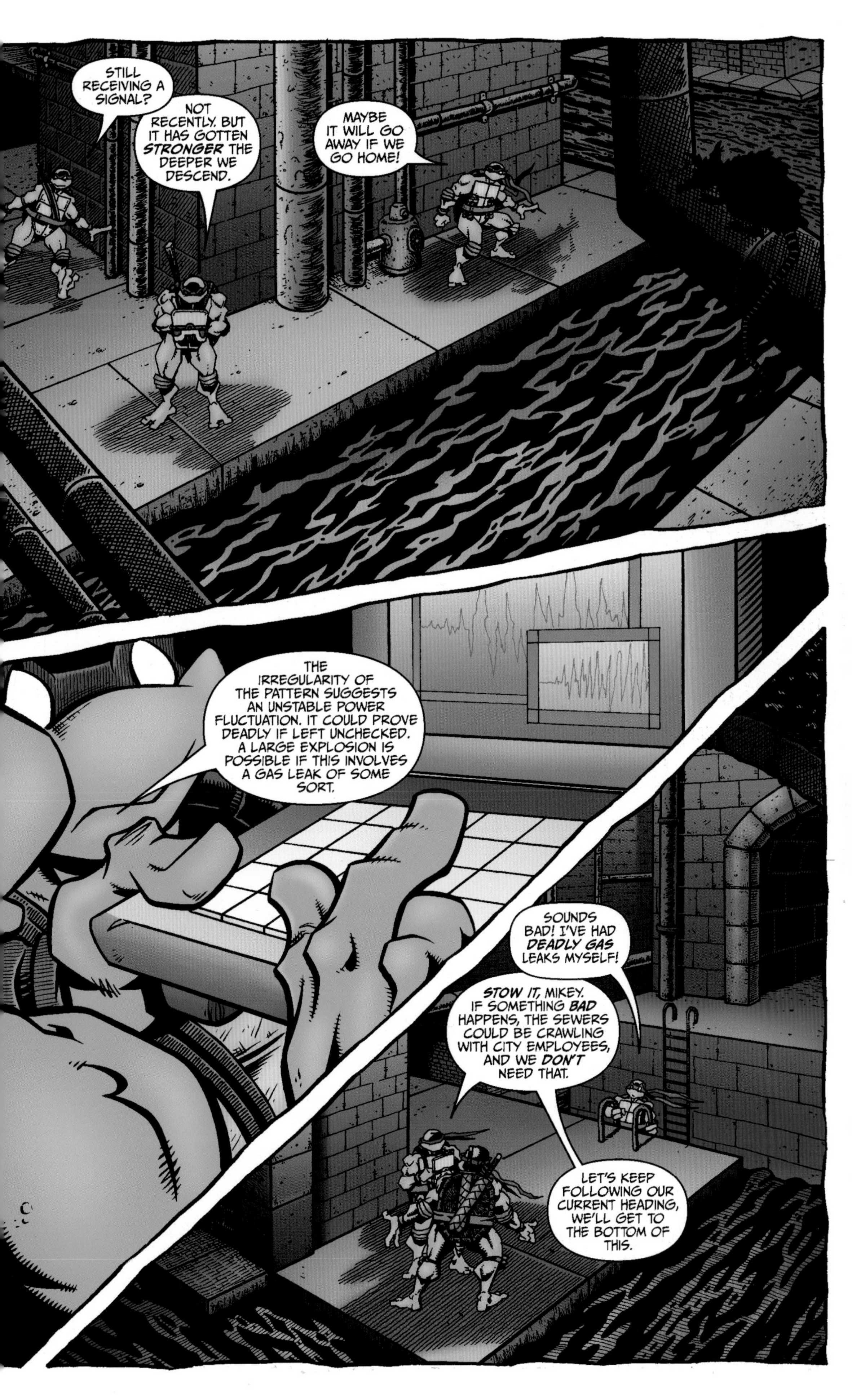
STILL RECEIVING A SIGNAL?
NOT RECENTLY. BUT IT HAS GOTTEN STRONGER THE DEEPER WE DESCEND.
MAYBE IT WILL GO AWAY IF WE GO HOME!
THE IRREGULARITY OF THE PATTERN SUGGESTS AN UNSTABLE POWER FLUCTUATION. IT COULD PROVE DEADLY IF LEFT UNCHECKED. A LARGE EXPLOSION IS POSSIBLE IF THIS INVOLVES A GAS LEAK OF SOME SORT.
SOUNDS BAD! I'VE HAD DEADLY GAS LEAKS MYSELF!
STOW IT, MIKEY. IF SOMETHING BAD HAPPENS, THE SEWERS COULD BE CRAWLING WITH CITY EMPLOYEES, AND WE DON'T NEED THAT.
LET'S KEEP FOLLOWING OUR CURRENT HEADING, WE'LL GET TO THE BOTTOM OF THIS.

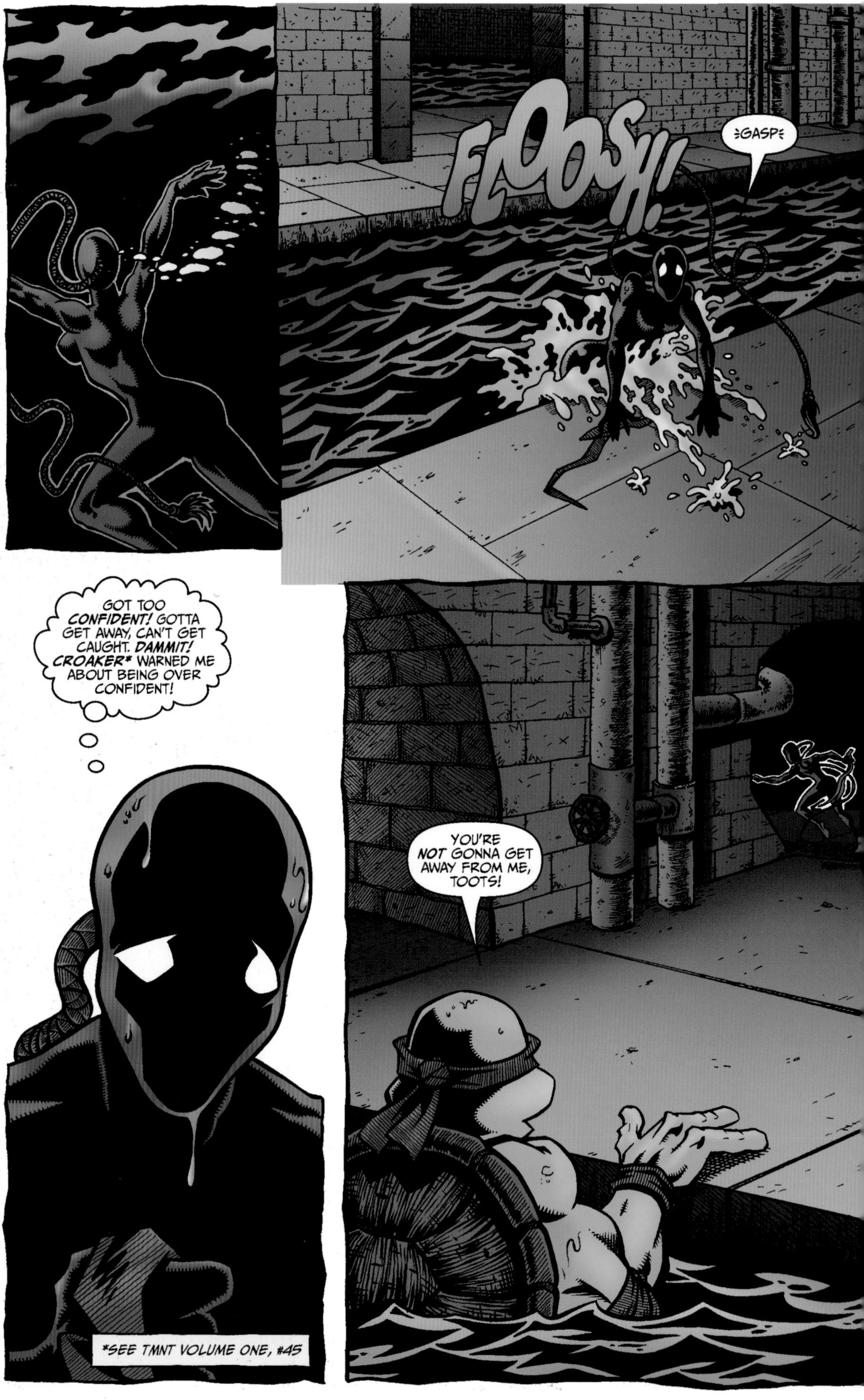
FLOOSH!
GASP
GOT TOO CONFIDENT! GOTTA GET AWAY, CAN'T GET CAUGHT. DAMMIT! CROAKER* WARNED ME ABOUT BEING OVER CONFIDENT!
*SEE TMNT VOLUME ONE, #45
YOU'RE NOT GONNA GET AWAY FROM ME, TOOTS!

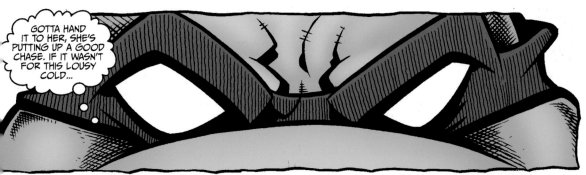

GOTTA HAND IT TO HER, SHE'S PUTTING UP A GOOD CHASE. IF IT WASN'T FOR THIS LOUSY COLD...

UGH! LAST THING I NEEDED WAS A COLD SWIM!

I SHOULDA JUST WENT TO BED AND SLEPT THIS OFF.

OH WELL.

TOO LATE NOW.

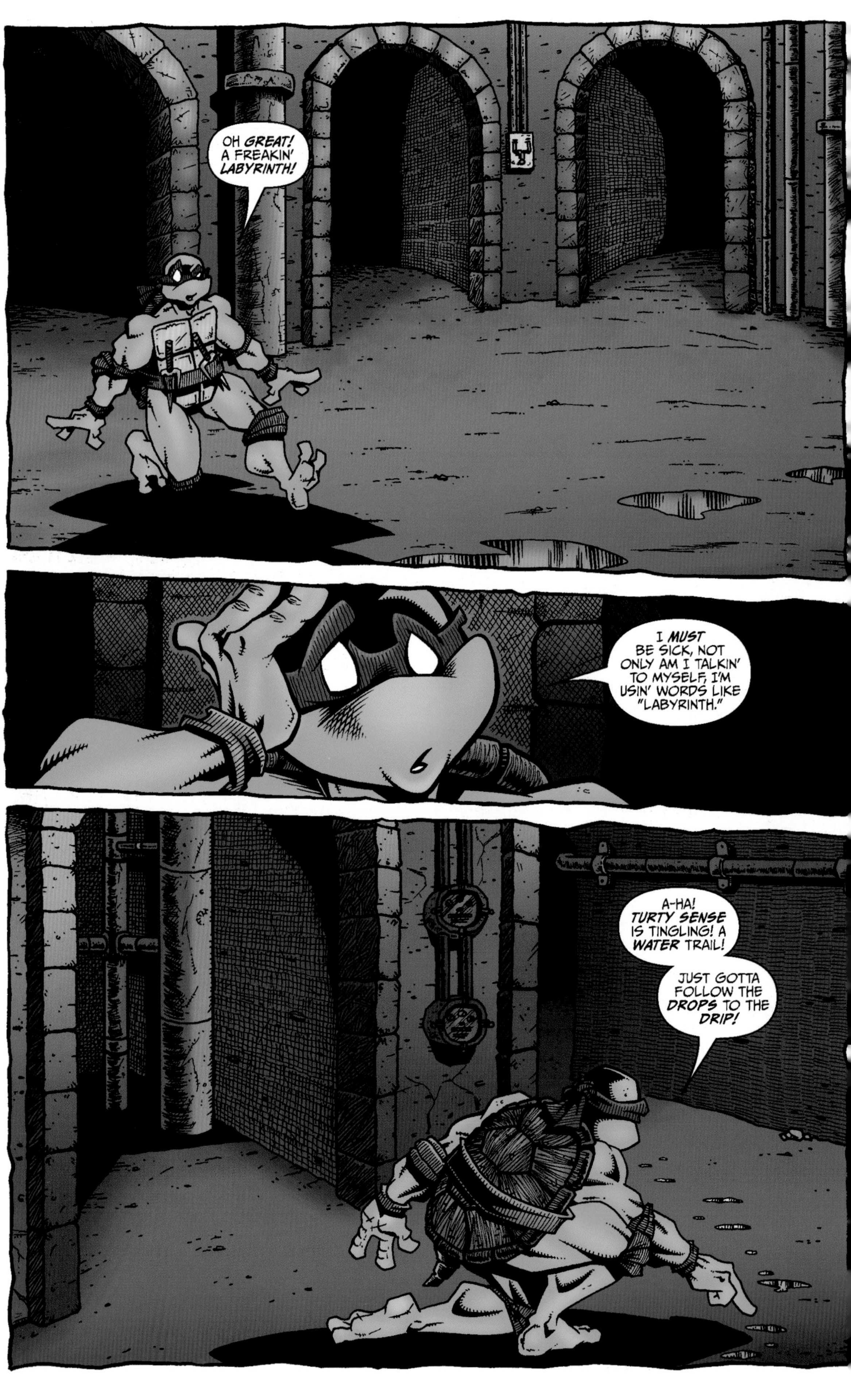

OH GREAT! A FREAKIN' LABYRINTH!
I MUST BE SICK, NOT ONLY AM I TALKIN' TO MYSELF, I'M USIN' WORDS LIKE "LABYRINTH."
A-HA! TURTY SENSE IS TINGLING! A WATER TRAIL!
JUST GOTTA FOLLOW THE DROPS TO THE DRIP!

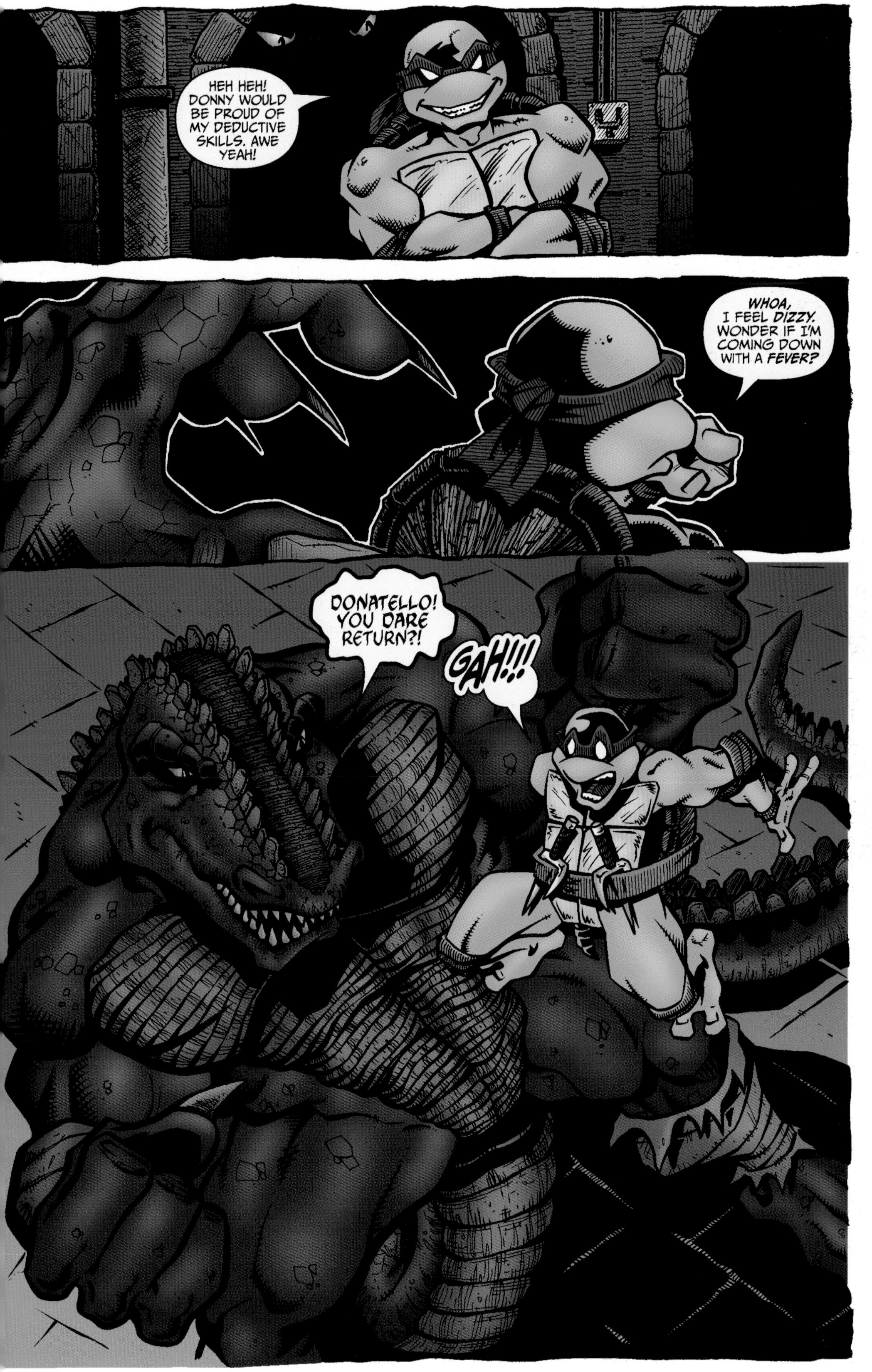
HEH HEH! DONNY WOULD BE PROUD OF MY DEDUCTIVE SKILLS. AWE YEAH!
WHOA, I FEEL DIZZY. WONDER IF I'M COMING DOWN WITH A FEVER?
DONATELLO! YOU DARE RETURN?!
GAH!!!

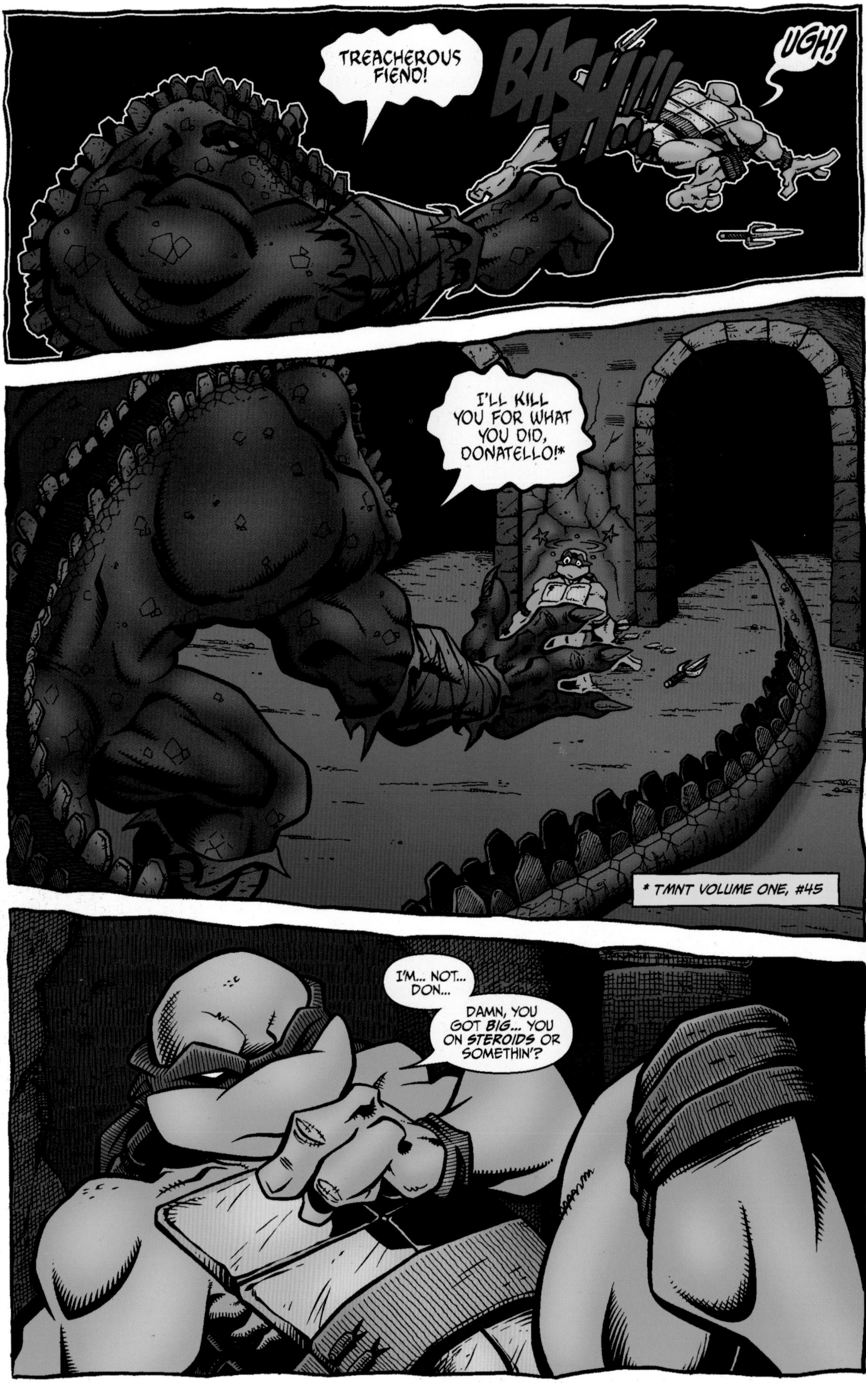
TREACHEROUS FIEND!
BASH!!!
UGH!
I'LL KILL YOU FOR WHAT YOU DID, DONATELLO!*
* TMNT VOLUME ONE, #45
I'M... NOT... DON...
DAMN, YOU GOT BIG... YOU ON STEROIDS OR SOMETHIN'?

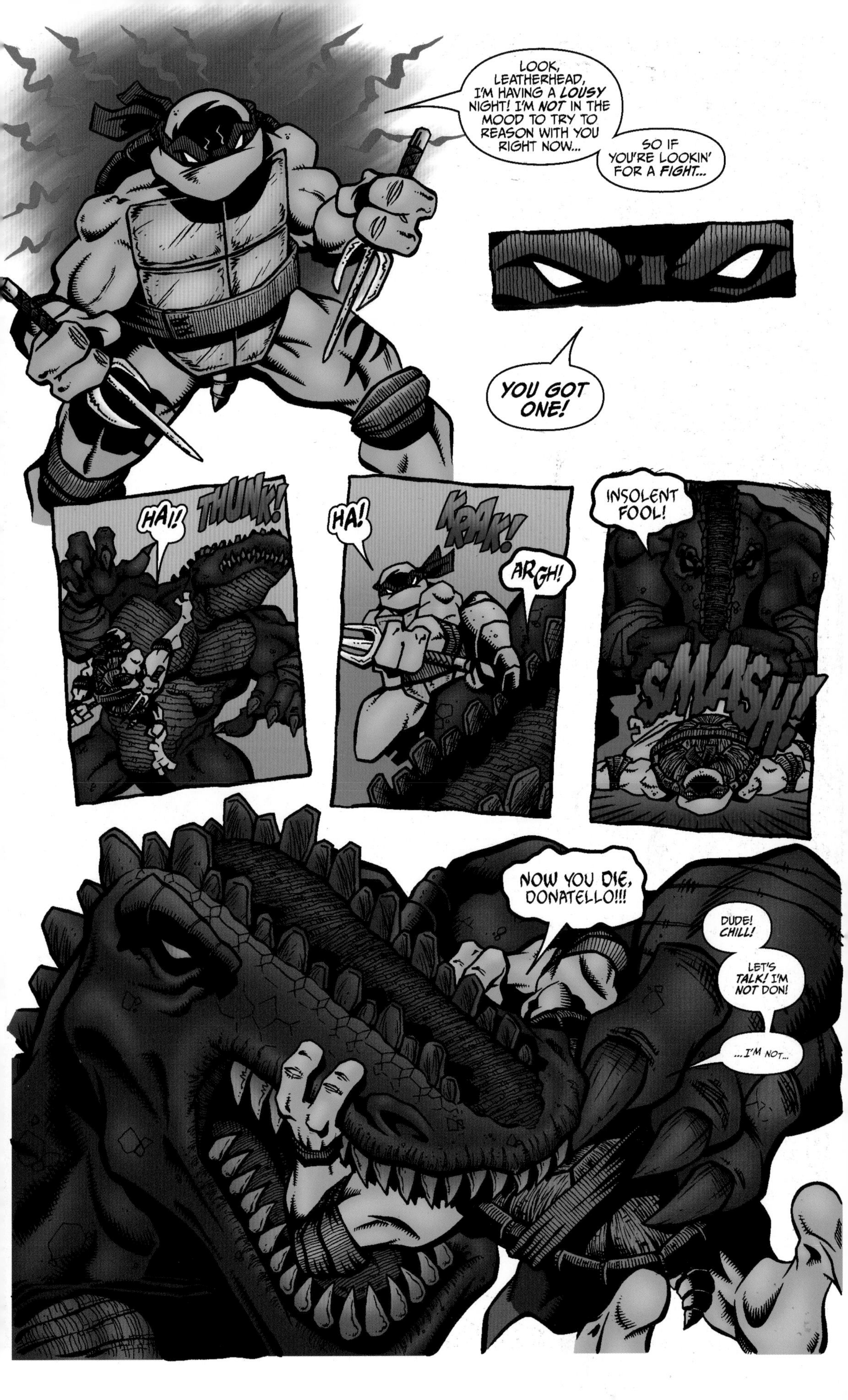

LOOK, LEATHERHEAD, I'M HAVING A LOUSY NIGHT! I'M NOT IN THE MOOD TO TRY TO REASON WITH YOU RIGHT NOW...
SO IF YOU'RE LOOKIN' FOR A FIGHT...
YOU GOT ONE!
HAI!
THUNK!
HA!
KRAK!
ARGH!
INSOLENT FOOL!
SMASH!
NOW YOU DIE, DONATELLO!!!
DUDE! CHILL!
LET'S TALK! I'M NOT DON!
...I'M NOT...

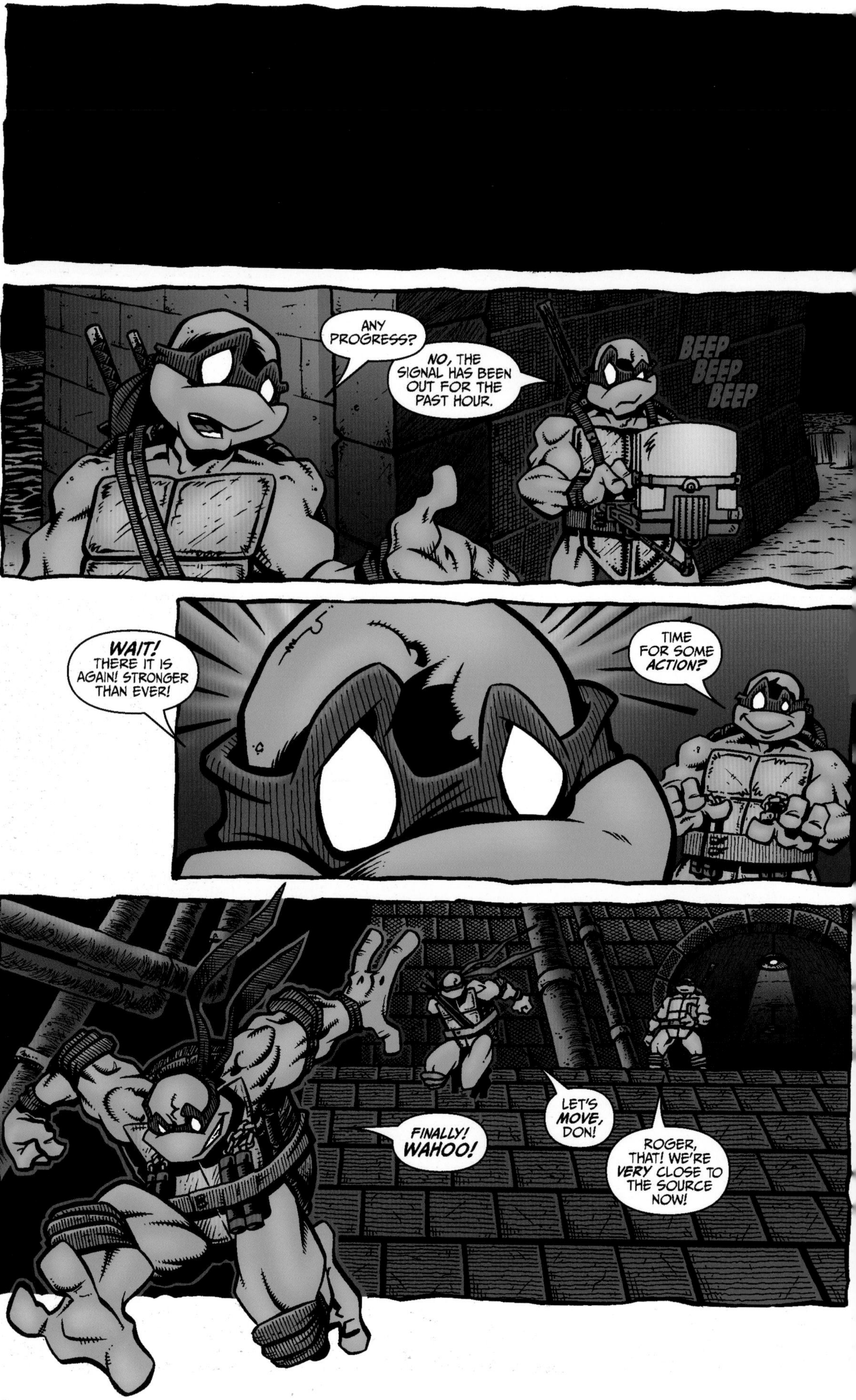

ANY PROGRESS?
NO, THE SIGNAL HAS BEEN OUT FOR THE PAST HOUR.
BEEP BEEP BEEP
WAIT! THERE IT IS AGAIN! STRONGER THAN EVER!
TIME FOR SOME ACTION?
FINALLY! WAHOO!
LET'S MOVE, DON!
ROGER, THAT! WE'RE VERY CLOSE TO THE SOURCE NOW!

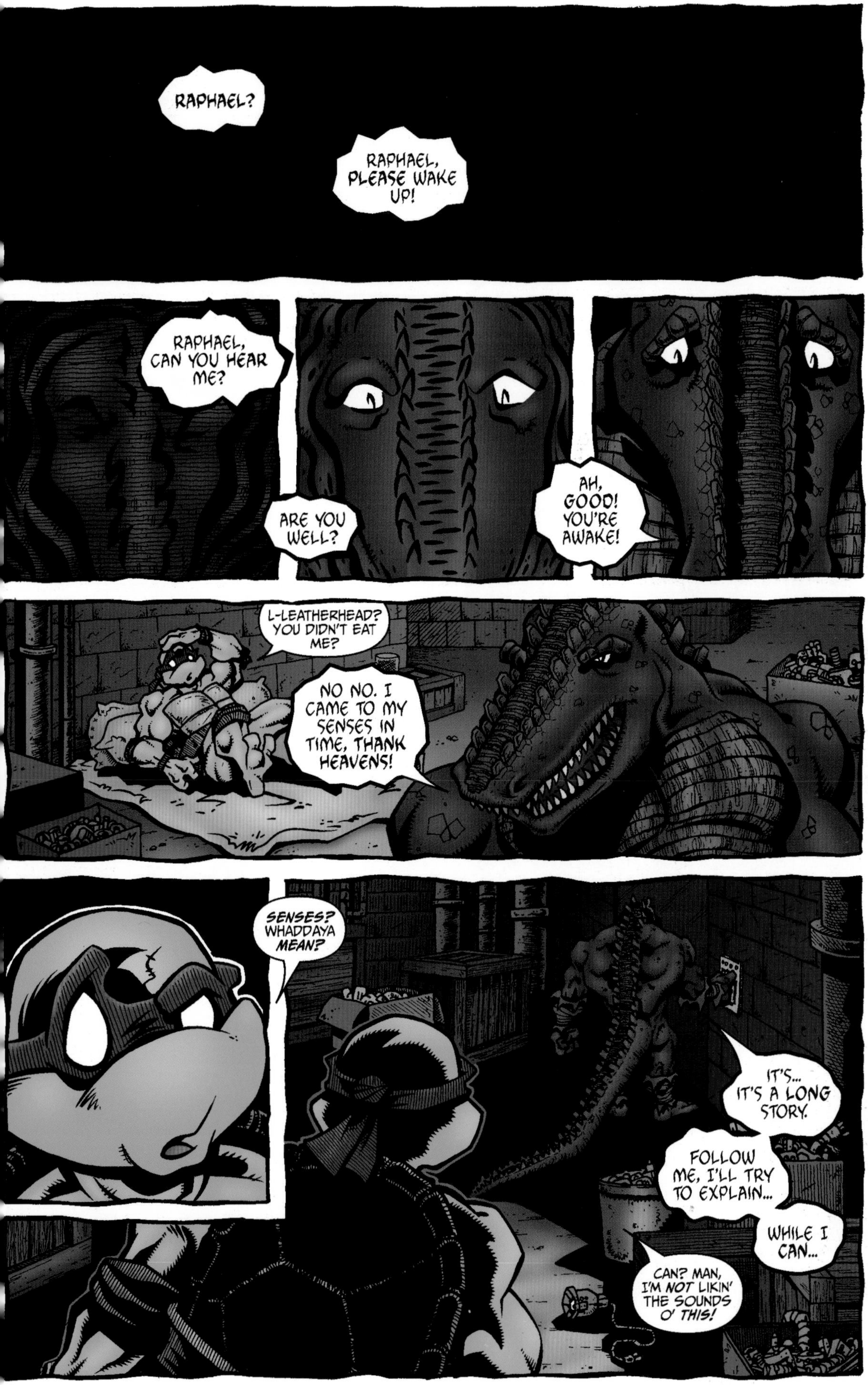
RAPHAEL?
RAPHAEL, PLEASE WAKE UP!
RAPHAEL, CAN YOU HEAR ME?
ARE YOU WELL?
AH, GOOD! YOU'RE AWAKE!
L-LEATHERHEAD? YOU DIDN'T EAT ME?
NO NO. I CAME TO MY SENSES IN TIME, THANK HEAVENS!
SENSES? WHADDAYA MEAN?
IT'S... IT'S A LONG STORY.
FOLLOW ME, I'LL TRY TO EXPLAIN...
WHILE I CAN...
CAN? MAN, I'M NOT LIKIN' THE SOUNDS O' THIS!

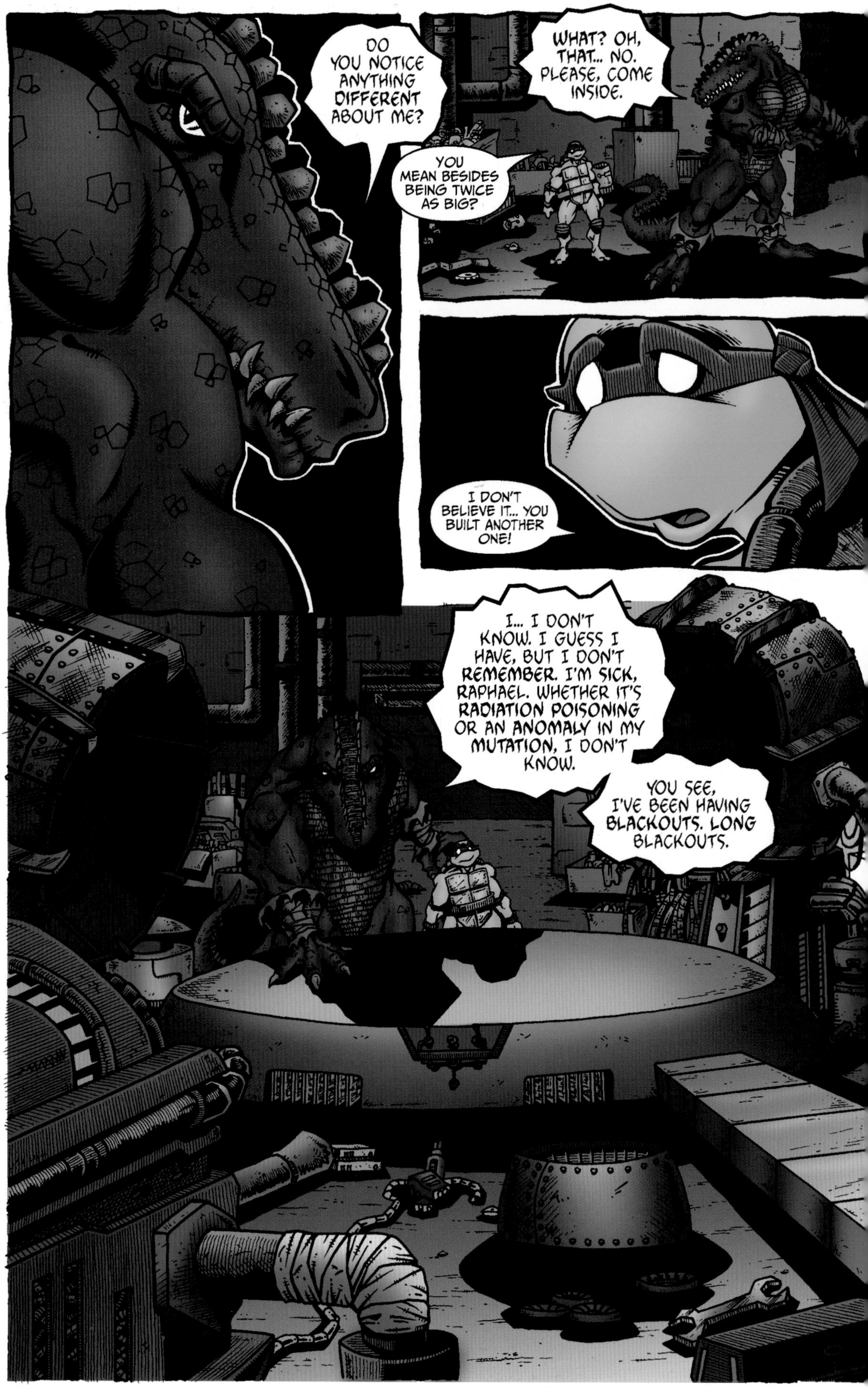
DO YOU NOTICE ANYTHING DIFFERENT ABOUT ME?
WHAT? OH, THAT... NO. PLEASE, COME INSIDE.
YOU MEAN BESIDES BEING TWICE AS BIG?
I DON'T BELIEVE IT... YOU BUILT ANOTHER ONE!
I... I DON'T KNOW. I GUESS I HAVE, BUT I DON'T REMEMBER. I'M SICK, RAPHAEL. WHETHER IT'S RADIATION POISONING OR AN ANOMALY IN MY MUTATION, I DON'T KNOW.
YOU SEE, I'VE BEEN HAVING BLACKOUTS. LONG BLACKOUTS.

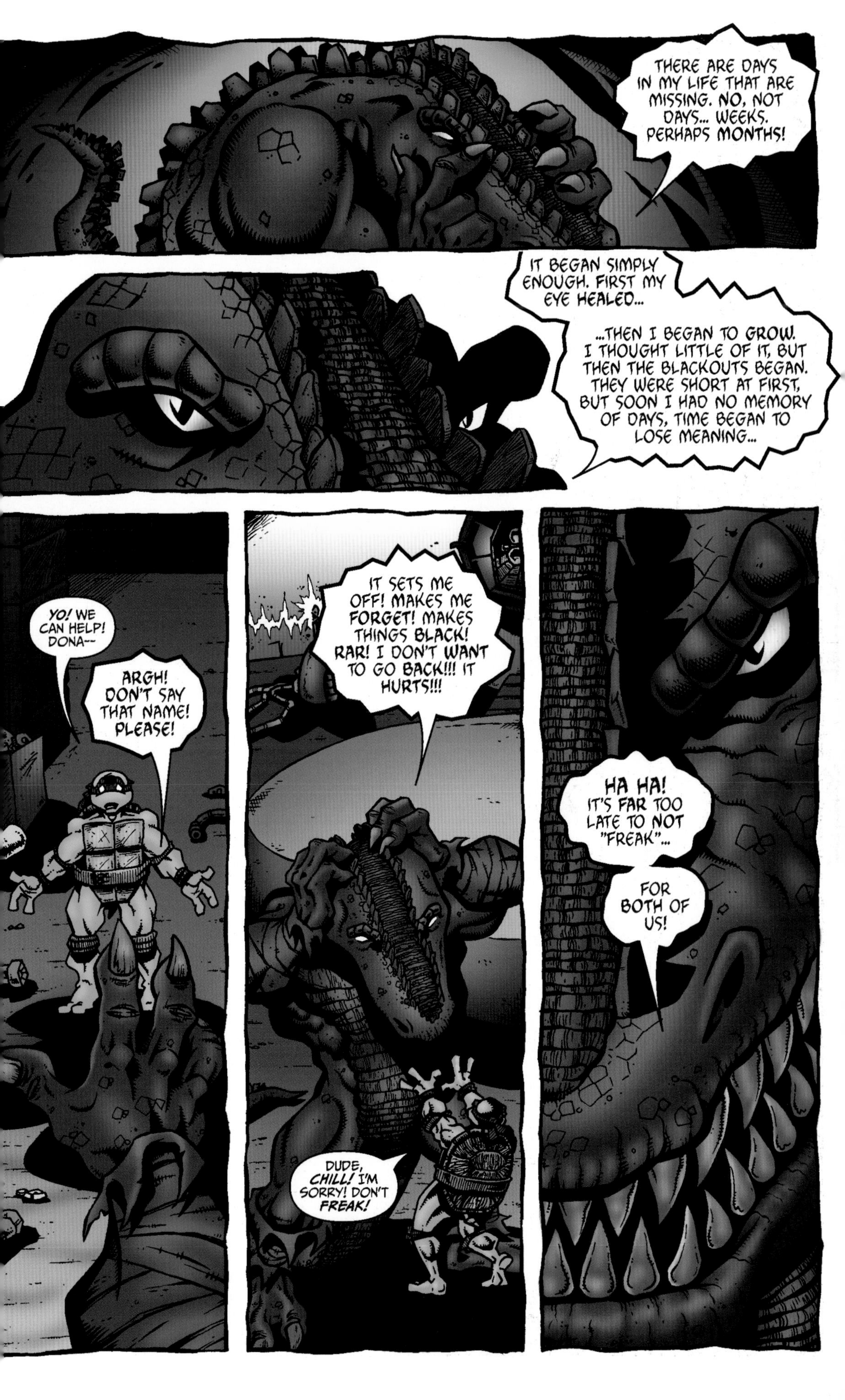
THERE ARE DAYS IN MY LIFE THAT ARE MISSING. NO, NOT DAYS... WEEKS. PERHAPS MONTHS!
IT BEGAN SIMPLY ENOUGH. FIRST MY EYE HEALED...
...THEN I BEGAN TO GROW. I THOUGHT LITTLE OF IT, BUT THEN THE BLACKOUTS BEGAN. THEY WERE SHORT AT FIRST, BUT SOON I HAD NO MEMORY OF DAYS, TIME BEGAN TO LOSE MEANING...
YO! WE CAN HELP! DONA--
ARGH! DON'T SAY THAT NAME! PLEASE!
IT SETS ME OFF! MAKES ME FORGET! MAKES THINGS BLACK! RAR! I DON'T WANT TO GO BACK!!! IT HURTS!!!
DUDE, CHILL! I'M SORRY! DON'T FREAK!
HA HA! IT'S FAR TOO LATE TO NOT "FREAK"...
FOR BOTH OF US!

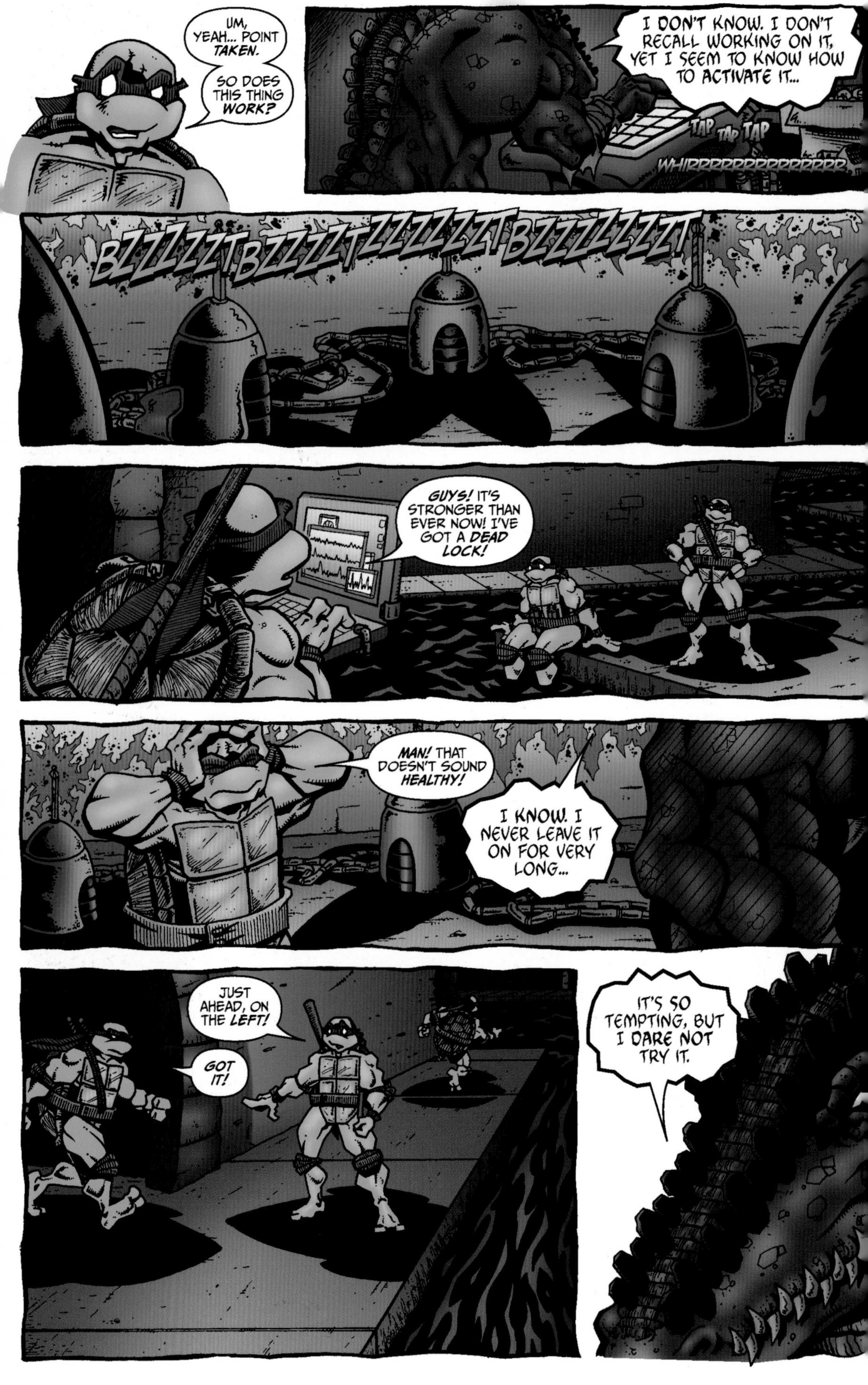
UM, YEAH... POINT TAKEN.
SO DOES THIS THING WORK?
I DON'T KNOW. I DON'T RECALL WORKING ON IT, YET I SEEM TO KNOW HOW TO ACTIVATE IT...
TAP TAP TAP
WHIRRRRRRRRRRRRRRR
BZZZZZTBZZZZZTZZZZZZTBZZZZZZZT
GUYS! IT'S STRONGER THAN EVER NOW! I'VE GOT A DEAD LOCK!
MAN! THAT DOESN'T SOUND HEALTHY!
I KNOW. I NEVER LEAVE IT ON FOR VERY LONG...
JUST AHEAD, ON THE LEFT!
GOT IT!
IT'S SO TEMPTING, BUT I DARE NOT TRY IT.

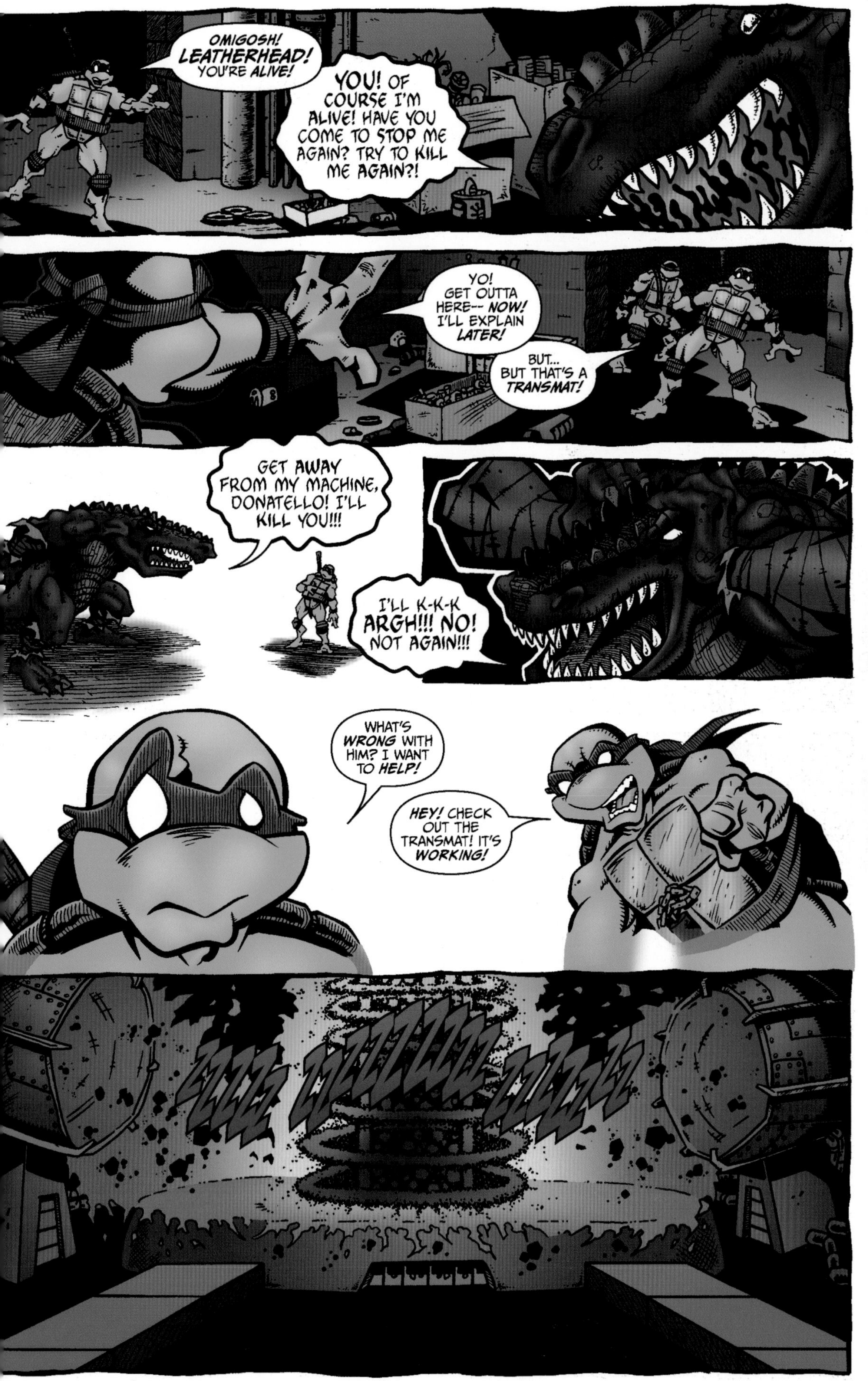
OMIGOSH! LEATHERHEAD! YOU'RE ALIVE!
YOU! OF COURSE I'M ALIVE! HAVE YOU COME TO STOP ME AGAIN? TRY TO KILL ME AGAIN?!
YO! GET OUTTA HERE-- NOW! I'LL EXPLAIN LATER!
BUT... BUT THAT'S A TRANSMAT!
GET AWAY FROM MY MACHINE, DONATELLO! I'LL KILL YOU!!!
I'LL K-K-K ARGH!!! NO! NOT AGAIN!!!
WHAT'S WRONG WITH HIM? I WANT TO HELP!
HEY! CHECK OUT THE TRANSMAT! IT'S WORKING!
ZZZZ ZZZZZZZZ ZZZZZZ

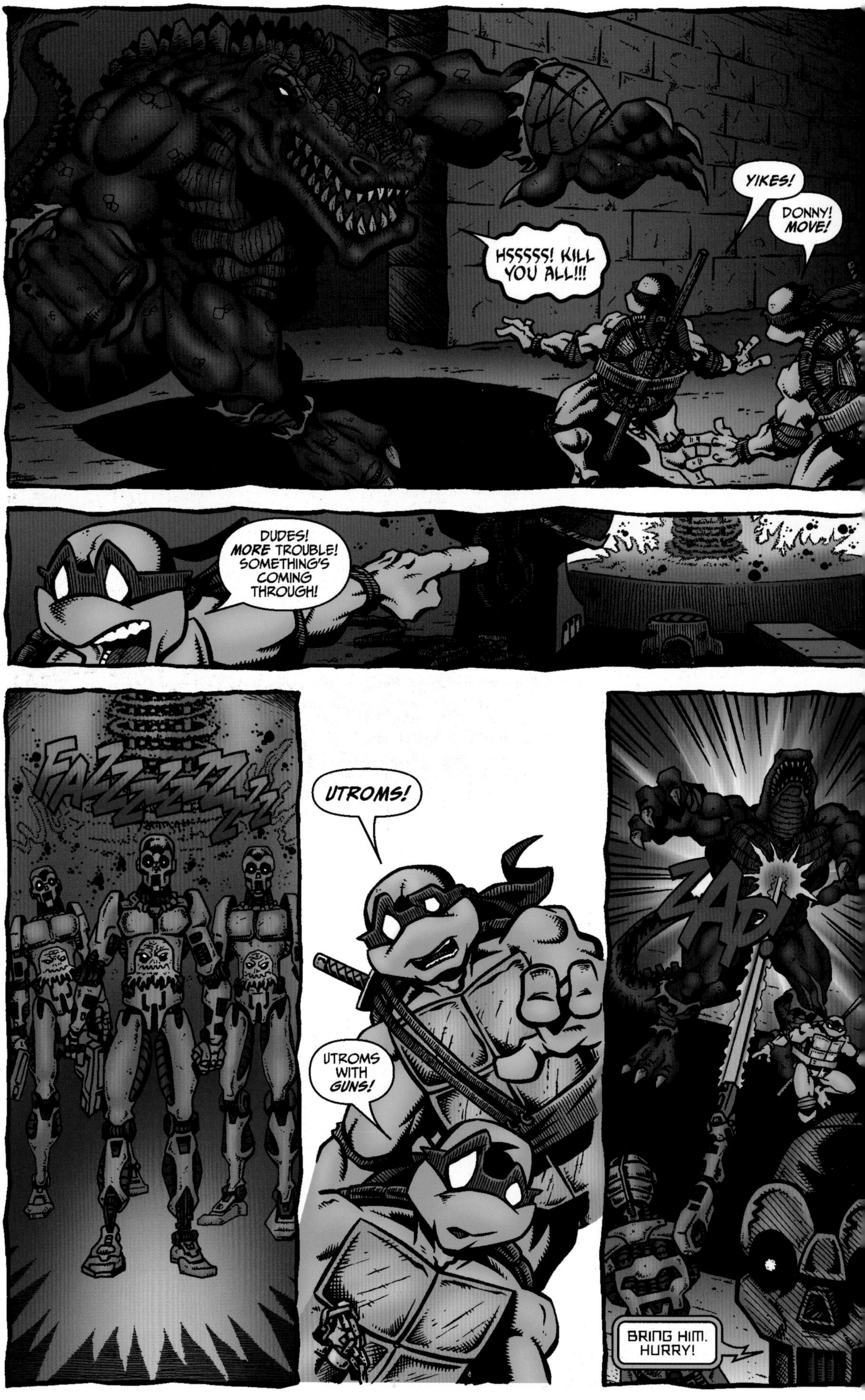
HSSSSS! KILL YOU ALL!!!
YIKES!
DONNY! MOVE!
DUDES! MORE TROUBLE! SOMETHING'S COMING THROUGH!
FAZZZZZZ
UTROMS!
UTROMS WITH GUNS!
ZAP!
BRING HIM. HURRY!

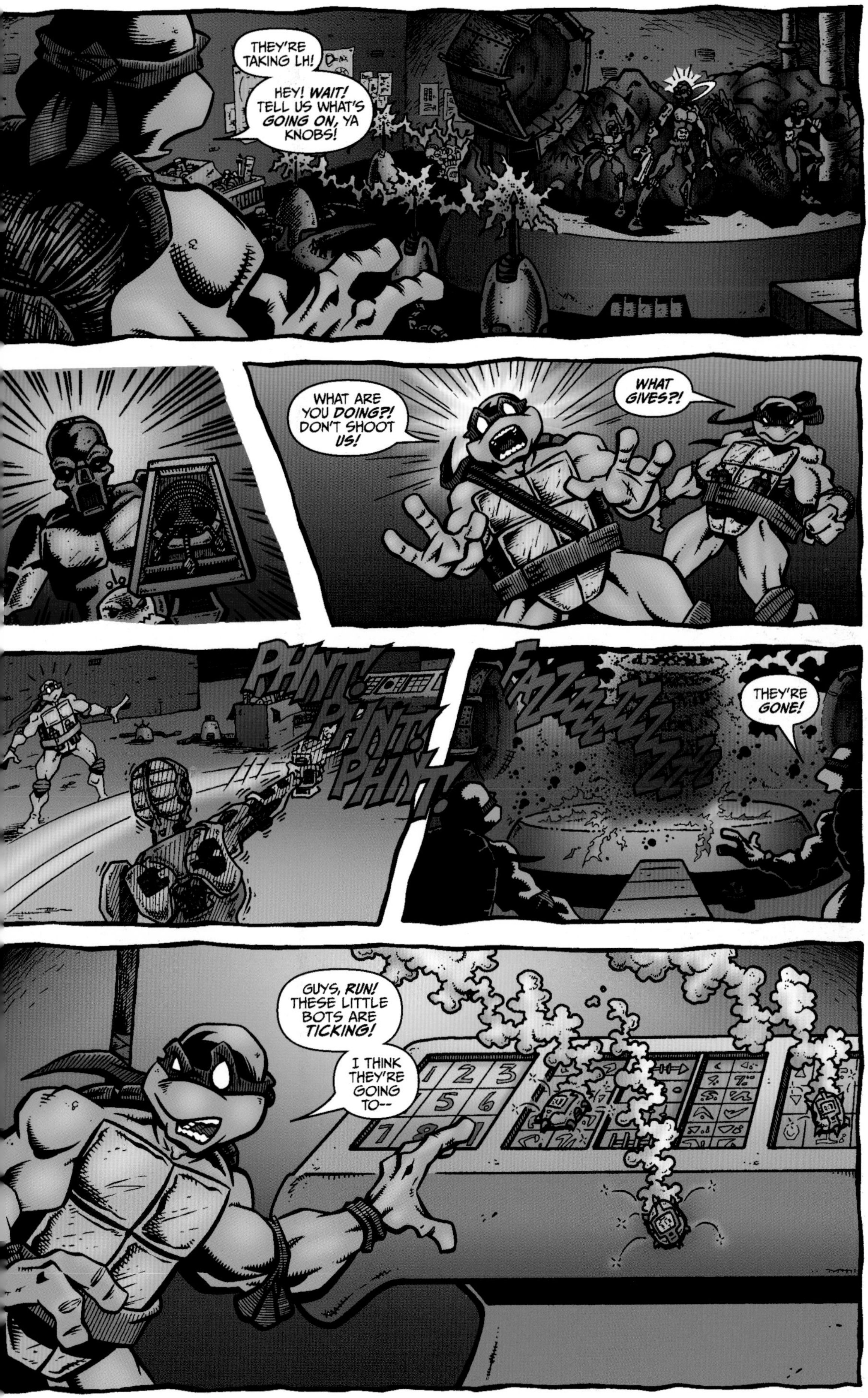

THEY'RE TAKING LH!
HEY! WAIT! TELL US WHAT'S GOING ON, YA KNOBS!
WHAT ARE YOU DOING?! DON'T SHOOT US!
WHAT GIVES?!
PHNT! PHNT! PHNT!
FAZZZZZZZ
THEY'RE GONE!
GUYS, RUN! THESE LITTLE BOTS ARE TICKING!
I THINK THEY'RE GOING TO--

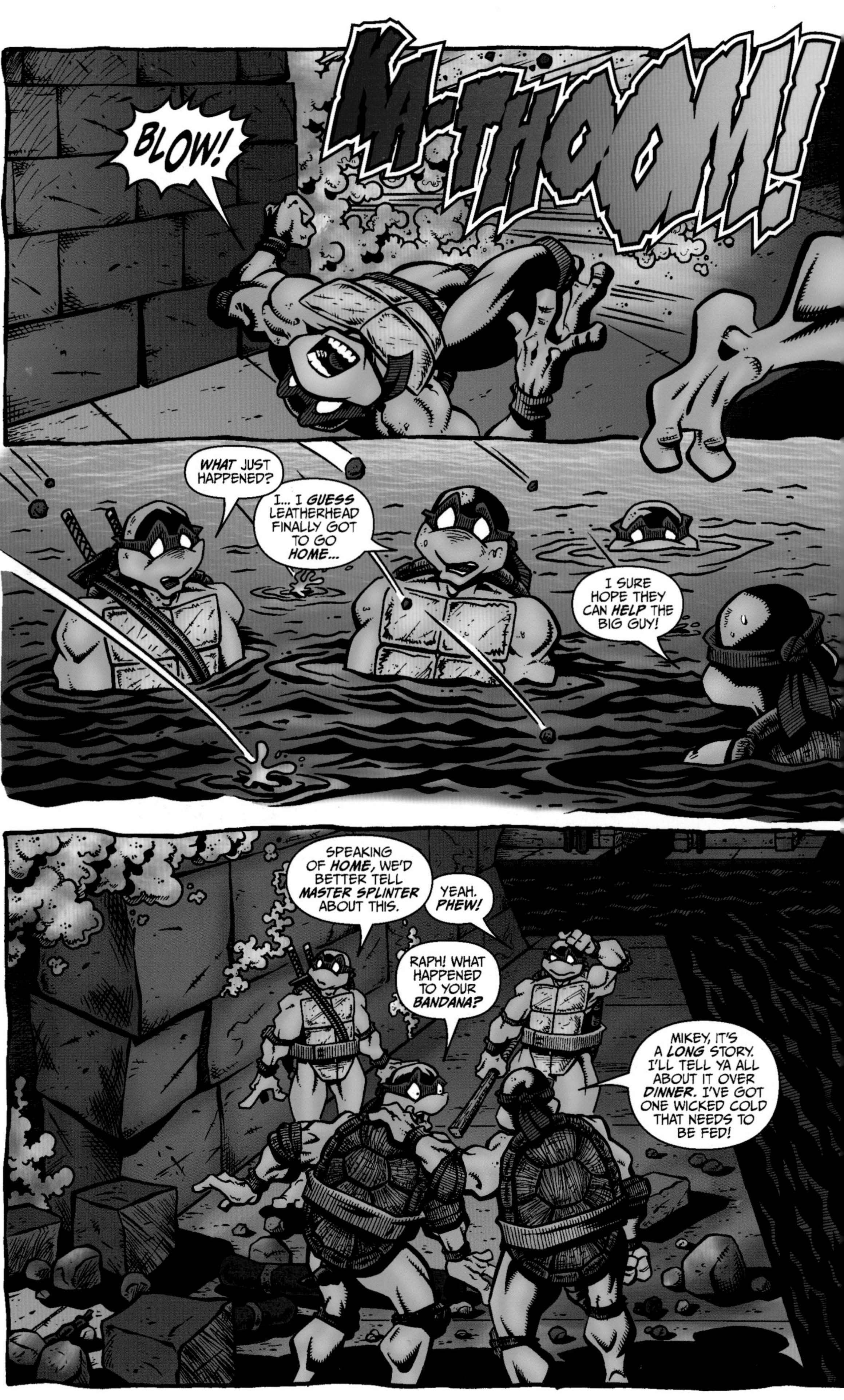

BLOW!
KA-THOOM!
WHAT JUST HAPPENED?
I... I GUESS LEATHERHEAD FINALLY GOT TO GO HOME...
I SURE HOPE THEY CAN HELP THE BIG GUY!
SPEAKING OF HOME, WE'D BETTER TELL MASTER SPLINTER ABOUT THIS.
YEAH. PHEW!
RAPH! WHAT HAPPENED TO YOUR BANDANA?
MIKEY, IT'S A LONG STORY. I'LL TELL YA ALL ABOUT IT OVER DINNER. I'VE GOT ONE WICKED COLD THAT NEEDS TO BE FED!

EPILOGUE

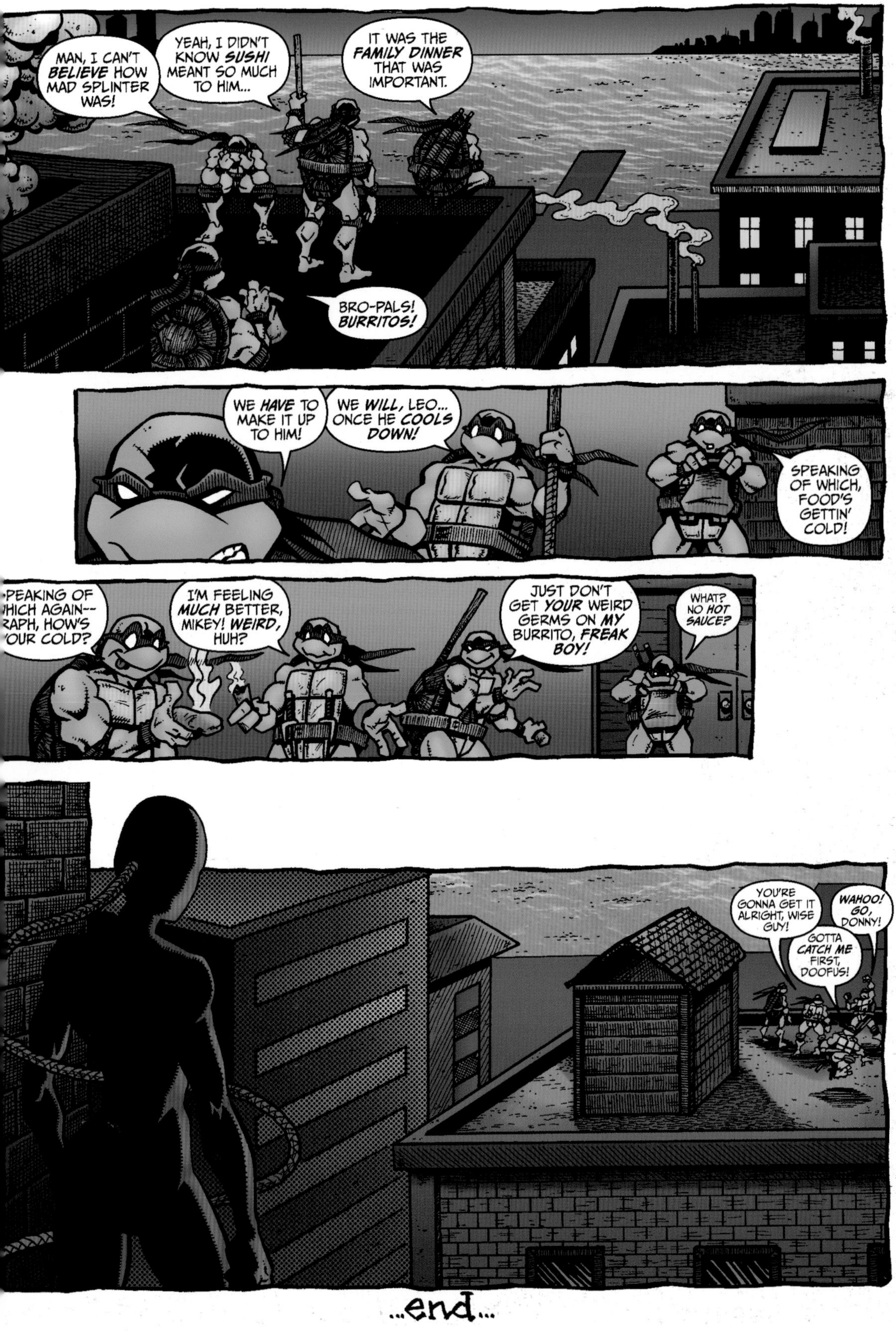
MAN, I CAN'T BELIEVE HOW MAD SPLINTER WAS!
YEAH, I DIDN'T KNOW SUSHI MEANT SO MUCH TO HIM...
IT WAS THE FAMILY DINNER THAT WAS IMPORTANT.
BRO-PALS! BURRITOS!
WE HAVE TO MAKE IT UP TO HIM!
WE WILL, LEO... ONCE HE COOLS DOWN!
SPEAKING OF WHICH, FOOD'S GETTIN' COLD!
PEAKING OF HICH AGAIN-- RAPH, HOW'S OUR COLD?
I'M FEELING MUCH BETTER, MIKEY! WEIRD, HUH?
JUST DON'T GET YOUR WEIRD GERMS ON MY BURRITO, FREAK BOY!
WHAT? NO HOT SAUCE?
YOU'RE GONNA GET IT ALRIGHT, WISE GUY!
WAHOO! GO, DONNY!
GOTTA CATCH ME FIRST, DOOFUS!

...end...

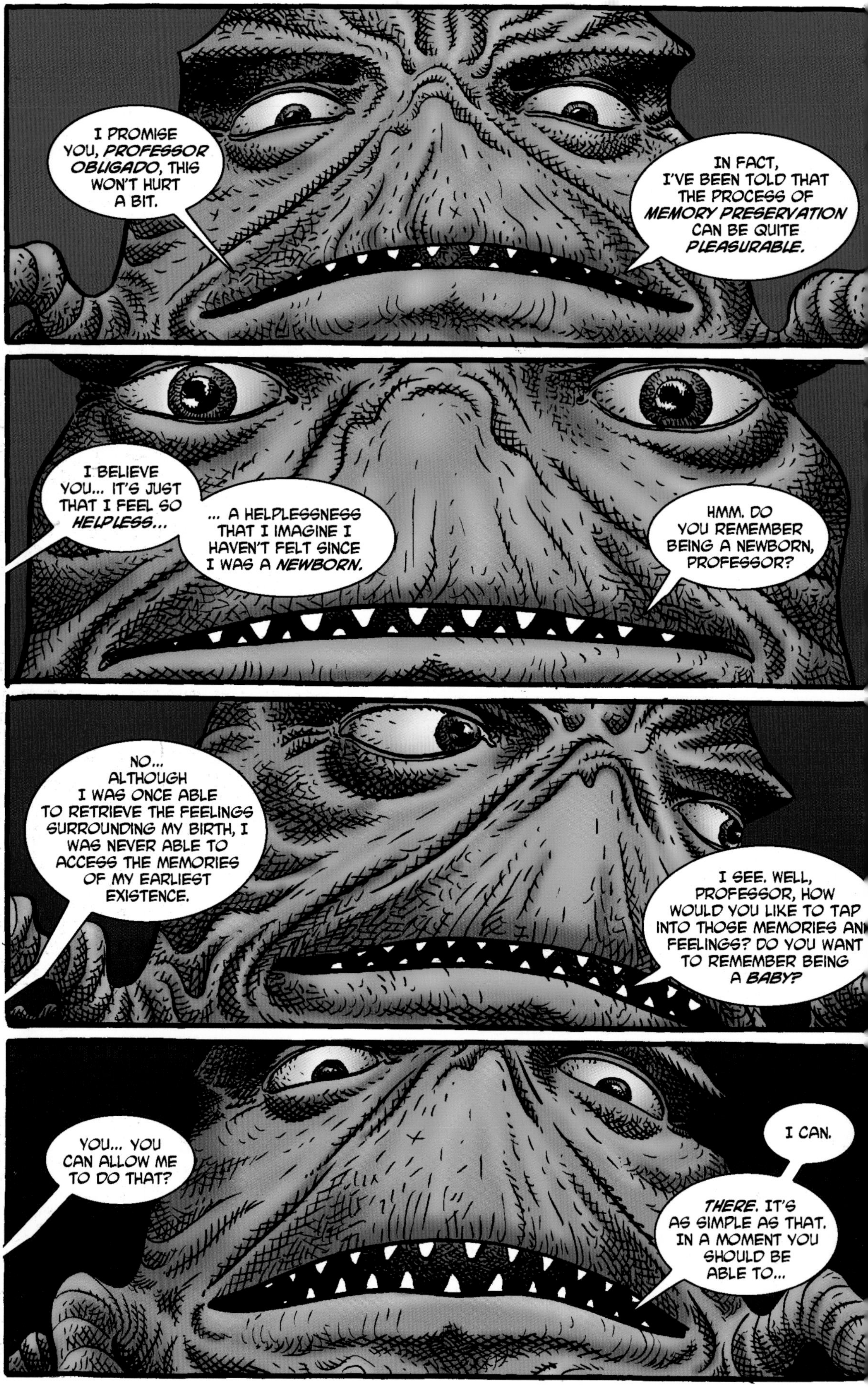

I PROMISE YOU, *PROFESSOR OBLIGADO*, THIS WON'T HURT A BIT.
IN FACT, I'VE BEEN TOLD THAT THE PROCESS OF *MEMORY PRESERVATION* CAN BE QUITE *PLEASURABLE.*
I BELIEVE YOU... IT'S JUST THAT I FEEL SO *HELPLESS...*
... A HELPLESSNESS THAT I IMAGINE I HAVEN'T FELT SINCE I WAS A *NEWBORN.*
HMM. DO YOU REMEMBER BEING A NEWBORN, PROFESSOR?
NO... ALTHOUGH I WAS ONCE ABLE TO RETRIEVE THE FEELINGS SURROUNDING MY BIRTH, I WAS NEVER ABLE TO ACCESS THE MEMORIES OF MY EARLIEST EXISTENCE.
I SEE. WELL, PROFESSOR, HOW WOULD YOU LIKE TO TAP INTO THOSE MEMORIES AN FEELINGS? DO YOU WANT TO REMEMBER BEING A *BABY?*
YOU... YOU CAN ALLOW ME TO DO THAT?
I CAN.
THERE. IT'S AS SIMPLE AS THAT. IN A MOMENT YOU SHOULD BE ABLE TO...

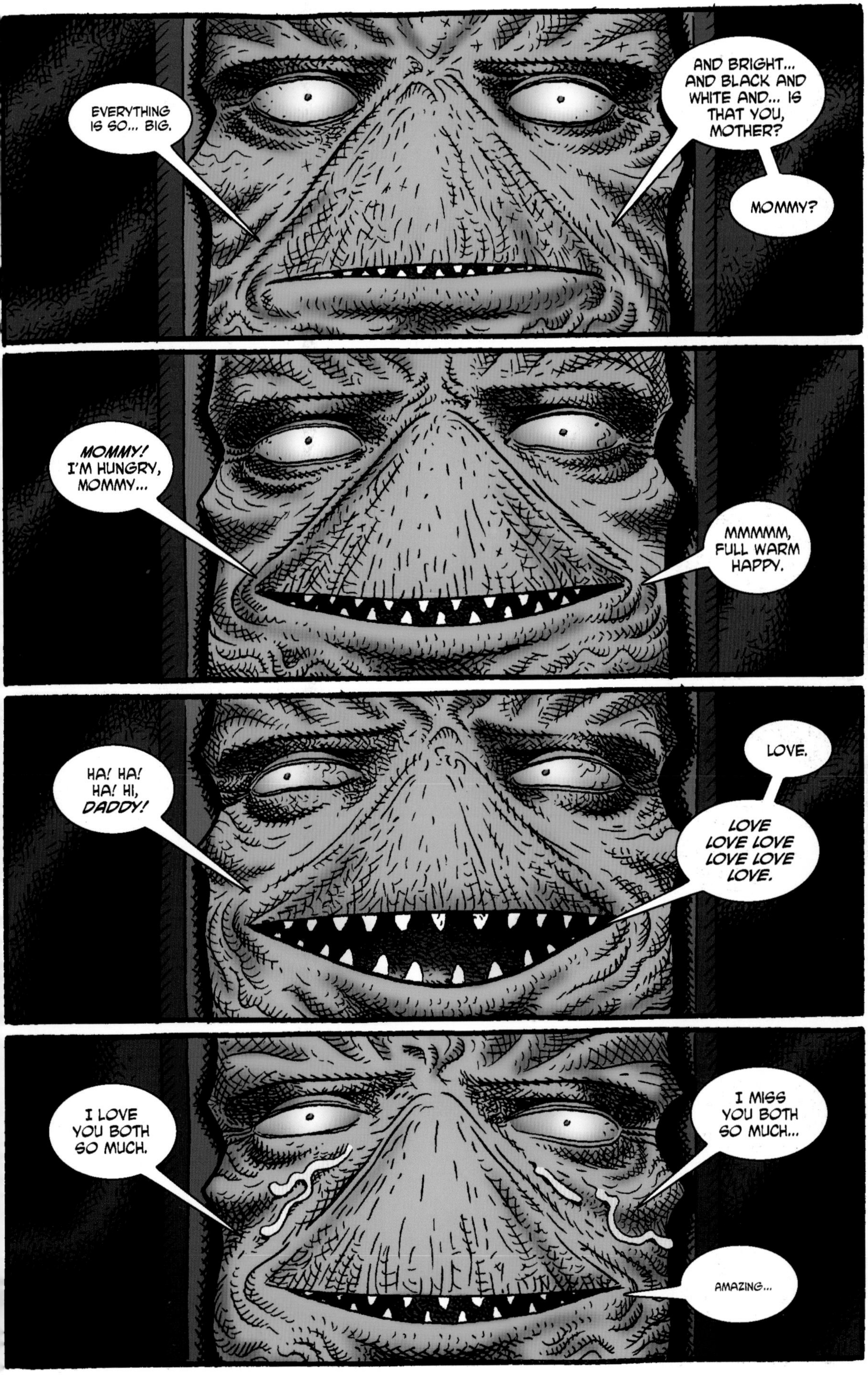
EVERYTHING IS SO... BIG.
AND BRIGHT... AND BLACK AND WHITE AND... IS THAT YOU, MOTHER?
MOMMY?
MOMMY! I'M HUNGRY, MOMMY...
MMMMM, FULL WARM HAPPY.
HA! HA! HA! HI, DADDY!
LOVE.
LOVE LOVE LOVE LOVE LOVE LOVE.
I LOVE YOU BOTH SO MUCH.
I MISS YOU BOTH SO MUCH...
AMAZING...

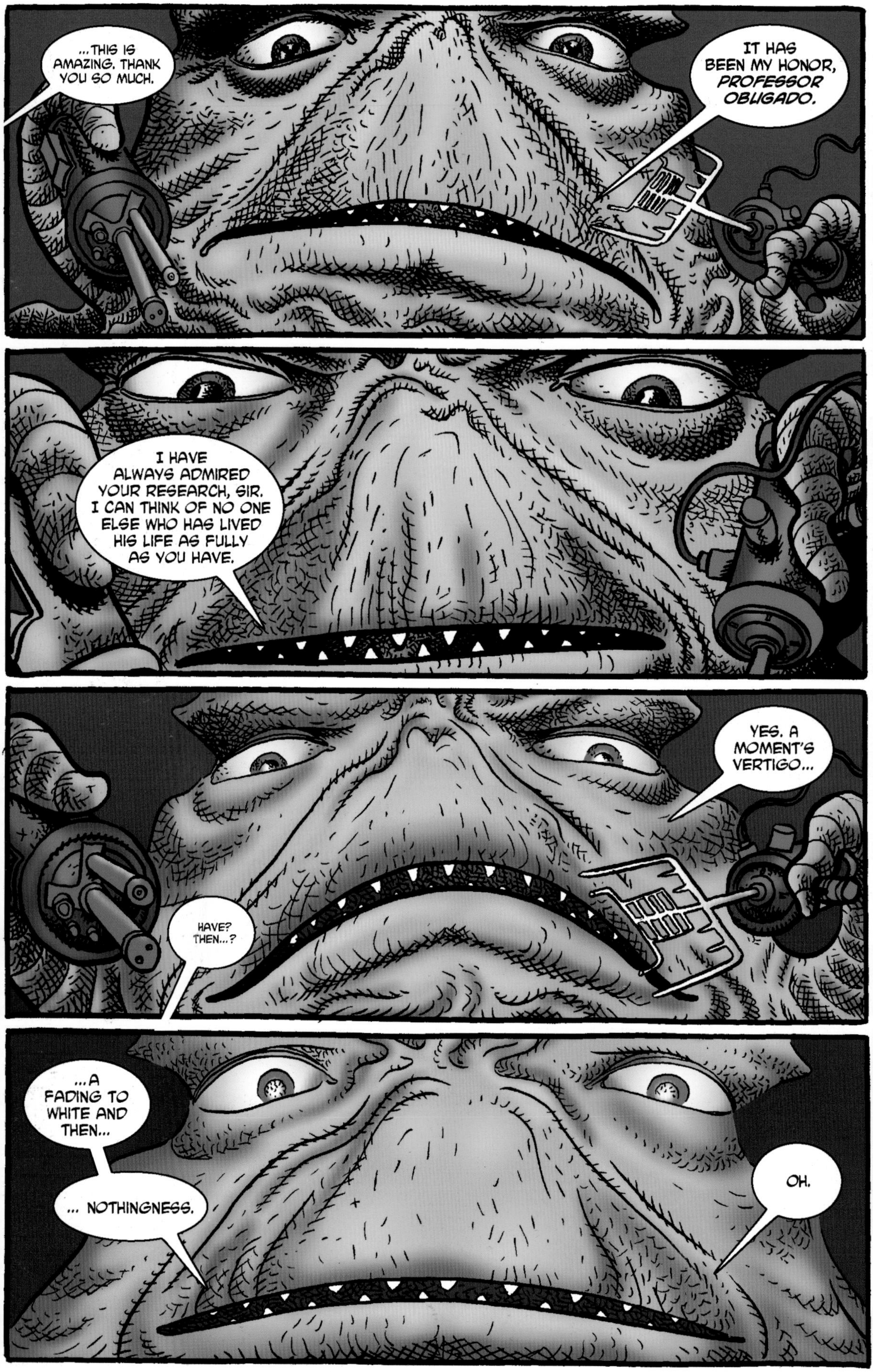
...THIS IS AMAZING. THANK YOU SO MUCH.
IT HAS BEEN MY HONOR, *PROFESSOR OBLIGADO.*
I HAVE ALWAYS ADMIRED YOUR RESEARCH, SIR. I CAN THINK OF NO ONE ELSE WHO HAS LIVED HIS LIFE AS FULLY AS YOU HAVE.
YES. A MOMENT'S VERTIGO...
HAVE? THEN...?
...A FADING TO WHITE AND THEN...
... NOTHINGNESS.
OH.

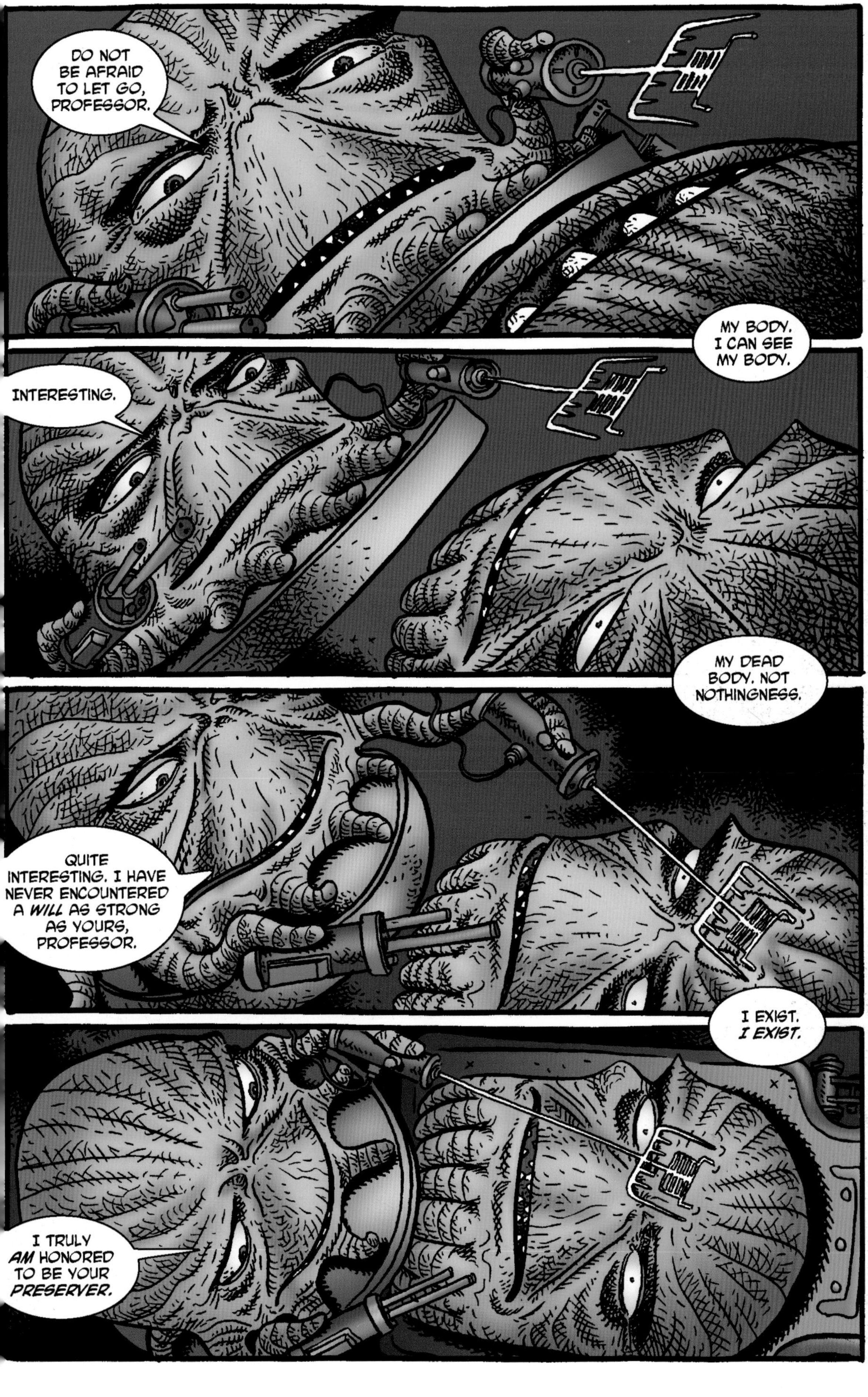
DO NOT BE AFRAID TO LET GO, PROFESSOR.
MY BODY. I CAN SEE MY BODY.
INTERESTING.
MY DEAD BODY. NOT NOTHINGNESS.
QUITE INTERESTING. I HAVE NEVER ENCOUNTERED A *WILL* AS STRONG AS YOURS, PROFESSOR.
I EXIST. *I EXIST.*
I TRULY *AM* HONORED TO BE YOUR *PRESERVER.*

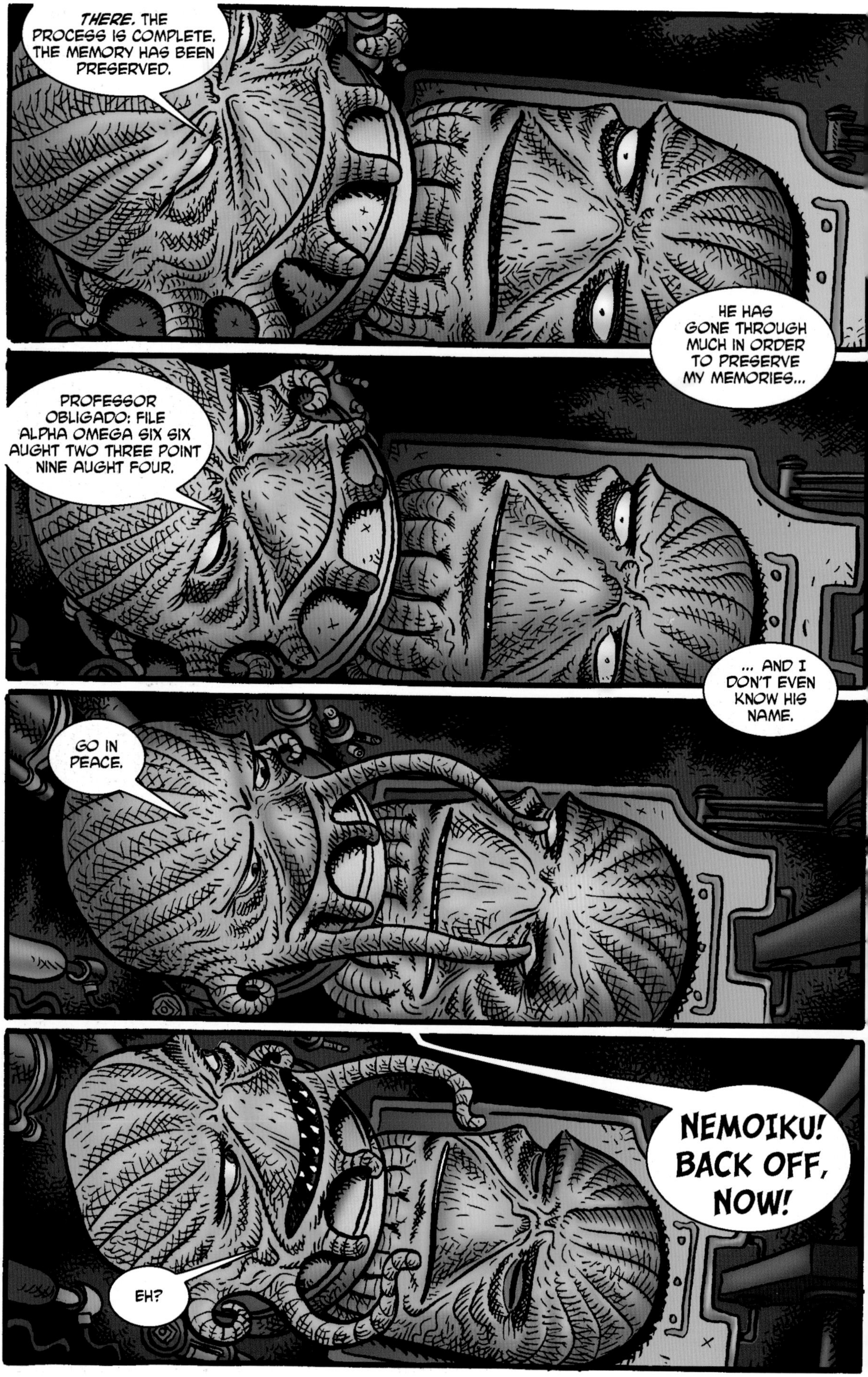
THERE. THE PROCESS IS COMPLETE. THE MEMORY HAS BEEN PRESERVED.
HE HAS GONE THROUGH MUCH IN ORDER TO PRESERVE MY MEMORIES...
PROFESSOR OBLIGADO: FILE ALPHA OMEGA SIX SIX AUGHT TWO THREE POINT NINE AUGHT FOUR.
... AND I DON'T EVEN KNOW HIS NAME.
GO IN PEACE.
NEMOIKU! BACK OFF, NOW!
EH?

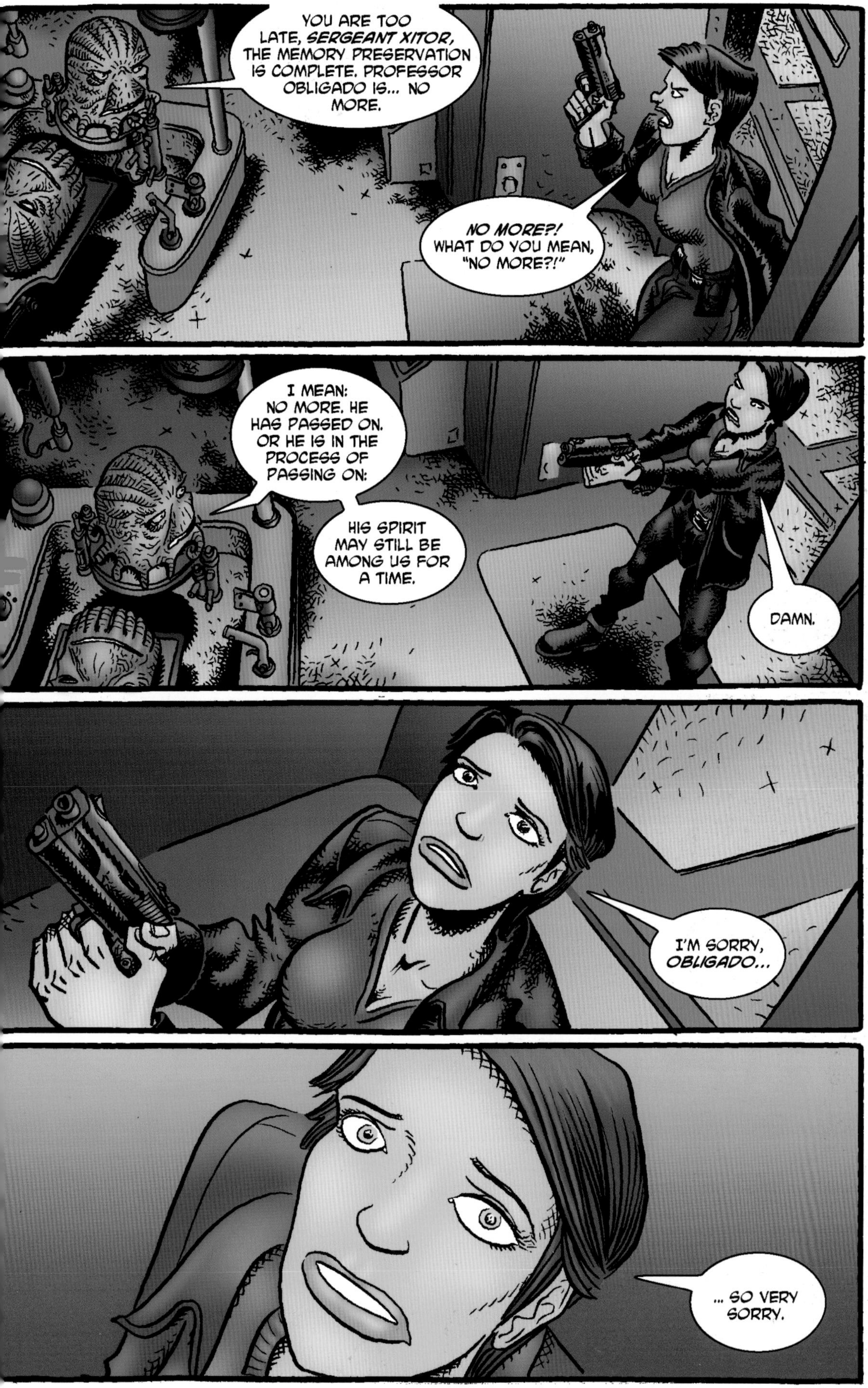
YOU ARE TOO LATE, *SERGEANT XITOR,* THE MEMORY PRESERVATION IS COMPLETE. PROFESSOR OBLIGADO IS... NO MORE.
NO MORE?! WHAT DO YOU MEAN, "NO MORE?!"
I MEAN: NO MORE. HE HAS PASSED ON. OR HE IS IN THE PROCESS OF PASSING ON:
HIS SPIRIT MAY STILL BE AMONG US FOR A TIME.
DAMN.
I'M SORRY, *OBLIGADO...*
... SO VERY SORRY.

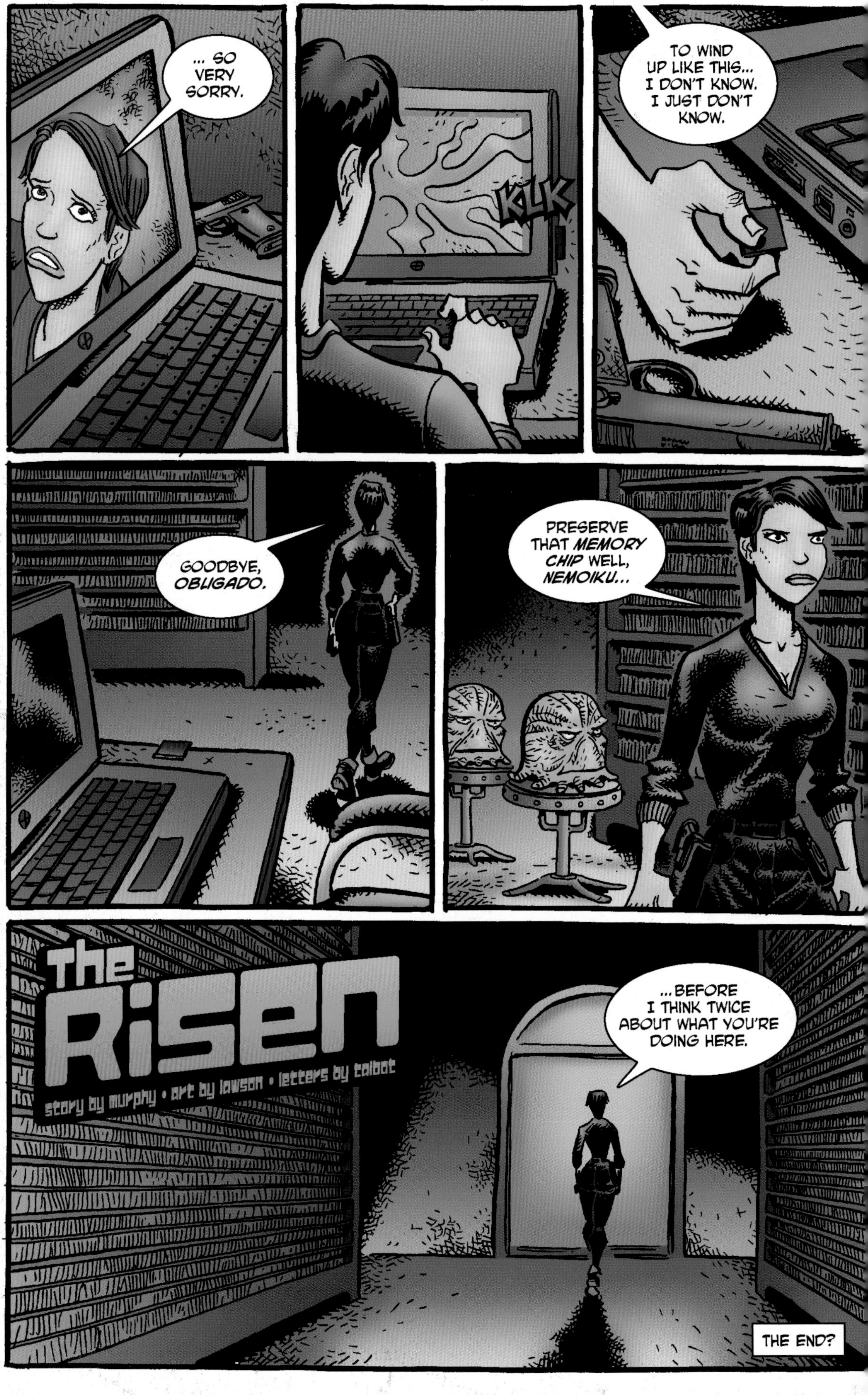
... SO VERY SORRY.
KLIK
TO WIND UP LIKE THIS... I DON'T KNOW. I JUST DON'T KNOW.
GOODBYE, OBLIGADO.
PRESERVE THAT MEMORY CHIP WELL, NEMOIKU...
The Risen
story by murphy • art by lawson • letters by talbot
...BEFORE I THINK TWICE ABOUT WHAT YOU'RE DOING HERE.
THE END?

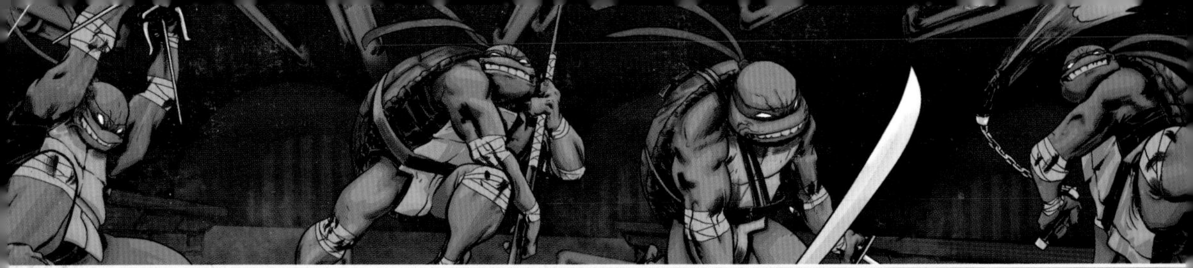

TEENAGE MUTANT NINJA TURTLES

MORE TURTLE ACTION!

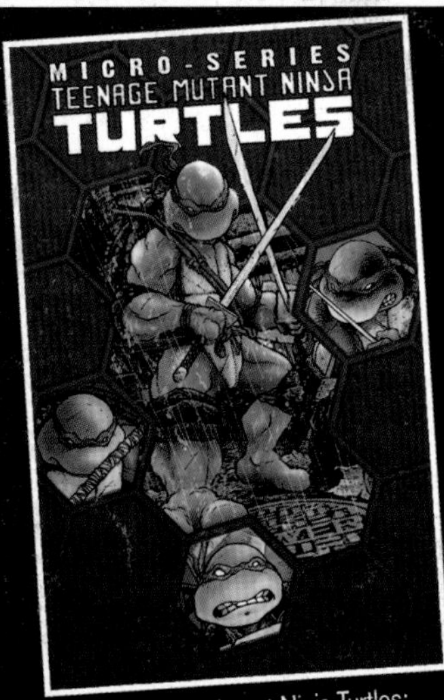
MICRO-SERIES
TEENAGE MUTANT NINJA
TURTLES

Teenage Mutant Ninja Turtles:
Micro-Series, Vol. 1
ISBN: 978-1-61377-232-4

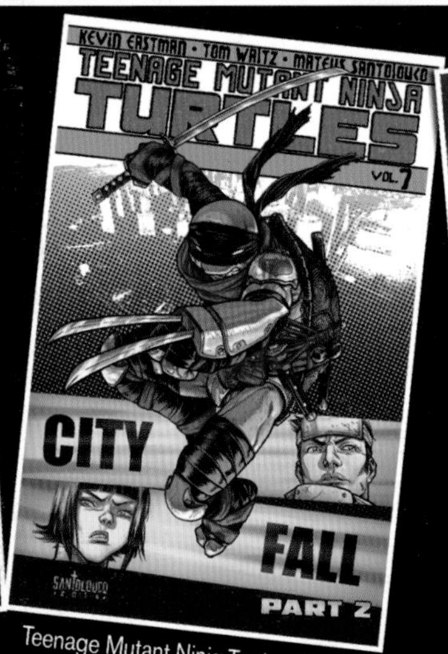
KEVIN EASTMAN · TOM WALTZ · MATEUS SANTOLOUCO
TEENAGE MUTANT NINJA
TURTLES
VOL. 7
CITY
FALL
PART 2

Teenage Mutant Ninja Turtles, Vol. 7:
City Fall, Part 2
ISBN: 978-1-61377-876-0

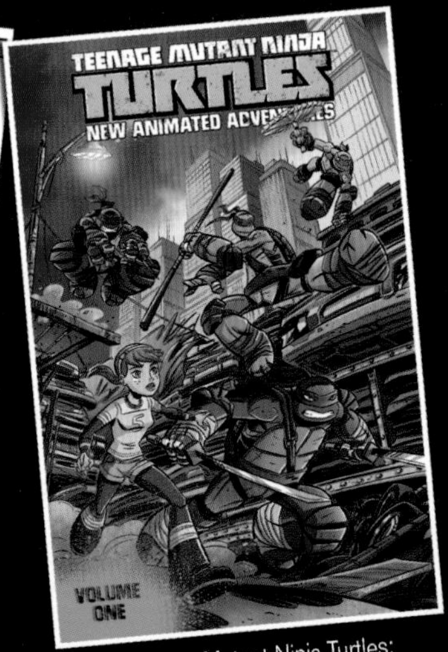
TEENAGE MUTANT NINJA
TURTLES
VOLUME ONE

Teenage Mutant Ninja Turtles:
New Animated Adventures, Vol. 1
ISBN: 978-1-61377-856-2

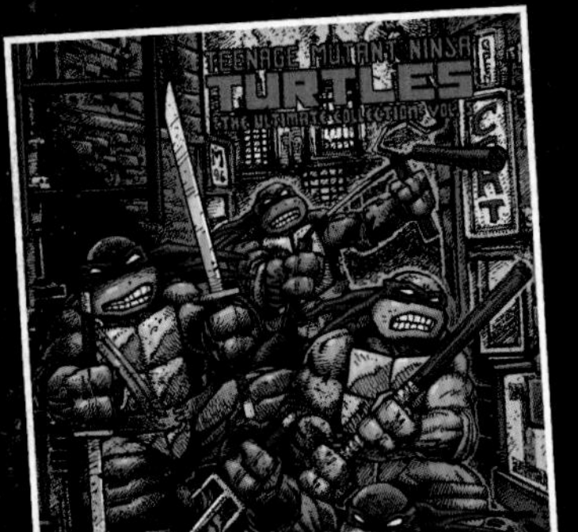
TEENAGE MUTANT NINJA
TURTLES

Teenage Mutant Ninja Turtles:
The Ultimate Collection, Vol. 5
ISBN: 978-1-61377-553-0

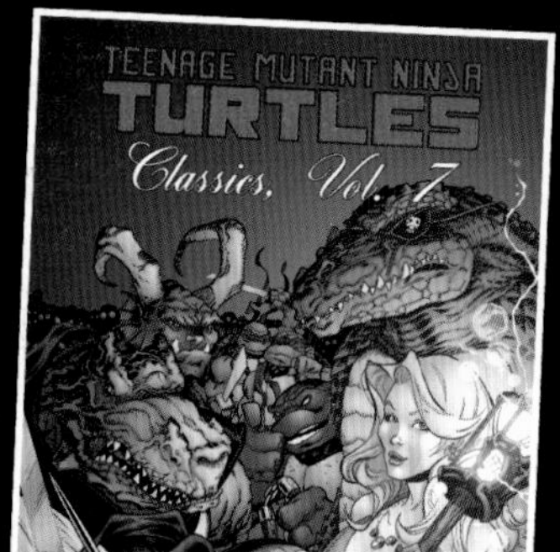
TEENAGE MUTANT NINJA
TURTLES
Classics, Vol. 7

Teenage Mutant Ninja Turtles
Classics, Vol. 7
ISBN: 978-1-61377-798-5

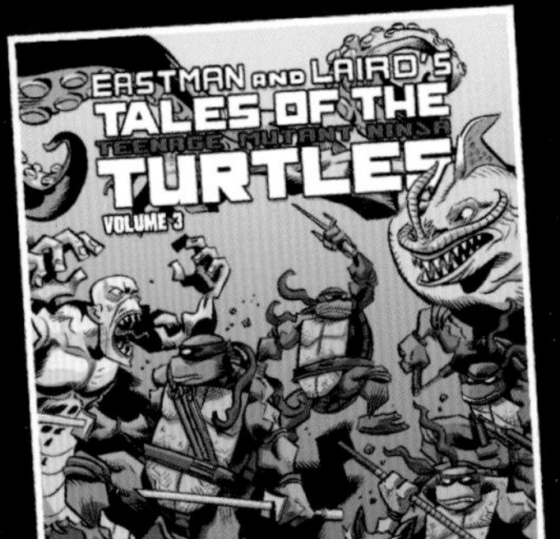
EASTMAN AND LAIRD'S
TALES OF THE
TEENAGE MUTANT NINJA
TURTLES
VOLUME 3

Tales of the Teenage Mutant
Ninja Turtles, Vol. 3
ISBN: 978-1-61377-762-6

ON SALE NOW

www.idwpublishing.com

IDW

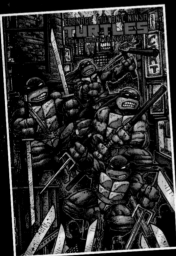

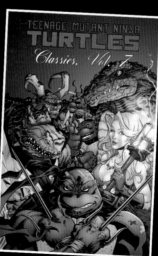

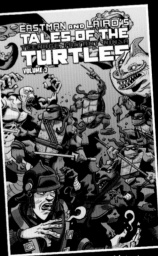